Nineteenth-Century Major Lives and Letters

Series Editor: Marilyn Gaull

This series presents original biographical, critical, and scholarly studies of literary works and public figures in Great Britain, North America, and continental Europe during the nineteenth century. The volumes in *Nineteenth-Century Major Lives and Letters* evoke the energies, achievements, contributions, cultural traditions, and individuals who reflected and generated them during the Romantic and Victorian period. The topics: critical, textual, and historical scholarship, literary and book history, biography, cultural and comparative studies, critical theory, art, architecture, science, politics, religion, music, language, philosophy, aesthetics, law, publication, translation, domestic and public life, popular culture, and anything that influenced, impinges upon, expresses or contributes to an understanding of the authors, works, and events of the nineteenth century. The authors consist of political figures, artists, scientists, and cultural icons including William Blake, Thomas Hardy, Charles Darwin, William Wordsworth, William Butler Yeats, Samuel Taylor, and their contemporaries.

The series editor is Marilyn Gaull, PhD (Indiana University), FEA. She has taught at William and Mary, Temple University, New York University, and is Research Professor at the Editorial Institute at Boston University. She is the founder and editor of *The Wordsworth Circle* and the author *of English Romanticism: The Human Context*, and editions, essays, and reviews in journals. She lectures internationally on British Romanticism, folklore, and narrative theory, intellectual history, publishing procedures, and history of science.

PUBLISHED BY PALGRAVE:

Shelley's German Afterlives, by Susanne Schmid
Romantic Literature, Race, and Colonial Encounter, by Peter J. Kitson
Coleridge, the Bible, and Religion, by Jeffrey W. Barbeau
Byron, edited by Cheryl A. Wilson
Romantic Migrations, by Michael Wiley
The Long and Winding Road from Blake to the Beatles, by Matthew Schneider
British Periodicals and Romantic Identity, by Mark Schoenfield
Women Writers and Nineteenth-Century Medievalism, by Clare Broome Saunders
British Victorian Women's Periodicals, by Kathryn Ledbetter
Romantic Diasporas, by Toby R. Benis
Romantic Literary Families, by Scott Krawczyk
Victorian Christmas in Print, by Tara Moore
Culinary Aesthetics and Practices in Nineteenth-Century American Literature, Edited by Monika Elbert and Marie Drews
Poetics en passant, by Anne Jamison
Reading Popular Culture in Victorian Print, by Alberto Gabriele
Romanticism and the Object, Edited by Larry H. Peer
From Song to Print, by Terence Hoagwood
Populism, Gender, and Sympathy in the Romantic Novel, by James P. Carson
Victorian Medicine and Social Reform, by Louise Penner
Gothic Romanticism, by Tom Duggett
Byron and the Rhetoric of Italian Nationalism, by Arnold A. Schmidt
Poetry and Public Discourse in Nineteenth-Century America, by Shira Wolosky

FORTHCOMING TITLES:

Trauma, Transcendence, and Trust, by Thomas Brennan
The Discourses of Food in Nineteenth-Century British Fiction, by Annette Cozzi
John Thelwall and the Wordsworth Circle, by Judith Thompson
Royal Romances, by Kristin Samuelian
The Poetry of Mary Robinson, by Daniel Robinson
Beyond Romantic Ecocriticism, by B. Ashton Nichols
Popular Medievalism in Romantic-Era Britain, by Clare A. Simmons
Coleridge and the Daemonic Imagination, by Gregory Leadbetter
Romantic Dharma, by Mark Lussier
Regions of Sara Coleridge's Thought, by Peter Swaab
Jewish Representation in British Literature 1700–1853, by Michael H. Scrivener

Poetry and Public Discourse in Nineteenth-Century America

Shira Wolosky

palgrave
macmillan

POETRY AND PUBLIC DISCOURSE IN NINETEENTH-CENTURY AMERICA

First published in 2010 by
PALGRAVE MACMILLAN®
in the United States—a division of St. Martin's Press LLC,
175 Fifth Avenue, New York, NY 10010.

Where this book is distributed in the UK, Europe and the rest of the world,
this is by Palgrave Macmillan, a division of Macmillan Publishers Limited,
registered in England, company number 785998, of Houndmills,
Basingstoke, Hampshire RG21 6XS.

Palgrave Macmillan is the global academic imprint of the above companies
and has companies and representatives throughout the world.

Palgrave® and Macmillan® are registered trademarks in the United States,
the United Kingdom, Europe and other countries.

ISBN: 978-0-230-10431-0

Library of Congress Cataloging-in-Publication Data is available from the
Library of Congress.

A catalogue record of the book is available from the British Library.

Design by Newgen Imaging Systems (P) Ltd., Chennai, India.

First edition: September 2010

10 9 8 7 6 5 4 3 2 1

Printed in the United States of America.

For Ariel

Contents

PREFACE: POETICS, CULTURE, RHETORIC

Contemporary aesthetic theory is a house divided between formalist and historicist trends. This aesthetic split persists in culture studies, with its renewed interests in society and culture after the twentieth century's emphasis on formalist poetics. The rise of formalism is in fact itself an historical phenomenon, out of and in response to social and economic transformations taking place throughout the nineteenth century and the position of art within these transformations. The challenge remains on how to pursue social-formalist readings without reducing poetry to the first or excluding history in the second. As Theodore Adorno commented in "Lyric Poetry and Society," in lyric poetry "the thinking through of a work of art justly requires a concrete inquiry into social content;" but this is not to say that lyric works be "misused as objects for the demonstration of social theses."[1]

Rhetoric opens an avenue across this divide toward a historicist-formalist approach. Rhetoric is the art of making claims. But it can also be claimed that the tropes and patterns of rhetoric themselves structure experience in so far as it is mediated by and expressed through language. Rhetoric therefore bridges the chasm between poetics and culture. Through shaping and re-patterning of the rhetoric that surrounds it, literature—including poetry—simultaneously reflects, interacts with, and intervenes in culture. Rhetoric provides a site where literature intersects with other forms of discourse, and not least public ones. The rhetorical modes of a culture penetrate literary representation; while literature derives its materials through such rhetorical matrices, doing so in ways that are more self-conscious, self-reflective, creative, and directed to its own ends.

As against the views of poetry as a self-enclosed art object that twentieth-century formalism projected, nineteenth-century poetry plays a vibrant and active role in ongoing discussions on defining America and its cultural directions. Here the mutual implication of rhetoric and literature takes on surprising power and significance. The notion of a self-enclosed poetic realm was not generally assumed in the nineteenth century except as an anxiety and looming threat within American culture itself. Instead, poetry directly participated in and addressed the pressing issues facing the evolving nation through its responses, circulation, and creative reflections on the rhetoric of national life.

In this study, poetry is treated as a distinctive formal field in which the rhetorics of nineteenth-century American culture find intensified expression, concentration, reflection, and creative generation. The literary force and genius of a writer often entail mastery of the rhetorical constructions widely available in his or her surrounding culture rather than a withdrawal from them into a pure or self-reflective aesthetic language. Poetic language and composition draw on, but also illuminate and redirect the rhetorics of social-cultural life. One argument of this study is that poetry gains both historical grounding and aesthetic coherence and force through the investigation of its transformative relationship to the rhetorics that surround it. This is not to collapse or deny all aesthetic difference. Poetic mastery itself may be measured in how a text deploys the rhetorics it responds to and remakes, its complexities across a variety of life-worlds. Such rhetorical analysis does not reduce literature to historical or ideological reproduction of social experience. Rather, , rhetorical analysis investigates the relations of literature to historical and cultural experiences through its own intrinsic practices, as mediated through linguistic patterns that engage and formulate values, attitudes, interests, and cultural directions at large in society. Investigating poetic structures such as voice, imagery, setting, self-representation, and address as they interpenetrate with rhetorical contexts and practices ultimately illuminates and affirms poetry's cultural importance and aesthetic power.

In pursuing the rhetorical intersections between poetry and public discourses, this study addresses both individually and in relation to each other, the writings of women and men, of Southerners and Northerners, and of genteel and elite across different regional, ethnic, racial, and religious identities. Particular attention is given to religious contexts, not merely as they are subsumed into the categories of race, gender, and class, as if religion were simply a derivative aspect of them, but also as itself a major force in the formation of American self-understanding penetrating social, political, racial, and gendered spheres. In poetry, as in speeches, sermons, fictions, and newspapers, nineteenth-century America's efforts at self-definition took shape through religious claims and counter-claims. The Bible, as a foundational text of American national identity, provided terms for articulating and arguing many different sides of American commitments.

Here the outstanding feature is the way the Bible in particular became a rhetorical base shared by even violently opposing interests and across a wide range of poetic undertakings.

One topic in which literary and cultural expression intercross through common and core rhetorical formations is modesty, a central parameter for defining both poetic and social conduct for women. Here I review and revise what have been traditional interpretive paradigms situating women and women's writing in private, domestic spaces as against public ones. Poetry in fact served as a major avenue for women's emergence into and participation in public issues. This is a context even for Emily Dickinson, whose writing addressed and contended with the cultural forces of when she lived despite–even through—her iconic privacy.

Nineteenth-century male poets more confidently regarded themselves as participating in public national formation, although they too faced questions about their status as artists. Their work particularly takes up the challenge of establishing American poetic languages, in both contradistinction against British antecedents and also as contesting regional claims and usages of common idioms and expressions that take on different courses and senses within varied American commitments. The issue of plural identities itself emerges as a defining and enduring American condition. Especially after the Civil War, poetry explores and offers new conceptions of America as a national framework and new conceptions of both the individual's and the community's place within it, including regional, ethnic, gendered, religious, racial, and economic identities. But nineteenth-century social transformations also involve an increasing domination of American culture by commercial interests, pressing to the side poetry and other cultural and civic involvements. By the century's end, there is evident a redrawing of poetic lines as a boundary against the active world, with the poem now emerging as a self-enclosed aesthetic object separate from public social life.

This study emphasizes poetry as it addresses, critiques, and participates in American cultural events. Poetry is presented as an art in its own right, but in terms of a rhetoric shaped by history and that shapes history in turn. This nineteenth-century public poetry finds its culminating figure in Walt Whitman, who at once asserts poetry's public power and also the threats to it posed by American cultural trends. Such public address in fact largely impels the nineteenth century's poetry, the role of which, as this study investigates, was to represent, articulate, and help define within its own unique terms and through its own unique modes and self-reflection issues fundamental to the emergence of American life.

*   *   *

I would like to acknowledge with heartfelt gratitude the following teachers, colleagues, and friends who have accompanied me through the writing and thinking of this book: Sacvan Bercovitch, Harold Bloom, Emily Budick, Beverly Haviland, Michael Kramer, and Cristanne Miller.

CHAPTER 1

MODEST CLAIMS

Anne Bradstreet inaugurated American poetry with a disclaimer. In her "Author to Her Book," she addresses her poetic offspring as a monstrous birth. Her "Prologue" concedes that, as a woman poet, she may be "obnoxious" to the many readers eager to cast "despite...on female wits." But both poems conduct their self-deprecation with consummate wit. The "Book" emerges as an impelling conceit of writing in the guise of childcare. Bradstreet's plea in the "Prologue" that she seeks no crown beyond one made of kitchen herbs both demonstrates her classical learning and constructs a counter-image to it: "Give thyme and parsley wreath, I ask no bays."

On this meek note Bradstreet launched not only her own poetically ambitious project, but also a rhetoric that continues through women's writing to this day. Feminizing the classical apologia, Bradstreet modestly denies her abilities. In doing so, however, she asserts her right to speak against those who would not even grant her that much. Reassuring her readers that she will not exceed her proper place, she enables herself, at least within these confines, to exercise her powers. But this in turn becomes a method and avenue exactly for broadening the narrow strictures allotted to her, as well as asserting a set of values not only imposed on women but embraced by them.

Bradstreet dramatizes the multiple faces of modesty. On one side, modesty surely imposes confinement, restriction, and boundary. On the other, however, it also marks, at least in women writers, an instability in those boundaries, their revision and even transgression as a feminine mode of entry into a wider world. In this double sense, modesty emerges as a central *topos* and stance of female writing. Indeed, while humility is a *topos* across gender, its contexts for men are usually religious: men humble themselves before God or his representatives within an ecclesiastical hierarchy. Women are modest in more social and generally defining ways.

Women's poetry of the nineteenth century follows a pattern of going out of print on the death of its authors, more or less causing its disappearance from literary history. New investigations into sentimental literature have especially worked towards recovering women's writing and redefining it not only as modestly circumscribed but also as modes of public engagement.[1] Yet modesty continues to be treated almost entirely as a lack of ambition, fear of fame, and mark of female submission.[2] The modesty *topos*, however, is more than a negative stance. It also structures ways in which women speak for and to female experience, their efforts to find a literary voice that will accord with their sense of themselves as women, and even articulate distinctive values and commitments. Instead of being viewed only as self-effacement in polar opposition to positive self-assertion, modesty within nineteenth-century female culture represents a complex negotiation between these two poles in ways that redefine both. Neither stark self-denial nor unlimited self-assertion represents for these women the ideal for personal or communal life. Theirs instead is a model of selfhood that defines itself through community values and commitments. Modesty registers a sense of self that is invested in social roles not focused on personal interests in opposition to community relationships. Modesty in this sense represents a positive set of values for women, in critical tension against definitions of self and society that threaten to fragment their experiences not only as women, but as Americans as well.

Modesty emerges as a core mode of female self-representation in literary terms from the colonial poetry of Anne Bradstreet to such twentieth-century poets as Marianne Moore and Elizabeth Bishop. Within the nineteenth century, modesty marks the work of women poets both popular and elite, accomplished and minor. Among these, it takes on different roles and carries differing degrees of force. Despite differences, however, modesty provides a lens for seeing into the diverse poetry produced by nineteenth-century women, as well as linking literary production to social conditions and cultural paradigms then and after.

Modesty, of course, is not only a literary stance. Perhaps more than any other quality, it has traditionally defined the quintessence of womanhood. Cotton Mather, in his *Ornaments for the Daughters of Zion*, names the "Purple of Modesty" as an indispensable adornment in the ideal female daily "Dress." As an early advice book puts it, modesty "is a very general and comprehensive quality. It extends to everything where a woman is concerned: conversation books, pictures, attitude, gesture, pronunciation." Indeed, through the myriad of etiquette books published from the late eighteenth and into the nineteenth centuries, modesty comes to extend well beyond an exclusive concern with female sexual behavior "to cover," as one advice book puts it, "the whole of experience." It "prescribes you a perfect rule of direction, how to behave yourselves in your whole course or conversation: In your very motion, gesture, and gate, observe modesty." As "the most indispensable requisite of a woman," it is urged as the quality most "essential and natural to the sex;" encompassing "your looks, your speech, and the course of your whole behavior, [which] should own an humble distrust of your selves."[3]

Modesty marks the complex structure of the "separate spheres" and the "Cult of True Womanhood," which, at least ideologically, shaped gender roles and relations in nineteenth-century America.[4] Within this construction, the lives of women and men were distinguished and assigned: the former to the private and domestic, the latter to the public, political, and economic.[5] Enforcing this division of social life were legal and political restrictions denying (married) women the right to inherit and own property, even their personal and household belongings; to have bank accounts and sign checks (treasurers of Female Societies had to be single or widowed); to sue, sign contracts, witness or judge in court; to hold office or to vote.[6] Extra-legal social norms reinforced legal ones, making it unseemly, for example, to speak publicly in mixed ("promiscuous") company or even to go out into public spaces unchaperoned or "improperly" dressed. Such norms established restrictions perhaps no less potent because they were not only imposed but also internalized. In this sense, the modest demeanor, status, and possibilities demanded of women served to enclose and subordinate them.[7]

And yet, modesty acted not only as a barrier, but also as a gateway of the women's sphere. While undoubtedly serving to keep women the prisoner (called "guardian") of the domestic hearth, modesty served as well to mediate and bridge private and public worlds. Its restrictive senses did not prevent it from becoming, in the hands of women writers at least, an avenue also leading out of the private domestic circle into the broader space of public and published expression. Modesty as a literary *topos* thus stands in complex relation to its social uses. Indeed, it serves as a manner not only of self-effacement but also of self-presentation and self-representation in both social and literary intercourse, which can be exploited to enlarge or intensify self-expression, as occurs in the hands of literary artists.

Modesty, then, is not just a mode of self- and social enclosure. It also defines parameters for expression, for venturing forth into the world. And the boundaries separating the domestic from the non-domestic, privacy from publicity, are neither as absolute nor as fixed as the ideology of the woman's sphere asserts. Norms of behavior, far from being self-evident and assured, were particularly vulnerable and uncertain through the nineteenth century, as the explosion of etiquette manuals itself suggests. People required so much instruction exactly because they were unsure what behavior was expected or acceptable. Nineteenth-century America is a period of extraordinary dynamism, transformation, and indeed rupture on almost every level, including demographic and economic as well as social and political structures. Urbanization, industrialization, and democratization all more or less radically changed the rules of conduct no less than re-organizations of work and financing, home-life, class divisions, and civic and political developments. Migrations to cities replaced the familiar intimacy of village life with the anonymity, mobility, production, and consumption of urban spaces. Life among multitudes of strangers required new norms of behavior for establishing—and avoiding—acquaintanceships, with a strong sense of social status mediating relations in both the world of business and the drawing room. The gentility that had been traditionally defined through social differentiations of inherited rank and titles became in industrializing America the aspiration of a middle class. Defining proper behavior thus became an urgent need, as new social situations and roles generated uncertainty about what genteel conduct consisted of as well as the desire to master it. At the same time, new technologies in communication, transport, material production, and publishing provided the means for disseminating a literature with instructions for doing so.[8]

Etiquette books, mass produced, rushed in to service this new demand for respectability. Gentlemen and gentlewomen, educators, editors, and journalists all were happy to inform young middle-class ladies what hours, companions, clothes, tones of voice, and topics of conversation were suitable for presenting themselves to what was called the World. As the much-reprinted *Lady's New Year's Gift* explained, venturing "out of your house into the world" is "a dangerous step...The Enemy is abroad, and you are sure to be taken if you are found struggling. Your behavior is therefore to incline strongly towards the Reserv'd part."[9] Besides offering what amounts to self-advertisement, this advice images the double face of modesty. Warning against the unknown "abroad," urging Prudence and Reserve and

"Close behavior," it nevertheless outlines, within accepted social norms, how to negotiate the world's dangers. This delicate balance is reenacted through the many available guides to manners. Strictures on modest dress ("never showy," writes Sarah J. Hale, and in keeping with the "prevailing fashion" so as to be "less conspicuous") and warnings against loud talk or laughter in company ("a young lady should never make herself conspicuous in public assembly" writes Eliza Ware Farrar in her popular *Young Lady's Friend*) also implicitly acknowledge new contexts and opportunities for women to appear in public. City streets offered new avenues for outings: although women's movements continued to be carefully overseen by specially demarcated semi-public places and many ordinances guarding public order, they were nevertheless granted a certain, albeit circumscribed, leeway.[10] This was especially the case with regard to the specific middle-class female contribution to the domestic economy (i.e., shopping). Department stores, a new creation of metropolitan space, generated in turn a "Ladies Mile" of shops in downtown New York, wherein it was permissible to walk, even alone. Eliza Farrar's is therefore a double message when she continues: "Always remember that a store is a public place; that you are speaking before and often to strangers, and therefore, there should be a certain degree of reserve, in all you do and say."[11]

Such genteel behavior in public was intended not least to distinguish women of the middle class from their working-class sisters, to say nothing of prostitutes. And behavioral codes remained restrictive. Still, American middle-class women enjoyed much more freedom of movement than did their counterparts in Europe, as De Tocqueville comments (one need only recall Daisy Miller, who died in Italy of a bad reputation). While falling far short of the women's rights envisioned and fought for by "ultraist" feminist political activists, middle class social roles also, it has been increasingly argued, strengthened female identity and enlarged female activity and power. The dual face of modesty coded as both suppressive and expressive in some sense mirrors an ambiguity and instability within the structure of the separate spheres themselves. Despite its ideological and, indeed, actual circumscription of female activity, the women's sphere also became an arena that made possible its own subversion. Feminist historians see the development of a specifically separate female sphere as constituting a distinctive culture in which nineteenth-century women shared events and intimate, highly supportive relationships, involving new female companionships and gaining new recognition and power.[12] The domestic sphere as properly women's own gave women one area of authority at least. A general increase in control over and within the family structure, measured by such factors as limitation in family size, is visible in what has been called "domestic feminism."[13] The family in this sense becomes a scene of social change, not only of conservative resistance to it. Nineteenth-century domestic confinement similarly frames the intense female friendships attested in letters and diaries, which in turn become one resource for female literary practices.

Furthermore, the intensification of the domestic sphere paradoxically also became the basis for involvement in activities beyond it. Even as the separation of spheres heightened gender-group identification and asserted limits on what was proper for women, it also militated against such strict boundaries, serving as a ground from which women could pursue worldly careers. There was, so to speak, a public side to domesticity, enacted through the extensive participation of nineteenth-century American women in societies and associations devoted to a wide range of social and political goals, including mission work, poor relief, hospital service, education, temperance, and, at the more radical extreme, abolition and legal reforms for the rights of women. These women's organizations marked a penetration into areas of public life from which women were ostensibly debarred. Besides setting up often elaborate business administration, including fund-raising, wages, incorporation, and distribution of benefits, the women "volunteers" also engaged in direct political activity, such as lobbying, petitioning, and financing and contributing to campaigns.[14]

These economic and political activities were justified as extensions, not revisions, of acceptable gender roles. Women were not so much liberated from the domestic sphere as they were enabled to enter social territories seen to derive in it. Social and political activities were viewed not as assaulting the whole (gendered) distinction of public/private, but rather as based within it. New ventures and rights were viewed as extensions of the traditional domestic roles of wife and mother and not alternatives to them. The achievement of new economic roles, the rise in women's education, as well as the increasingly public social roles associated with various reform projects were seen as based in, and applications of, home values.[15] Female education was justified as enabling women to educate children and to provide their husbands with more fit companions.[16] Social action was directed toward improving the material and moral conditions of the poor, immigrant groups, orphans, the ill, and perhaps above all, the men: agitation against drink, prostitution, and gambling included attacks on the saloon, not only as the site of these nefarious activities but as a man's world away from, and threatening to, his domestic obligations.

Women could present these social programs as intended to safe-guard the home against evil, even if doing so led out of the home and into the world. It accorded, moreover, with feminine images of nurturing self-sacrifice and moral purity, even as it expressed social values women actively upheld. The essentially conservative element in reform projects can be measured by their popularity compared to more radical feminist goals such as the suffrage, which posed a much greater threat to the separate spheres by implicitly defining women as individuals rather than as members of a household. Abolition, too, was a less popular cause than temperance, and was often justified in the name of the destructive effects of slavery on the family.[17] Yet many other women's activities cannot be described as domestic extensions. Prison reform, Indian rights, urban planning of parks and sanitation, libraries, and women's suffrage do not resemble, or extend, activities performed at home.

Moreover, even if education, economic rights, and social reform began as extensions of the domestic sphere, they nevertheless insti-tuted changes often unforeseen in their beginnings. Such tensions are exemplified in a figure such as Catherine Beecher. Beecher was a devoted advocate of female education, health, dress, and domestic economy—all expressions of the home as a private domain of vir-tue removed from and safeguarding the marketplace. Beecher thus saw domestic identity as the basis for a special role for women. Yet her work finally exceeded and helped to unravel the separate spheres as defining feminine possibilities. By strengthening female identity, insisting on the need for and right to education and remuneration, and establishing the authority of women over issues before given to men, even if only within the home, Beecher ultimately challenged the perimeters of the domicile and the domestic restraints on female authority. As her father, Lyman Beecher, instructively complained, her public advocacy could only be at the cost of "that female delicacy, which is above all price." Thus, although attacked as conservative by contemporary feminist suffragists, Beecher has come to be seen as another avenue of development for women's rights.[18]

Another prominent conservative of the woman's sphere who still contributed to breaching its boundaries was Sarah J. Hale. Author of the unruly "Mary Had a Little Lamb," Hale was the editor of the wildly successful magazine, *Godey's Lady's Book*. Conservative val-ues helped promote her popularity, but they also became her ground for support of female education, property rights, athletic prowess, and moral power.[19] In the advice book she published in 1862, she promotes women's "healthy, innocent sports" against a "premature ladyism." Inventing the term "Domestic Science," she urged a professionalism in women's undertakings with a concomitant investment in education, including advocating female admission to medicine; not on the basis of personal advancement, however, but as "daughters of the Republic" who should be able to serve the "public weal."[20]

Hale ultimately endorses the "indirect influence" by which women could effect events through moral suasion, although Hale herself (like Beecher) preferred the career of giving this advice to one of taking it. "Greatness is most perfect," she writes, "when it acts with the least reference to the self; power is most efficient when moving the will [of men] through the heart."[21] At issue is whether indirect influence, like other paradoxes of the woman's sphere as at once women's base and confinement, was ultimately socially transforming or a further entrenchment of female limitation.[22] Does indirect influence, at a remove from direct economic or political intervention, trade off more power than it gains? Restricting women's effective power, even rhetorically, to a moral, interior, and private appeal rather than to concerted, public, and organized pressure may only reaffirm the problems and divisions it sets out to overcome. Yet there is also a question of the definition of selfhood and its sources of value as self-referring or contributing to larger concerns.

Modesty not only respects, but negotiates and redefines the relations between public and private spheres, in ways that penetrate and question their very meanings, and not only for women. This is especially the case in the context of literary production. As a mode of public appearing, publishing was explicitly seen as an issue of modesty. The Puritan suspicion against publication, registered in the anonymous printing of Anne Bradstreet's poetry and her characteristic claim that it was done without her knowledge by her brother-in-law, persists centuries later (as one Puritan contemporary of Anne Bradstreet wrote in condemnation of his sister, "Your printing of a Book beyond the Custom of your Sex, doth rankly smell."[23]). Concealments of authorship under male pseudonyms or anonymity concede publishing to be immodest exposure.[24] As one lady author put it, she might have named herself "had not her modesty absolutely forbid it." *An Essay in Defense of the Female Sex* (1696) writes that nothing could "induce me to bring my name upon the public stage of the world." Publishing extends more general norms against women's speaking. Richard Allestree, whose *The Ladies Calling* was much reprinted, opens it with a section "Of Modesty" that warns against a young girl being "too forward and confident in her talk." Richard Brathwaite's *The English Gentlewoman* sums up: a woman's "modest disposition" urges the lady "to observe rather than discourse."[25]

Modesty here verges on silencing, an extreme that women writers by definition resist. Yet it is significant that women writers do not merely abandon modesty references, but make them the basis of their claims, incorporating them into complex literary personae, styles, motifs, and ventures. At issue is not hypocrisy—the especially Protestant concern with "true inner" modesty as opposed to a merely "external" appearance of it—on which some recent discussions have focused.[26] Modesty is, in both society and literature, above all a convention, whose display constitutes its very existence and measure. That is, modesty occurs as a mode of presentation, of appearing before the self and others, within a system of social or literary encoding. As such, distinctions between interiority and exteriority are much less relevant than are questions of conformity, manipulation, and transgression. Nor is reticence, if this is taken to mean invisibility and silence, exclusively at work.[27] Modesty is multiply constituted and cannot be reduced simply to self-erasure, submission, powerlessness, or, for that matter, sexual chastity. If chastity correlates in Victorian America with "passionlessness," modesty in contradistinction remains a sexual mode, in which partial concealment suggests partial exposure to erotic effect.[28] Similarly, the modesty *topos* as a literary event does not reduce to invisibility and submission, but rather works as a vehicle of assertion: deploying such public opportunity as was available to women within specific cultural norms. As has been claimed more generally of the "separate spheres," modesty must be multiply constructed: as an ideology imposed on women, but also as a culture created by women; as a repressive and limiting condition, but also as a scene of female values, activities, and identity.[29] Modesty retains these dual aspects and, especially in literature, contributes to a complex composition of female personae, style, images, and roles.

These contradictions of modesty are written large in the work of Sarah Hale's sometimes partner, Lydia Sigourney. Sigourney's biography reads like one of the plots so popular in nineteenth-century women's fiction. Born a poor girl in 1791 in Norwich, Connecticut, she was educated and sponsored by the patrician family her father worked for to publish, teach, and finally marry into the middle class. This last triumph, however, rather undermined the earlier ones, as her new husband did not approve her publishing. As she wrote upon marrying: "Thou too, my harp! and can it be / That I must bid adieu to thee?" But failure came to her aid. As with many women writers of the nineteenth century, the impetus to a literary career originated in and was justified by financial need. With business reversals, Sigourney began to provide for her family by publishing her works: first anonymously ("I wish," she dutifully writes, "to avoid notoriety"), but then with increasingly lucrative publicity.[30] With this plea, she cheerfully moved from anonymity to advertising, and through her career did not hesitate to fully exploit the commercial value of her authorship. Besides fantastic sales of her own books, Sigourney was paid top dollar for features given to magazines, eventually selling her name for use in Sarah J. Hale's *Lady's Godey's Book* until a quarrel ended this financial arrangement.[31] The tensions her work created in her marriage were finally resolved with her entry into a protracted and satisfactory widowhood, lovingly surrounded by former students and hailed as the Sweet Singer of Hartford until her death in 1865.

Sigourney's immense popularity during her lifetime did not prevent her poetry from going out of print and her reputation fading away after her death, a characteristic pattern in women's literary history. She has been dismissed as a sentimental and cloying writer ("valueless and trite" in the words of one recent critic) whose obsession with dead women approached necrophilia.[32] In her own time, too, Poe, whose own favored topic was also dead women, describes her as not a real poet but only a "domestic" authoress.[33] Sigourney's consolation poetry was presumably Mark Twain's model for Emmeline in *Huckleberry Finn*, the gentlewoman poet of obituary verse who died because the undertaker got there first. Others, however, have begun to urge Sigourney's recognition not only as significant within her historical context, but as herself an "historian" who "constructs a view of the public sphere and aggressively comments on it."[34] Sigourney in fact succeeded in becoming, with Longfellow, what to us seems almost an oxymoron: a best-seller poet. She is perhaps best placed in the context of the similarly popular women novelists also dismissed as sentimental—Hawthorne's mob of scribbling women.

Like these women novelists, Sigourney's is very much what has been called a "female world" with its attachments and anxieties.[35] The "dead babies" and other poems of mourning so often mocked today evoke this intimate female world, not least through a variety of threats to it in which death often acts as an image for other forms of separation, vulnerability, and conflict. Death functions as a complex trope for anxieties and commitments generated by changing social conditions both in general and specifically within nineteenth-century female culture. It is in the context of greater investment in children as birth rates declined, and a women's new role as educator,

that infant mourning intensifies.[36] But the death scenes also register ambivalence, conflict, and guilt over women's changing roles.
Courtship and marriage are not infrequently depicted as death scenes
(one recalls Dickinson's "Because I could not stop for Death") in
separating daughter from mother. "To an Absent Daughter" opens
with a funereal "Lamb, where dost thou rest?" which, it turns out
means the married daughter now lies "On stranger-bosoms" (i.e.,
her husband's). The "Forgotten Flowers to a Bride" die when they
arrive at the daughter's new home. In "The Bride," the mother ultimately commends the bride to the "ministry of Death." Death similarly shadows girls who leave home in pursuit of other activities, who
either die themselves, as in "On the Death of a Sister while Absent
at School," or guiltily miss the deaths of those at home, as in "The
Mourning Daughter."

These commemorative verses, as Nina Baym has argued, may
generally be seen in the aspect of public elegy and memorial.[37] But
Sigourney also wrote directly public poems without abandoning her
domestic resources. Her poems address and portray the world of
female activism. Sigourney's is in many ways the poetry of the Female
Benevolent Society. Her poems in "Appeal of the Blind." poems on
temperance, and other "Benevolence" poems praise women's causes
as the best investment, giving "the famished food, the prisoner liberty, light to the darkened mind, to the lost soul a place in heaven."
Her particular cause was Indian removal. She devoted tracts and
prose works, lyrics and a full epic *Pocahontas* to the plight of the
Indians. "Indian Names," a poem that has become anthologized,
names the Indian places that define, through an erasure she exposes,
American white settlement. Sigourney's intense lobbying efforts to
protect Indian rights and lands were, of course, unsuccessful. But the
extent to which she made poetry a vehicle for expressing such social
and political positions suggests a different sense of both women's and
poetry's place and purpose than the aesthetic that later refused her
recognition. As with her treatment of gender, she mainly represents
the Indian cause through scenes of family rupture.

Sigourney's work offers important documentary material for wom-
en's history, both in recording events and also in the feminized viewpoints that ordinary history has so often overlooked. She writes about
the nation's westward expansion, about war through the experiences
of women and the effects on family life. Poems such as "The Western
Emigrant" and "Death of the Emigrant" imagine the dislocations and
challenges of new settlement through tender conversations, illnesses,
and deaths within isolated families. Sigourney's Unionism pictures

the nation as a "Thriving Family," and she objects to factional strife as the "shame 'twould be to part / So fine a family." War, and the male attraction to it, is denounced as anti-family in "The Volunteer." Slavery, too, is represented as personal assault and anguish. Sigourney pictures the nation as one large family, with each historical concern or event figured as within a domestic scene. In the witty and elaborate "On the Admission of Michigan into the Union," each new state admitted to the union is figured as a "little sister" bringing her dowry and joining the original colonies, here depicted as maiden aunts in a way that displaces the masculinity of the Founding Fathers. Sigourney in this recalls the trend of women to feminize male organizations, founding, for instance, a female counterpart to the George Washington Union as the Martha Washington Union.[38] In this witty poem, the effect is less one of a Ladies' Auxiliary than of an inversion and even displacement of gender conventions. Here domesticity becomes the arena, not the retreat from politics, with national life at large reconceived through feminized images and relationships.

Sigourney's feminizations reenact ambivalences inscribed in the "separate spheres" themselves. On one hand, her feminized representations seem to retreat from political structures. Yet on the other, they establish a female domestic realm as the truly defining one, feminizing political and national life. Here, as elsewhere, conservative and progressive impulses intercross in complex ways. Sigourney was a writer of conduct books for young ladies, through which she not only supported but also helped to shape the woman's sphere. The popularity of her work, both in verse and prose, is due in part to its support of traditional female roles. Yet, she claims for them a special dignity and significance in opposition to the "World" as the masculine sphere that she critiques. A poem such as "To a Shred of Linen," although resolutely set within domestic life and its tasks, emerges as a historical portrait of the changes in women's roles, with the linen itself a trope for "the thread of discourse" of Sigourney's own poetic activity. Far from being another trivial moment in Sigourney's "gemmy" world in which "inanimate objects busy themselves with every sort of domestic activity,"[39] the poem is a highly crafted reflection on its own status, as this in turn represents wider women's issues. This includes a double-edged modesty. The poem's end commends the linen into the hands of a "worthier bard" than herself. This concession, which is also self-undoing, signals the self-consciousness and self-irony seen also in her wry comment that "If there is any kitchen in Parnassus, my muse has surely officiated there as a woman of all work, and an aproned writer."[40] Her poetry thus enacts the fundamental instability in the boundaries drawn by the ideology of the woman's sphere. The world it encloses increasingly speaks for a viewpoint, value system, and identity that spill from the privacy of the home into the public domain. But this also undermines the basic ideology of female against male, domestic against public divisions, if only in muted ways.

Modest self-representation in literature in effect renegotiates the boundaries and definitions of public and private spaces. Through it, concession frames assertion, disclaimer launches claim. Encompassing textual units both large and small, it amounts to a complex rhetorical mode. As such, it is a stance not just imposed but also deployed: a self-insisting claim that makes voluble its own reticence, an appropriation of demur strictures against writing in order to write, an assertive call to expose one's own concealment, and also, finally, a value genuinely informing female identity in ways that direct energy towards communal responsibility and public activity and away from purely self-interested self-assertion.[41] It is in this sense that Addison and Steele define modesty as "the virtue which makes Men prefer the Publick to their Private interest."[42]

Modesty emerges, then, both as a barrier to be negotiated and as an avenue to self-expression; as a challenge, but also a medium, for female representation. Nor is this entirely or always a matter of calculation and strategy. As part of nineteenth-century female self-definition, modest representations may genuinely assert feminine values often critical of the broader society, as part of an authentic voice for an historically constituted female identity. Instead of a stark opposition between submission and assertion in feminine identity, especially that of writers, modesty offers ways of negotiating between these two poles in critical redefinition of each of them.[43] Although modesty embodied society's restrictive pressures on women, it also came to serve as a mode for developing and expressing a complex feminine voice.

CHAPTER 2

EMILY DICKINSON AND
AMERICAN IDENTITY

Emily Dickinson seems, and in many ways is, the most private of poets. Her retreat into her father's house around the age of thirty cut her off from direct social intercourse with her surrounding world. Her texts similarly seem to draw a circle around themselves, in interrupted and apparently inconsistent expression. Even phrases or words are fragmented and isolated by her idiosyncratic dashes, which substitute for the integrating medium of punctuation. All of these almost compel an image of Dickinson's poetry as a closed and impervious, if also a provisional and fragmentary, world.

But Dickinson's work reflects and enacts the cultural concerns and challenges of the world in which she lived. Removal from public life is certainly suggested by her severe textual obliqueness, as well as by her riveting refusal either to appear in public or to allow the publication of her work. In another sense, however, Dickinson's texts are scenes of cultural crossroad, situated within and acting as an arena for the many profound transitions taking place around her. This includes gendered ones. Dickinson brings to a kind of consummation trends and contradictions within women's evolving social and literary positions. In her, modesty can be said to take on its intensest form; as at once fulfilled and transmuted. Dickinson in her reclusion inhabits the domestic sphere with a vengeance. This is not simply to overturn gendered norms. Yet at the same time she resisted other gender expectations, such as motherhood and marriage (although this was not such an anomaly: Dickinson's was generally a period of high single womanhood).[1] Arguments for Dickinson's reclusion as a "strategy" by which she gained the autonomy to write poetry against gender roles urging marriage and motherhood exaggerate on the side of strength.[2] Arguments describing her reclusion as an evasion born of frustration, anxiety, and madness make her into a mere victim and exaggerate on the side of weakness.[3] Dickinson's self-enclosure gained her some degree of control over her world, yet the very extremity of her withdrawal measures severe conflict with it.[4] Her reclusion is ultimately a highly contradictory act of explosive compliance: a challenge in the guise of extreme fulfillment of expected female cultural paradigms. It registers to an acute degree both her profound marking by social norms and her equally severe resistance to them.[5]

But Dickinson's conflictual relation to her culture extends beyond gender—or rather, extends gender into a wide terrain. Her identity crises may be said to reflect the nation's; the severe transformations surrounding her take specific formation in her work. This includes not only the political turmoil over slavery and its ultimate eruption in war, but also the radical religious transformations as pluralist denominationalism and secularizing trends challenged traditional authority and theology; and the broad social and cultural trends redefining the position of the self in the face of new economic configurations.

In Dickinson's work, these several cultural tensions and the strands of American identity that make them up emerge through characteristic figural systems that are at once mutually interwoven and yet also dissonant, discordant, and mutually contesting. These systems, which each also represent or engage an aspect of Dickinson's identity, can be distributed as: gender; religious concerns—which, contrary to many twentieth-century readings, remained a potent force from which she never completely divested herself; Dickinson's identity as a poet concerned with poetry, language, and art; and, perhaps surprisingly but persistently and pervasively, an American identity consisting of economic, political, and cultural images and references. These systems, or dimensions, are Dickinson's central engagements, defining her own identity and also her culture's. Her poetry can be seen as a battlefield of their clashing and conflicting impulses and commitments, with each text offering its own configuration and contest among them, as do poems against and with each other in the ongoing project of her work. Some poems focus on one concern, others on another. Dickinson's most powerful and accomplished texts bring all these dimensions to bear on each other.

But this is not to say that Dickinson offers a vision that creates correlations among these several dimensions of experience. Her poetry recalls, but ultimately diverges from, religious and literary traditions of metaphorical analogue and correspondence, in which different spheres are brought into correlation with each other through types, metaphors, and conceits. Instead, it is Dickinson's peculiar genius to assemble but then open fissures and inconsistencies between elements, rather than reveal sudden or harmonious links between them. Dickinson's are highly structured texts of extreme density. A poem or group of poems will propose a number of figural systems on a number of different levels. These invite or promise a complex orchestration of the different figures deployed. The texts seem to set up elaborate metaphorical equivalences, reminiscent of the intercrossing figural levels of Renaissance metaphysical poetry. Different levels of experience seem to be images or metaphors for each other, to represent each other in an architectonic structure. However, close attention to Dickinson's language often discloses that the figural levels do not fully correlate with one another. A process of what might be called figural slippage, or "mismatch," instead occurs. On the one hand, Dickinson's poems seem to establish a structure that brings their multiple levels into correlation. She gathers into her texts different engagements, seeming to promise they will serve as figural correlatives for each other.[6] But instead, through ambivalent or contradictory representations they come into collision in ways that question or undermine their full correspondence. The promise of systematic, tight, even highly ornate correspondences is stymied. What is in fact experienced is a resistance to just such alignments. Figural correlation becomes figural slippage.

Dickinson's characteristic textual conduct works toward this resistance or defeat of analogical figures, even while invoking them. Her interrupted syntax, off rhymes, dashes, and punning words whose meanings point in disparate directions work to fracture rather than convene the many fields and areas her work assembles. This is one reason that reading Dickinson involves severe textual challenge. Patterns that seem promised instead come apart, so that texts often seem to work backward, undoing whatever designs they seemed to have offered. Dickinson's texts seem to both say and unsay; claim and disclaim; desire and decline; offer and retract; assert and deny; defend and attack; gain and lose; define and circumvent definition.[7] Different options seem to demand exclusive choices and sacrifices, often painfully, and almost always at great cost.

This textual multiplicity and contradiction, however, is not a detached indeterminacy or open-ended ambiguity, as is sometimes claimed.[8] It deploys and brings into mutual confrontation personal and cultural forces that remain deeply at stake for Dickinson. Her positions remain irreconcilable. Hers is not a poetry of conversion and redemption, where negative experiences characteristically become justified and transformed into positive ones, although this can happen. Nor is the artwork or language itself typically proposed as site of resolution and deliverance.[9] Nor is she content with open indeterminate possibilities. Dickinson's instead is a poetry of disputation. While some texts do offer moments of ecstatic fulfillment, these remain in counter tension against the many that do not. These contradictory stances in Dickinson's work are by no means merely random moments of changing mood or attitude.[10] Rather, they are moments in an ongoing critique that Dickinson never brings to completion. Suspicious of cultural claims, sensitive to cultural contradictions, Dickinson's work explores and exposes, challenges and contests. Opposing possibilities contend with each other with greater or lesser violence, and each imagined resolution is ultimately judged unsatisfactory.

Thus in Dickinson, figure clashes against figure, selfhood against selfhood, claim against claim. These conflicts are not merely private and idiosyncratic. They represent a cultural dissension whose components are often violently at odds with each other. One overriding element of such cultural contradiction is gender. Dickinson's poems offer a rich variety of feminine figures. There are female speakers and actors, female bodies, sexuality and dress, images and sites, activities and objects. Throughout there is also what can be called a feminized form of presentation and self-representation. This involves intentional obfuscation in Dickinson's textual practices. Her writing is conducted in profound self-concealment. Indirection is not necessarily female, but in Dickinson it evokes both reclusion and the modesty that so marks nineteenth-century female writing. These, however, expand into a powerful rhetoric of duplicity, entrapment, and assault. In some sense, modesty becomes Dickinson's pivotal trope. To hide, to be hidden, is central to both her life and work. But modesty is in Dickinson a trope of extreme complexity. It both concedes and contests female self-definition. In her work, its various claims and disclaimers become modes in which Dickinson confronts, re-appropriates, and contests cultural paradigms surrounding her.

Gender is therefore entangled in Dickinson's language at the most fundamental levels of textual imagery and conduct. This in turn underlines the role of language itself in forming cultural constructions, for gender but also other Dickinsonian concerns. She particularly shows how social ideologies are articulated through gendered ones, in alliance with religious and economic orders. Modesty remains a pivotal term in what Dickinson exposes as scenes of contest rather than legitimate hierarchies, with gender being one component in what proves to be a series of mutually sanctioned disciplinary structures. The poem "I Meant to have but Modest Needs" (J 476 / Fr 711), for example, makes modesty less a concession than a challenge and confrontation, exposing social subordinations as authorized by religious ones. The poem opens with the speaker apparently praying for "modest needs," asking to be granted "Content—and Heaven—/ Within my income—these could lie / And Life and I—keep even—." The seemingly modest request for "Content and Heaven" proves, however, to be an exposure of both, with the very rhetoric of plea launched as a form of attack rather than appeal to God. For what the speaker requests is "A Heaven not so large as Yours, But large enough—for me." Competition, not petition, is set into play, pursued in terms of an economic imagery that so pervasively recurs in Dickinson's work in only apparently tangential ways. The "modest needs" are described as "income." The prayer is a way of keeping accounts "even." Describing the spiritual in economic terms is a familiar rhetoric, perhaps especially in America. But in this text there is a question of whether "Content and Heaven" can "lie" in balance, or whether such a balance is a "lie." The poem's modest request becomes an assertive one for personal independence and earthly satisfaction, competing against, and displacing, a heavenly one. But this is denied her. "A Smile suffused Jehovah's face," but not in beneficent response. Instead of a benefactor, God appears as a swindler who the poet, now suspicious, learns not to trust.

A whole series of relationships are called into question in this text. The poet is female in her modesty to a male authority; childish in her appeal to a God; therefore filial to his parental role as Father and also economically vulnerable to his manipulations, figured as financial. But, as in the poem "I Never Lost as Much but Twice" (J 49 / Fr 39), where God is addressed as "Burglar! Banker—Father," God's different privileged roles confirm each other, and do so at her expense. The authorized structures of relationship within society, including familial, religious, and economic orders, all work against her. Indeed, she shows their claim to protect and serve those below them in the social chain of being as validating their authority to be a fiction. Theirs is not a benevolent hierarchical order distributing the good or goods, as Aristotle claimed hierarchy to be in the *Politics*. Instead it is a structure of domination. Dickinson shows that the alignment between economic, divine, familial, and male authorities is in fact a mode of complicity. And she doubts that her gendered place in these structures is just or benevolent. Power is seen to withhold, not to bestow, indeed to establish its dominance by withholding. The alignment of the masculine, the economic, and the divine is no system of mediated need, but a naked structure of control.

Modesty in this poem does not accede to the structure of power but rather is a mode of resisting it. If, as Dickinson puts it in another poem, Heaven is "Bashful," then she in turn can "Hide—too—from thee—" (J 703 / Fr 733). Her shyness is thus challenge and accusation. This is a modesty that resists even while adopting gender roles. And God and/as Father is only one of Dickinson's gendered opponents or counterparts. She also confronts powerful Husband/Lover figures. Dickinson's opus includes a cluster of "Wife" poems, all the more acute in that she speaks in them from a position firmly not her own. The figures of love, sexuality, and marriage have attracted more discussion than perhaps any others in Dickinson discourses. For decades critics have pursed the identity of the "Master" to whom Dickinson addressed three passionate letters found among her papers. In recent years, attention has turned to Dickinson's intense emotional attachment to Susan Gilbert Dickinson, with its questions of sexual identity.[11] But Dickinson's images of love are highly resistant to interpretation and cannot easily be resolved as romance of whatever kind or sentimental religion.[12] Love relationships perhaps especially remain embroiled in the social conventions that comprise them and the identity issues that they both define and threaten. Dickinson's emerges as a deep ambivalence by which she both pursues and evades a figure of love whose power she yearns toward even as she fears it will engulf her.[13]

One text from the group of "Wife" poems thus ambiguously declares that the "World—stands—solemner" since the speaking "I" in the poem was "wed," in that "A modesty—befits the soul" now undertaken in marriage (J 493 / Fr 280). But in the course of the poem modesty becomes increasingly suspect rather than sacred. The poem describes "A doubt—if it be fair—indeed—/ To wear that perfect—pearl." The opening declaration devolves into "doubt" in language that puns on "fair," as to both the beauty and justice of her condition. The woman herself seems to be reified as "pearl," a traditional image for purity, but which in the poem is described in language of possession and enclosure, as what "The Man—upon the Woman—binds—/ To clasp her soul—for all." It is as if the woman herself is clasped like a piece of jewelry. The "modesty" that "bears another's—name" comes to involve erasing her own.

Dickinson's work, as seen here, critiques the position of woman in a male authority structure. But this does not mean that she wishes to take up a male place to claim for herself. Readings of Dickinson as complaint that her gender restricted her or excluded her from male positions don't fully acknowledge the extent to which she puts such power structures into question. Dickinson is concerned with feminine restriction. In another "Wife" poem, she compares being "wife" to being "Czar—I'm "Woman" now—/ It's safer so –" (J 199 / Fr 225). But "Czar" is not a very good image for wife. Male, Russian, and royal, it is quite unlike a female, subordinate, and American wife. What the false comparison underlines is the feminine paradox that the apparent fulfillment of one's nature and social position as "Woman" is also the moment of losing one's own authority and, under coverture, even legal identity to a husband's as wife. Figuring female authority is itself an almost paradoxical undertaking within Dickinson's cultural arrangements.

That women are not self-governing is cause for complaint and protest. Yet Dickinson's work also points to problematic aspects of the conception of independence, autonomy, and self-determination as this was emerging in America as a male model that carries with it isolation. Dickinson's poems are full of declarations of self-reliance, recalling not only Emerson, but also a whole discourse of individualism central to American culture. But in Dickinson autonomous selfhood comes with hidden costs. Texts that seem to assert autonomous power and sufficiency almost always take strange twists that rebound on their claims. Dickinson texts do sometimes show enclosure to open into infinity and renunciation to lead to fulfillment or transcendence. But these are structures that overall Dickinson treats as very problematic. Dickinson similarly treats autonomous selfhood in ways that implicate it as gendered, as well as in terms of ideological commitments particularly American.

It is very tempting to see Dickinson's retreat into the self as accession to power, converting limitation into expansion, intensity into extension, and constrictive circles into infinite circumferences. In a number of poems, Dickinson does this. The model of retreat/expansion is one she would have liked to accomplish. Yet what occurs most often in her texts is the collapse back to retraction rather than its conversion to transcendent wholeness. "The Soul selects her own Society," but "Then—shuts the Door—" to find itself in something like a prison, with "the Valves of her attention" closed, deathlike, "Like Stone" (J 303 / Fr 409). If "A Prison gets to be a friend," it does so not by opening into expansive transfiguration, but by its "narrow Round" exchanging "Hope—for something passiver." "Liberty" in this poem, far from being achieved, is "Avoided—like a Dream" (J 652 / Fr 456). If "The Soul unto itself/ Is an imperial friend," it is equally "the most agonizing Spy— / An Enemy—could send" (J 683 / Fr 579). The "chamber" of the self is "Haunted," a frightening self-enclosure concealing "Ourself—behind Ourself" in multiplying self-fragmentation, not unity (J 670 / Fr 407). The "Consciousness that is aware / Of Neighbors and the Sun" is a Soul hunted, "condemned to be—/ attended by a single Hound / Its own identity" (J 822 / Fr 817).

In such texts Dickinson gestures toward a release she fails to attain. But the reader falls into her trap. We see "Renunciation" as "Virtue" rather than as "piercing," in a poem whose syntax and structure makes its correlations and contrasts, gains and costs, almost impossible to distinguish (J745 / Fr 782). Our stubborn American presuppositions direct us to see self-sufficiency as the ideal we should strive for.[14] Nor is Dickinson's own exclusion from autonomous independence as female her only objection. Rather, her gender may allow her a critical stance on ideologies of the self that dissociate it from social, cultural, or religious commitments that in other ways are constitutive of identity and, while on one level limit the self, on others extend it beyond its own boundaries. The burden of self-sufficiency, as Dickinson shows, can be crushing.

Emerson, whose *Essays, Second Series* (1844) Dickinson read in 1850, uses specifically gendered language in his imagery of self-reliance.[15] In "Self-Reliance," he urges that a "true man belongs to no other time or place, but is at the center of things." "Every true man is a cause, a country, an age; requires infinite spaces and numbers and time fully to accomplish his design." It is the "life of man" that Emerson describes as "a self-evolving circle." But Emerson ignores, or accepts, the implications of its "rush[ing] on all sides outwards to new and larger circles," whose final term is to press "onward to the impersonal and illimitable" ("Circles"). This is a destabilizing vision that abandons prior ties and commitments. It is, as Joyce Appleby remarks, a singularly male vision, one which has founded the American ideology of liberal individualism:

> Obviously the liberal hero is male. Less obviously liberalism relied on gender differences to preserve the purity of its ideal type. Dependency, lack of ambition, attachment to place and person—these qualities were stripped from the masculine carrier of inalienable rights and conferred upon women...This allowed the unsentimental, self-improving, restlessly ambitious, free, and independent man to hold sway as a universal hero.[16]

In Emerson, it is the "true man" who is at the center of things; the "life of man" that rushes on all sides outwards. And if, as he adds, the "only sin is limitation," it is a peculiarly female sin: by social custom, religious stricture, education, or legal rule. This applies to Dickinson, who, unlike Emerson's Self-Reliant calling to "shun father and mother," remains, for all her solitude, profoundly enmeshed in family life, in a personal network of friendships and in the domestic duties of cooking, baking, and sewing. "God," she wrote in one letter," keep me from what they call households" (L 36); but He did not. Yet Dickinson also writes out of the strength of her ties, which she holds precious. It is her protest against their rupture that leads to many of her accusations against God, who, she felt, could have arranged matters differently if He had so chosen rather than, as she describes it in one poem, "Proceed—inserting Here—a Sun—/ There—leaving out a Man –" (J 724 / Fr 747). Emersonian, liberal notions of autonomous selfhood contrast not only against female social realities and roles, but may also run counter to fundamental conditions in the world, fundamental needs of society, fundamental needs of the self itself.

Dickinson's poetry of selfhood, especially her use of circular imagery that recalls Emerson's, calls into question his shape and boundaries of the self, and does so in particularly feminized ways. The circle of selfhood unravels in "I felt a Cleaving in my Mind" in imagery of mismatched patchwork, where Dickinson tries to rejoin pieces of her self "Seam by Seam—But could not make them fit –" (J 937 / Fr 867). Her sewing of poems into fascicle booklets connects her domestic to her poetic arts. Indeed, the dashes that at once mediate and disrupt her flow of syntax suggest the sewing thread on which she strings her words, yet in doing so dramatizes the fragile connections they weave.[17]

There are in Dickinson apparently ecstatic poems, at times associated with what she calls "Circumference." It is, for example, "Out upon Circumference" that she ventures when she sets out "alone" on a cosmic "Speck of Ball...Beyond the Dip of Bell" (J 378 / Fr 633). Emerson, in his essay on "Circles," speaks of "dislocations which apprise us that this surface [of nature as concentric circles] is not fixed, but sliding." But he presents the sudden "rushing from the center to the verge" as inspiriting and expansive. Dickinson here, too, ventures "Out upon Circumference," or, as she writes in a similar poem, "beyond the estimate / Of Envy, or of Men—" out "among Circumference" (J 798 / Fr 853). But to be "Beyond the Dip of Bell" is in Dickinson's poem as alarming as it is exhilarating. She describes the "Heavens" she verges into as "stitched," as if in pieces, feeling its "Columns close" in threatening claustrophobia. Indeed, the poem opens: "I saw no Way." There is as much loss of orientation as ecstatic release. Here as generally Dickinson and Emerson stand in something like inverse ratio, where the skepticism that is muted or suppressed in Emerson emerges in Dickinson as her central tone. "I saw no Way" associates the adventure of circumference with cataclysmic imagery of worldly dissolution. Emersonian circles become severed demi-spheres as the "Earth reversed her Hemispheres" and the universe slides away. The self "alone" is nothing more than a "speck upon a Ball," almost lost in an immense space that is does not contain or represent.

Emersonian circles take another severe gendered turn in "Severer Service of Myself" (J 786 / Fr 887). Dickinson in this poem undertakes the service to the dead that were women's to perform, but also to herself as she reels under the "Awful Vacuum" left by death. She is left with "Wheels" in herself that do not match nature's, out of step and link with the cycles death has interrupted: "I worried Nature with my Wheels / When Hers had ceased to run—." Circles here are neither expansive nor inclusive. Dickinson finds not infinity but interrupted, dissociated moments. Here, retreat into the self is undertaken in painful response to a world that is beyond the self's control. It is called in the poem, as Dickinson's reclusion is often said to be, a "stratagem." But here it is not a successful one. "Affliction would not be appeased." The stratagem confirms the darkness rather than dispelling it. As to "Consciousness," it does not offer freedom, independence, or self-definition beyond mortal conditions, but is itself a malady: "No Drug for Consciousness—can be—/ Alternative to die." Death is both problem and self-defeating solution. Dickinson's self does not have easy access to an Emersonian universal being beyond individual limitation and tribulation. She instead questions this possibility. Her poems of selfhood propose an autonomy of the self by itself, without need and world. But they also enact a clash between such American, romantic, liberal self-definitions and the self as defined and conditioned through relationships and commitments beyond it. These are dramatized here in a female attendance on the dead, including a pun on masculine heir as inheriting property, which in the poem becomes feminine "Hair" of personal memento: "some dull comfort Those obtain / Who put a Head away / They knew the Hair to."

The sense of conditioned selfhood no doubt reflects in part Dickinson's exclusion, as female, from the liberal paradigm of self-fulfillment as one's highest possibility, along with the freedom to pursue it. These do not extend to her as a nineteenth-century woman. But she also questions this paradigm. Dickinson's poetry contests the

American model of self-reliance not only as gendered male, but also as incomplete, untrue to experience, and psychologically, metaphysically, and morally vulnerable. The power of her poems of selfhood reside not in the extent to which they fulfill the dream of American selfhood, but in their contention against this model whose fissures she exposes.

But Dickinson's concerns extend beyond the self. Her questions about death and suffering, about justice and divine order, are not her private ones alone. They belong to her wider community. It is, oddly, where poems are most personal in terms of suffering, that they are also most culturally engaged. For the problem of suffering is, in the Christian scheme, essentially the problem of history. Attempts to find religious justifications for violent, historical events would have been, in Dickinson's context, completely current. It is more than a coincidental curiosity that Dickinson began writing intensively, and wrote over half of her poems, during the American Civil War—a war that was interpreted urgently in its time in theological as well as political terms.[18] The Civil War reached levels of carnage before unknown, made possible both by new technologies and new strategies of total warfare in combination with profound ideological conflicts in American national claims and self-identity. To Dickinson, the war focused her need for interpretive transfiguration in order to put together a world that was breaking apart, quite literally, in American sectional strife and ideological warfare. The image of Dickinson as incarcerated in her room, cut off from the world raging around her, is highly distorted and may itself be gendered. Her father served as treasurer to Amherst College and Amherst civic leader. In 1838 he was elected as Representative to the General Court of Massachusetts (where he came to know Herman Melville's father-in-law, Judge Lemuel Shaw, who Dickinson retains in her quarrel with God in Poem 116: "Jove! Choose your counsel—/ I retain "Shaw.""). He was twice elected Massachusetts State Senator in 1842–1843; was a Whig delegate, and was then elected to Congress in 1852. Many of Dickinson's friends were influential and politically active journalists and editors.[19] These include Samuel Bowles, editor of the *Springfield Republican*, with its column through the war on *Piety and Patriotism*; Dr. Josiah Holland, editor of *Scribner's Magazine* and one of Lincoln's first biographers; and Thomas Wentworth Higginson, famous for pronouncing Dickinson unpublishable, but himself a radical Northerner, supporter of John Brown, activist in abolition and women's rights, and colonel of the first black regiment in the Union Army.

Dickinson's work makes numerous references to the war, both in letters and in poems. Some of these references are oblique, using martial imagery that belongs to religious as well as political contexts—although this nexus of theo-politics is the case not only in Dickinson's work but also in Civil War rhetoric linking the national conflagration to sin, purgation, and ultimately redemption.[20] The war was an intense scene of mission as well as military activity. Politicians called for fast days and churches organized intense prayer meetings for the war effort both in the North and South. Dickinson's famous letter to Thomas Wentworth Higginson, asking if her verse "breathed," was sent to him while he was posted to South Carolina as commander of the first Union black regiment, and in just such a national religious context: "I trust you may pass the limit of War, and though not reared to prayer—when service is had in Church, for Our Arms, I include yourself" (L 280). Civil War rhetoric resonated with calls to holy war and religious drama. Dickinson's father himself wrote a plea in 1855: "By the help of Almighty God, not another inch of our soil heretofore consecrated to freedom, shall hereafter be polluted by the advancing tread of slavery."[21] Even Lincoln, with his exquisite restraint, appealed for public religious rituals throughout the war, beseeching Union victories as "the gracious gifts of the most high God, who, while dealing with us in anger for our sins, hath nevertheless remembered mercy" (October 3, 1863).[22]

America's women played their own significant role in the war effort, organizing supplies and providing health care. Dickinson refers to this womanly provisioning, but to contrast it with her own work: "I shall have no winter this year—on account of the soldiers— Since I cannot weave Blankets, or Boots—I thought it best to omit the season—Shall present a "Memorial" to God—when the Maples turn" (L 235). Dickinson's "Memorial," however, is deeply equivocal. The war seemed to her a more intensive image of the disorder, violence, and threatened collapse of meaning in the world. As she wrote to her Norcross cousins after learning of the death of Frazer Stearns from Amherst: "I wish 'twas plainer, the anguish in this world. I wish one could be sure the suffering had a loving side" (L 263). In 1864 she writes the cousins again: "Sorrow seems more general than it did, and not the estate of a few persons, since the war began; and if the anguish of others helped with one's own, now would be many medicines (L 298). The war represented a further tearing in the fabric of a world that in any case seemed to Dickinson rent by contradictions and resistant to interpretation.

Dickinson's verse tracks this encounter between her imagination and an historical reality she felt deeply resistant to. Doubts as to inherited religious accounts were exacerbated by war. One poem of appeal, accusation, and disappointment—"At least—to pray—is left—is left"—concludes by turning to Christ in a gesture at once imploring and accusatory: "Thou settest Earthquake in the South / And Maelstrom, in the Sea . . . Hast thou no Arm for Me?" (J 502 / Fr 377). The "earthquake" in the "South" surely has political-geographic significance, and if Christ is responsible for it, then what "Arm" can he offer her? There are in Dickinson many such subtle political references: canny electoral puns, as when the "Soul selects her own society" as if by a "Majority" chosen "from an ample nation."(J 303 / Fr 409). In another poem, the "Heart" is the "Capital of the Mind" while "The Mind is a single State." In this body politic, "One" is a "Population / Numerous enough" for the "ecstatic Nation" of the "self" (J 1354 / Fr 1381). Denying distinctions of "Color—Caste—Denomination," death works democratically (J 970 / Fr 836), treating "The Beggar and his Queen" with full equality (J 1256 / Fr 1214).

As to the war, it enters Dickinson's texts in many ways: as brief moments of imagery, as a general structure; as elegies for the particular dead, as religious confrontation, as interior battles. It would be difficult to compile an exhaustive list.[23] Natural events are described in martial imagery, as when a storm effects a "Massacre of Air" against "martial Trees" whose "Armies are no more" (J 1471 / Fr 1505). Sunsets appear as "Whole Gulfs—of Red, and Fleets—of Red—and Crews—of solid Blood" (J 658 / Fr 468), or like war uniforms, as "A slash of Blue—/ A sweep of Gray" speckled with "scarlet patches" (J 204Fr 233). Conversely, soldiers "drop like flakes" or "Like Petals from a Rose" (J 409 / Fr 545), comparing warfare to natural events thus rendered traumatic. Or war is interiorized, as a "Battle fought between the Soul / And No Man" (J 595 / Fr 507), a "Campaign inscrutable / Of the Interior" (J 1188 / Fr 1230), a soul "Garrisoned . . . In the Front of Trouble" (J 1243 / 1196). To "charge within the bosom / The Cavalry of Woe" is "gallanter" than "To fight aloud" (J 126 / Fr 138). Her own death is "one Battle more," "A Foe whom I have never seen / But oft has scanned me o'er" (J 1549 / Fr 1579).

Dickinson's opus includes a number of poems apparently written as specific war elegies. "When I was small, a Woman died" (J 596 / Fr 518) seems addressed in memory of Francis H. Dickinson, the first of Amherst's war dead. The largest number is (probably) connected with the death of Frazer Stearns, the son of the president of Amherst

College: "His big heart shot away by a 'minie ball'" (L 255). One, "Robbed by Death" (J 971 / Fr 838), describes dying in war as being "Robbed by Liberty," a contradiction within Liberty's core meaning of Lockean self-ownership and freedom (J 971 /Fr 838). "My Portion is Defeat Today" (J 639) imagines herself, woman though she is, on the battlefield among the bodies of the dead whose eyes show "scraps of Prayer." In "Victory comes late," (J 690 / Fr 195), the fact of victory does not justify or redeem the loss of life. Dickinson goes on to ask: "Was God so economical?" Invoking the biblical promise that God oversee the fates even of "Sparrows," Dickinson does so only to counter that this is an "Oath" he fails to keep, leaving the sparrows of "little [divine] Love" to "starve." Economic imagery here joins with biblical reference to question both divine mercy and justice. In "It feels a shame to be Alive / When Men so brave— are dead—," she similarly compares the lost "lives" to "Dollars" that must be piled up. In "He gave away his Life," the self expended in war is a "Gigantic Sum," which, granted its heroism, still "burst the Hearts" (J 567 / Fr 530).

The personal, the historical, and the religious infuse and contend with each other in Dickinson, but also in her culture, with a clash among them as to which claims priority on what terms. In the context of an increasingly commercial American society, Dickinson's rendering of redemptive history, construed through terms of sacrifice and mercy, in monetary terms, gives the economy of God, a standard theological concept, a problematic twist as parsimony. Dickinson's peculiar poetic territory is the relationship between these different theological, historical, and economic spheres. The promise of cultural analogy confronts inconsistencies and cracks between these realms of experience. Dickinson's is thus a constant effort to read her world according to the codes available to her, and the constant defeat of her attempt to do so. Her poems become conflictual scenes of promise and revocation, across a complex of cultural investments: in redemptive history, material prosperity, personal fulfillment.

The poem "Success is counted sweetest / By those who ne'er succeed" (J 67 / Fr 112) stages these conflicts between pattern and meaning as a war scene. As often occurs in her texts, Dickinson engages in balancing gain against lost. Yet as often occurs, what appears to come out even in fact shows a deficit. This text fails to convert negative into positive experience, despite invoking a structure for doing so. It may be that success counts sweeter for "those who ne'er succeed," but this is little comfort to them, the painfully acute consciousness of something denied them.

This failed balance between desire and fulfillment, hope and a defeat that sneakingly displaces realization, subtly substituting despair for contentment, is posed in the poem's first stanza in general terms. But it is striking that Dickinson then chooses military imagery to elaborate it. "Not one of all the purple Host" of victors know in fact what "Victory" is as does the one who is left on the battlefield defeated—dying –," for whom the "strains of triumph" remain "distant" and "agonized," but thereby all the more "clear." Although the poem has been dated to 1859, before the outbreak of the Civil War, aggressive and pugilist language was increasingly shrill throughout the final pre-war years. Here the gains of war, even in victory, slips through Dickinson's grasp, tragically defeating the patterns that promise to justify them. The perverse and self-defeating best that can be said of "Dying," as she writes in yet another war poem, is that it "annuls the power to kill" (J 358 / Fr 616). Even "Triumph" is embittered in view of the "finished Faces" of victor and vanquished alike, in a poem that issues a general cry against the blindness of time and the impossibility of binding its wounds through some appeal to grand schemes, providences, or retributions. "Could Prospect taste of Retrospect," she writes, "The tyrannies of Men / Were Tenderer—diviner." But past and future do not exist in any such integrated economy, at least not for humans—to divine the future, she implies in a bitter pun, is a privilege of divinity. And yet, the poem continues, even if we could see backwards, could know "Prospect" as "Retrospect," the suffering would still remain unredeemable. As the poem concludes: "A Bayonet's contrition / Is nothing to the Dead" (J 1227 / Fr 1212). Compensation cannot extend to those for whom it is intended. The circle of justification is broken, its pattern either fragmentary or irrelevant.

In "Success is counted sweetest," the imagery of victory and defeat is by no means exclusive to military battles. On the contrary, the poem evokes personal and spiritual, no less than historical experience, and the struggle to construe suffering into some meaningful and valid configuration extends to each and all of these levels. A further American sense in the poem lurks in the opening word, "Success." This dominant American value, increasingly becoming the measure of all others, had been privileged in the rhetoric of the Puritan fathers, with their notion of earthly calling as sign of spiritual election, and more and more explicitly in an evolving nineteenth-century entrepreneurial rhetoric of promise. Dickinson may intend, using a martial setting and male gender ("he"), something specifically masculine in this measuring of self against success, which is here "counted." A poem that closely follows it (J 68 / Fr 112) begins with a reference to "Ambition." Perhaps she intends a comparison between the competitive scene of success and warfare. But in any case, here there is no triumph to offset defeat; only a dying without restitution, a success measured by its utter failure to be achieved. This failure of justification is, in Dickinson generally as in this poem, "agonized," a painful agonistic contention between opposing claims. The military scene opens into wider tensions between pursuit of success and its costs; the gap between those who lose and those who gain; between those who are excluded and those who are triumphant in a culture where triumph, success, itself more and more is what "is counted," as if by number or economy, displacing any other sort of spiritual or cultural value. Economy, religion, gender, selfhood itself, work against each other in ongoing contention.

These conflicts in Dickinson's texts, as in her culture, ultimately reflect back into her poetic discourse, in its self-unraveling image systems, figural slippage, and its very language construction through syntactic slips, clashing terms, dashes and fragmentation. Her poetic thus constitutes not a formalist self-reflective aesthetic, but a register of her world.

CHAPTER 3

PUBLIC AND PRIVATE: DOUBLE STANDARDS

Nineteenth-century women's verse has long been assigned as poetry of the separate spheres. From its time of writing to its going out of print almost immediately upon the death of its authors, and through its gradual recovery by literary history, it has been largely seen as private and domestic, albeit with varying judgments. In the nineteenth century, regarding the poems as domestic and private made them acceptable, popular, diminutive, and safe. As with many other women's activities, women's writing could be consigned to the comforting and appropriate domain of the woman's sphere.

Yet even in this guise, the poems signaled women's entry into new areas before closed to them. Barriers had been gradually undermined, firstly in terms of gaining the literacy necessary to take one's place in literature, that is, being able to read at all, and then to gain sufficient access to cultural capital so as to be able to contribute to it. Such opportunity only arose to large extent because of the American Revolution, with the establishment—first in Philadelphia in 1787—of secondary education to women in the form of female seminaries. Such educational initiatives already entailed a political and civic dimension. If women were not yet permitted to vote and hold office, they nonetheless married and mothered male citizens who could do so.[1] Education became part of their republican participation, soon as teachers as well as mothers. Immediately, it gave to women the tools for literary endeavor, which is why the nineteenth century witnesses a woman's poetry movement of extent previously unknown.

What ensued was a veritable riot of circulation. Women's sphere in this way, at least as a perceived category, opened to women the avenue down which they could make their poetic way—not least to being acceptable to publishers.[2] As Rufus Griswold, the poetmaker (or, as in Poe's case, unmaker) of the period's literary respectability, warns in introducing his groundbreaking *Female Poets of America* (1848): "We are in danger of mistaking for the efflorescent energy of creative intelligence, that which is only the exuberance of personal 'feelings unemployed.'" In such manner was women's poetry promoted and dismissed.

Recent assessments, first for prose and then also for poetry, have begun to puncture the "narrow circle of domestic interests and duties" with which De Tocqueville described American women's lives. Domesticity, however, remains in many ways the model for approaching women's poetry, even in the expanded terms that have come to be applied to it. First, there has been a reevaluation of the fact of publication itself: an emergence into print that was enormously consequential, not only in publicizing women's words beyond the home but also in bringing, through print, public experience into the home. Here, however, "public" often has meant publication itself: the bringing to view, through print, of the private lives of women in the domestic sphere—"private woman" made visible on the "public stage" of print.[3] New analyses of sentimental writing, first in prose and now also in poetry, have reinterpreted domestic writing not as mere effusion of private emotion, but as an approach to pressing public matters.[4] The focus, however, largely remains on domestic representation, even if it is now seen in its complexity and variety, and acknowledges that all sentimental poetry was not simply complicitous with the women's sphere but also attempted to extend and even to critique it. Domesticity itself may have been incorporated into ideological projects such as American expansion, in what has been called "Manifest Domesticity."[5] Not all women's writing, however, was domestic, and not all domestic writing was complicitous politically.[6] In general, in the American context, conservative and progressive impulses are often inextricably intertwined and cannot be reduced to simple oppositions. Conservative intentions often prove unable to limit progressive outcomes, while radical impulses may oddly intercross with conservative values.

Debates about domestic writing in fact echo debates about the woman's sphere itself and indeed about different kinds of feminism. On the one hand, the nineteenth century witnessed transformations in women's status and activities, including their emergence into authorship. On the other, to the extent that women continued to understand themselves and to be understood by others within the terms of the separate spheres, they betrayed the possibility of genuinely breaking out of these spheres into fuller public engagements and roles. This limit is seen to have prevented the triumph of a genuine feminism of equality, drawing instead on women's sense of difference that finally curtailed their possibilities of advancement. Instead of claiming rights, women pledged themselves to duties seen to hem them into their domestic and private world.[7]

But the terms difference and equality, domestic and political, private and public set up stark oppositions that leave no exit. The terms themselves entrap. They reproduce rather than illuminate social distributions and their gendering as represented and addressed by women's writing. The very categories of "public" and "private" need themselves to be rethought across a variety of features and purposes, commitments and interests. Private and public prove to be ideological and indeed gendered terms. Nineteenth-century women and their poetry are regarded as private even when they address and engage social and political issues, which they do to a surprising degree.[8] A review of this women's poetry does not support the distinction between public and private that has largely governed analysis not only of women's writing, but of nineteenth-century women's history and political theorizing as well. This is not to question the historical fact that women have been assigned to the private domain in cultural and political discourse, indeed long before the nineteenth century. These are distinctions reaching far back in political and social history.[9] Moreover, nineteenth-century women themselves largely adopted the distinction, conceiving and describing their situation within its terms. Nevertheless, the poetry shows the public/private distinction to be highly unstable, open to revision and reconfiguration. It raises questions regarding just what is private, what is public, and how these are aligned as female and male in terms of social, political, economic, and civic distributions. Such areas in practice intercross in ways that do not correspond with the gendered opposition between male and female. Thus women's poetry, rather than programmatically fulfilling public/private distinctions, calls them, and their gendering, into question.

The domestic category ultimately covers only a portion of women's writing. Women were involved in a wide range of activisms, reflected in a range of poetic norms that only with difficulty can be characterized as domestic or private. Some of these resemble things women did at home; others do not. As women raised children at home, so they educated them in schools and orphanages; as they cared for the sick, so they organized hospitals and sanitation. Abolition, too, was partly based in sexual outrage and against the assault on families, as was moral reform and temperance. But these activisms, as well as those closer to domesticity, are hardly private. And other activities cannot be called domestic, either geographically or substantively, such as the founding of libraries, urban planning, or prison reform, which do not take place in the home nor extend the activities conducted there. It is only when women pursue these activities that they are called private; when men do them they are public. That is, it is not that women do private things; it is that what women do is seen as private. The terms are tautological.

Rather than observing divisions of private and public, the activities of women—and strikingly, their writing—address and reflect a different line of demarcation. The nineteenth century is one of wrenching transformation. A largely agrarian culture became urban and industrial, with new forms of transportation and communication. Material interests and economic individualism had been present from the first American venture: the Pilgrims were not only religious utopians but also holders in joint stock companies. But it is in the nineteenth century that economic interests become increasingly dominant, challenging and pushing to the side both the religious culture that had been fundamental to America's founding and the civic, republican political culture that had flourished in and fueled the country's Revolution. The division of private and public against the background of these social, political, and economic markers is not domestic as against non-domestic—with the former female and the latter male—but rather commercial interest as private, as against community values—with the former male and the latter increasingly in the hands of women. Women in the nineteenth century can be said to have inherited the civic virtue that had been a basis of revolutionary America.[10] Their sphere is not private-domestic, but civic-communal; and not only as sentimental representations, but as public forms.[11]

This redrawn map of social alignment is attested in the wide variety of poetic ventures undertaken by women in the nineteenth century. These include documentary poems depicting historical trends and events, such as westward expansion and war, often from a woman's viewpoint otherwise difficult to access. Poetry here, with other literary forms, provides rare historical material. There are also poems that are directly political, social, religious, and prophetic concerning the vision of America. Women were neither professors nor journalists, neither ministers nor politicians, nor lawyers nor judges. Literature remained their major form of public discourse. Within this poetic conduct, the categories of private domesticity and sentimental verse are therefore limited, even as a description of women's poetry. They are also problematic in reproducing the very terms they seek to analyze, continuing to project a division into private and public life that is already gendered. The concerns of women's verse instead can be approached as critical regarding commercial, private self-interest as against contribution to civic life and the common good. Women's writing in fact emerges as one of the core voices critiquing the American pursuit of material prosperity to the exclusion of other values and commitments.

The division between private interest and public interest—whether in domestic or nondomestic settings—emerges under many guises. In her "A Loyal Woman's No," Lucy Larcom, who worked at the experimental Lowell Mill that tried to accommodate domesticity to factory work, gives voice to a woman taking her own political stance in opposition to her suitor's and the domesticity he offers:

> Not yours, because, in this the nation's need,
> You stoop to bend her losses to your gain,
> And do not feel the meanness of your deed;—
> I touch no palm defiled with such a stain!

The speaker disapproves not only of her suitor's lack of commitment to the Northern cause but also of his placing his own self-interest before the Union's. This is a poem at once political and historical, but it reads through distinctive definitions of both selfhood and America that are also interestingly gendered. It is the man who pursues private interest against the woman's political dedication. Such a split in values and gender emerges in poems that offer documentary windows into westward expansion from the woman's viewpoint. In Alice Cary's (1820–1871) "Growing Rich," the man's pleasure in his prosperity is not shared by his pioneer wife, who not only mourns her lost attachments to the family she has left behind but also does so in the framework of economic and social critique rather than sentimental terms: concern for her "brother Phil," who still works in the "coal pit," and "Molly," whose hand "was cut off in the mill." The cost of American production and expansion is recognized and portrayed. Alice Cary ("The West Country"), Frances Harper ("Going East") and Lydia Sigourney ("The Western Emigrant") all offer poems on the difficult lives of women on the western frontier. Poems of the city show "The Homeless" (Alice Cary) wandering "Alone in the populous city," or follow a "Charitable Visitor" (Julia Ward Howe) as she leaves her "city palace" to enter "a bewildering alley, with ashes and dust thrown out," populated by beaten children, drunken men, and hungry, angry wives. Sarah Piatt's angry, anti-religious, and anti-nostalgic repudiation of a former lover at his graveside sets his betrayal of the woman speaker against the historical backdrop of civil war ("the ghastly field where the fight had been that day") and also their own social-economic injustice: the man sings to a "woman in jewels and lace" while indifferent that "close to us, down in another street [are] children crying for bread and fire" ("Giving Back the Flower"). Helen Hunt Jackson's "The Money-Seekers" charts the way money has begun to define the American world through a series of inversions and oxymora in which gain really is a form of loss and material status proves unreal and shameful:

> What has he in this glorious world's domain?
> Unreckoned loss which he counts up for gain,
> Unreckoned shame, of which he feels no stain,
> Unreckoned dead he does not know where slain.

Just so, Ella Wheeler Wilcox's ironic "Hymn of the Republic" similarly attests: "I have seen the money-getters pass unheeding on the way…And I marveled, and I wondered, at the cold dull ear of greed."

Ella Wheeler Wilcox, born in Wisconsin and writing late in the century, first made her name through the scandal over her *Poems of Passion* (1883), which sold 60,000 copies after (or because of) being rejected by a publisher for obscenity. But Wilcox's work shows how sexuality itself faces not only inward to individual sensibility but also outward towards socio-cultural concerns. Sexuality in fact received wide treatment throughout the century: less in terms of a new freedom for women than of their betrayal, through seduction, ruined social status, and prostitution. That is, women throughout the century were concerned with sexuality as a site where the so-called private world of morality and the public world of economic system problematically collude. At issue is the double standard which, as Keith Thomas demonstrates, is deeply rooted in a long legal and economic history treating female chastity as "the property right of the woman's father or husband," safeguarding a male line of inheritance.[12] This battle against a double standard that restrains female but not male sexual behavior took specific form as social action in the social purity movements of the 1830s and then in moral reform movements that followed them. These campaigns were immediately directed against prostitution, which had reached new levels due to urbanization, immigration, and industrialization. As such, the reform movements retained a strong conservative element, trying to legislate sexual morality while continuing to assert the ideology of the separate spheres. They defined women as moral guardians and justified public intervention in the name of protecting the sanctity of the home. These campaigns were quite ineffective; their legislative successes, attempting to criminalize not the prostitutes but their patrons, were few and empty.[13] But they stage on the woman's body the complex intersections and conflicts between questions of individual liberty, social action, and gender; at once from conservative and radical positions. Moral reform attempted to alter women's sexual-economic status and played an important role in women's political emergence through the century, as an avenue for their participation in public discussion and legislative activities. It became a base for activism towards women's rights in employment, which would offer alternatives to prostitution for the destitute and desperate.

But most fundamentally, the reform movements, in raising questions about the sexual double standard also questioned the wider gendering of social powers that it expressed.[14] Sexual codes emerge not only as personal or "moral," but as a social and economic gendered status. And they raise questions concerning social and economic inequalities in American life, as these more and more betray public responsibility and the public good. In these senses, the double standard can stand not only for the divergent rules governing male and female sexual behavior, but also the increasing split between private and public life that took on gendered dimensions as moral concern as against increasingly dominant self-interested power.

The sexual double standard itself emerges as a recurrent topic in women's verse. The women poets explore both its moral, ideological, and economic implications, opposing not only the fallen woman against the fancy-free seducer, but also dependence against independence, and poverty against wealth. These poems dramatize seduction, betrayal, and prostitution, providing one striking arena for a critical attack on an exploitative society in the name of feminine values. Julia Ward Howe's "The Soul-Hunter" pictures a lurid haunter of the night, setting a "Devil's bait" for an as yet "sinless" maiden. In Howe's "Outside the Party," a girl hovers before the window, looking at "the fine gentleman, grand in his glory" who has left her with a baby "akin to him, shunned and foresaken." Alice Cary represents the double standard within the Gothic-balladic conventions she favors. Her "Spectre Woman" endlessly haunts the churchyard in grave clothes, mourning her seducer while she "bend[s] down fondly, but without a mother's pride / Over something in her bosom that her tresses can not hide." Frances Harper's "The Contrast" juxtaposes the "wrecked and ruined" girl whose fate is irremediable against the socially approved seducer:

> They scorned her for her sinning,
> Spoke harshly of her fall,
> Nor lent the hand of mercy
> To break her hated thrall

Christian charity is denied the girl. But "he, who sullied / Her once unspotted name" dances "Through the halls of wealth and fashion / In gaity and pride" with his new "fair and lovely bride." Harper pursues this nexus of seduction and sin into its consequences in prostitution in her poem, "A Double Standard." The poem's writing in the first person of the fallen girl is a strategy that might bring its middle-class readers into greater sympathy with the fallen speaker. The text is constructed as the girl's accusatory questions against her accusers. First oblivious that "Beneath his burning kiss / The serpent's wiles" lurked, she asks of her turn to prostitution:

> Can you blame me that my heart grew cold
> That the tempted, tempter turned;
> When he was feted and caressed
> And I was coldly spurned?

The sin here is society's, not the girl's.

Born free in Baltimore, Frances Harper was active in abolition and the Underground Railroad, and after the Civil War, freedman's education and women's rights. Her 1854 *Poems on Miscellaneous Subjects* were of a piece with these campaigns, going through twenty editions and selling 50,000 copies.[15] As in Frederick Douglass' famous oration, asking, "What to the Slave is the Fourth of July?" Harper shows the double meanings of American celebrations and rhetoric for slaves as opposed to free whites. Harper invokes slogans of the American self-image, showing how these fail and are betrayed in actual history. Slavery makes American freedom an oxymoron (a "proud country's shame") as the star-spangled "banner in mockery waves" over the fugitive mother, hunted as she flees ("Eliza Harris"). In a poem called "Free Labor," Harper makes free labor an exposé of its counterpart, slave labor, which grounds whole areas of American production as if: "no toiling slave / wept tears of hopeless anguish;" "no cry to God," "no stain of tears and blood." The "Eden" and "Zion" of American promise are smothered by "Slavery's scorching lava-tide" ("Lines") and vitiated by the right "to bind with galling chains the weak and poor" and "hunt the slave" ("The Dismissal of Tyng"). Harper picks up the language of American mission ("Build me a nation, said the Lord") but then shows it to be a scene of betrayal: "Men grasped the prize, grew proud and strong / and cursed the land with crime and wrong" ("Then and Now"). In her mouth, "Bury me in a Free Land" makes that American epithet ironic in what is actually the "land of slaves."

In Harper, the double standard encompasses slave and free, as well as male and female, in mutually implicating economics. As is common in anti-slavery verse, she portrays the horrors of slavery through its assault on the integrity of the family. Harper's "The Slave Auction" depicts young girls as "defenseless in their wretchedness," while "mothers stood with streaming eyes / And saw their dearest children sold." "The Slave Mother" opens with a "shriek" and a "heart breaking in despair," as her sold away "boy clings to her side." These sentimental images are, however, themselves radical in claiming for the slave the emotions and attachments that the slave system would deny. To be a chattel slave was by definition to be reduced to a status governed by economic forces. Harper's insistence on the private and personal, on feelings of sentiment and family devotion among slaves is already to deny their reduction to economy and property and to assert their status as cultural beings with human rights.[16]

Harper has been suspected of accommodating herself to genteel norms of the white middle class, in a conservative commitment to "inner virtue through cultivation of proper thoughts and feelings, proper sentiments, fine and pure, noble and tender, refined and correct, including self-restraint."[17] But Harper demonstrates the way conservative and radical commitments can intercross. As is strongly the case among African-American writers, Harper draws on religious norms and traditions as part of her critique of America and of American Christianity itself. America's failure to live by its supposed Christian values runs as a bass chord through many texts. "The Dismissal of Tyng" mocks a missionizing America that sends Bibles to far "heathen lands" while failing in its own Christian commitments. Nor are benevolent society women spared. "An Appeal to My Country Women" shows them to be more concerned with the exotic "sad-eyed Armenian" and "exile of Russia" than with slavery in their own nation.

The critique of American life as betraying its own principles is in various ways shared by conservative and radical women, as an issue where these two ends of the political spectrum meet. Ella Wheeler Wilcox, despite her early notoriety as sexually daring, has come to be suspected for her conventional marriage and her "continued ideal of renunciation and self-sacrifice."[18] She in fact does retain traditional paradigms of "Motherhood" and its "holiest purpose" with women in "Lord, Speak Again," specially appointed by God to represent Him, "to go forth throughout all time...And make my world what I would have it be." But this grants to women special authority (not to mention criticizing God for having fudged His job). And if woman are the moral agents, then what are men? This is a feminism that critiques America as increasingly empty of morality and community commitment; a society that reduces women, but also all Americans, to social exploitation and indifference. Social life is portrayed as increasingly betraying basic tenets of American norms. This betrayal was by no means the exclusive concern of women. It is no less central to works as different as *Walden* and *The Education of Henry Adams*. In women's poetry, however, it becomes specifically gendered. The separate spheres become spatial configurations for general bifurcations within American culture. A double standard opens not only between men and women, but also in the broad diversion of economic and political life from moral responsibility and communal commitments. Rather than proposing that women enter this man's world, Wilcox examines "The Cost" of doing so, in a poem of that title. There the woman leaves behind sentiment and domesticity, to enter, successfully, the man's world:

> She wept no more. By new ambition stirred
> Her ways led out, to regions strange and vast...
> Still on and up, from sphere to widening sphere,
> Till thorny paths bloomed with the rose of fame...
> She stood triumphant in that radiant hour,
> Man's mental equal, and competitor.

But the poem, instead of embracing the woman's economic transformation and success, runs up against its "cost": "From out the heart of her / Had gone love's motive power." The poem's economic title is not accidental. What the woman has earned is also the price she must pay, the reduction of self to monetary measure.

The mutual implication of economy, sexuality, woman's place, and American values is at the core of the expressly ideological poetry of Charlotte Perkins Gilman. Best known today for her story "The Yellow Wallpaper" and its painful exploration of domestic confinement as an imprisoning form of madness, Gilman in her own time was most famous for her tract, *Women and Economics*. There she traces the connections between gender roles, economics, and their broader social consequences, arguing that the current relationship between men and

women is an economic one where "woman's economic profit comes
through the power of sex-attraction." This makes the "open market of
vice" only relatively different from marriage, which is the "same economic relation made permanent, established by law, sanctioned and
sanctified by religion, covered with flowers and incense and all accumulated sentiment." This female economic dependence culminates in
"the full flower of the sexuo-economic relation—prostitution."[19] In
her poetry, Gilman treats this sexual double standard directly in the
poems "One Girl Of Many" and "Unmentionable," which address
the institution, and then evasion, of prostitution:

> And yet it is as common in our sight
> As dust or grass;
> Loathed by the lifted skirt, the tiptoe light,
> Of those who pass.

The separate spheres of home and work explode in Gilman's many
poems on household drudgery. Wider social histories in which home
is work are evoked in regard to women immigrants, a burgeoning
population through the century, who are:

> Exiled from home. No mother to take care
> That they work not too hard, grieve not too sore;...
>
> To toil for alien household gods she comes;
> A servant and a stranger in our lands,
> Homeless within our homes.

The distinction between public and private blurs when alienated work
is in the home, where the domestic servant is paradoxically "homeless"
in terms of interrelationships, regardless of domestic geography.

Gilman's central poetic technique is one of rhetorical play of voices.
She characteristically represents the dominant voices of society in
ways that expose and then undercut their positions. Or she represents
the suppressed, muted voices of women, at once giving expression to
their lives in a public poetic record and yet also recording the extent
to which they have internalized the views that dominate, subordinate,
and silence them. In Gilman's poem "Homes: A Sestina," the separate sphere itself speaks in its full rhetoric, with the "Homes" voicing
their complacent assignments. Regarding women, the homes say:

> And are we not the woman's perfect world,
> Prescribed by nature and ordained of God,

Beyond which she can have no right desires
No need for service other than in homes?

At the same time, men have no other need in life:

Than to go forth and labor in the world,
And struggle sore with other men therein?
Not to serve other men, nor yet his God,
But to maintain these comfortable homes?

The spheres, by way of their own rhetoric, are shown to split apart both society and each individual person. They are a reduction and betrayal of each, and destructive to the society as a whole. Society becomes bifurcated between lives sacrificed to others and lives self-ishly consumed—a configuration that is gendered but also economic. And Gilman's solutions are economic and social. Poems such as "Unsexed" and "Females" insist that only full participation by each gender in productive economic life can reform and transform men and women. Yet her goal remains social participation, not private gain. Her poem "Nationalism" pledges itself to a quintessentially Jeffersonian vision, urging individual participation in the republic. What America requires is

the sum of all our citizens,
Requires the product of our common toil...
Our liberty belongs to each of us;
The nation guarantees it; in return
We serve the nation, serving so ourselves.

Adrienne Rich in *Of Woman Born* speaks of a "womanly splitting of the self" between "the unfree woman, the martyr" as against a self-image that is "individuated and free."[20] But nineteenth-century womens' senses of self neither simply dismiss service as martyrdom, nor simply elevate pure individual freedom. For nineteenth-century women, as expressed in their writing, fundamental senses of identity entailed a connection to family, to community. These are commitments nineteenth-century women would want not only to retain but also to defend. Indeed, it is part of their critique of society that they see it as increasingly assaultive, in its hegemony of commercialism, on commu-nity concerns both within and outside the family. Their insistence on values of responsibility for and to others, as opposed to unmitigated competition between isolated individuals vying for economic gain, makes their self-definition in relation to others an attack against the evolving American industrial, urban, and political culture.

The result is often an ambivalence about their own ambitions, evident in recurrent poems devoted to this topic: Alice Carey's "Fame"; Adah Isaacs Menken's "Aspiration"; Henrietta Cordelia Ray's "Ambition" and "Aspiration"; Helen Hunt Jackson's "Opportunity"; Ella Wheeler Wilcox's "Opportunity" and "Individuality"; and Emma Lazarus's "Success." These poems remain torn between personal ambition and suspicion against it. But in this, the modesty that on one hand acts as a constraint on female aspiration on the other hand serves as an avenue of critique, and not simply against the social restriction of women. Modesty is not only a negative value, but also a positive one directed against developments of culture that women were among the first to recognize, deplore, and protest. Women's protests against the limits of their sphere did not necessarily mean endorsing the male "world" and wishing to enter it, in which ambition was fast becoming the defining and paramount value, pursued through unbridled competition, with its offshoots of corruption, exploitation, and impoverishment in American life.

Mary Wollstonecraft devoted one section of her *Vindication of the Rights of Woman* to "Modesty Comprehensively Considered and Not as a Sexual Virtue," which she intended as a refutation to advice-book rules of comportment. There, Wollstonecraft distinguishes modesty first from chastity, then from humility (which is a "kind of self-abasement"), then from bashfulness, timidity, innocence, and ignorance. Modesty instead represents for her "the reserve of reason," the ability to conceive "a great plan and tenaciously adhere to it, conscious of [one's] own strength," and, in sum: "a simplicity of character that leads us to form a just opinion of ourselves, equally distant from vanity or presumption, though by no means incompatible with a lofty consciousness of our own dignity."[21] Wollstoncraft here attempts to transform modesty from an emblem of female restriction to a powerful self-definition, which would oppose unrestrained self-assertion no less than self-abasement. At issue is no longer a specific and restrictive female virtue, but a general moral stance closely tied to what, in political history, may be called "civic virtue." Viewed from this angle, the social involvements, reform movements, charity work, and other social services undertaken by nineteenth-century women do not merely represent an extension of private, domestic roles into a public sphere. Instead, these activities can be seen as communal and indeed public work in the tradition of the disinterested civic virtue associated with America's revolutionary ideology.[22] It may be argued that it was nineteenth-century women who inherited this tradition, while men increasingly through the century came to pursue an economic interest that can properly be called private. The inheritance by women of civic virtue also signals, however, the relative devaluation of social and communal concerns in an America increasingly devoted to economic values and private material gain.

CHAPTER 4

GENTEEL RHETORIC, NORTH AND SOUTH

Mid-century women poets came from a wide range of social classes and groups: Eastern and Western, poor and privileged, ill- and well-educated within the terms available to them, and with ethnic, religious, and racial variation as well. Men poets of the same period form a narrower assembly: mostly Protestant, mostly middle class, mostly schooled, mostly Eastern and white. Each, moreover, took upon himself the possibility or desire to be what Emerson in "The Poet" called "representative": to speak for Americans and America, indeed to define who and what these are and mean. Particular to this task was to create a literature that would realize and equal what they saw, in the wake of the American Revolution, to be the promise of a new society in the New World.

This task began with the language itself. Noah Webster's attempt to invent an American English by codifying it through a dictionary, a reader, and the *Blue-Backed Speller*—which sold over a million copies by 1783—was consciously devoted to helping create an American identity. To him, "a national language" would act as a "band of national union," making his lexicons of American usage, spelling, and vocabulary an object "of vast political consequence" (*On Being American*, 101).[1] His work was nation building: he undertook to "throw his mite into the common treasure of patriotic exertions" in order "to promote the honour and prosperity of the confederated republics of America" (*OBA*, 25). To fulfill its destiny, the American continent would come to be "peopled with a hundred millions of men, all speaking the same language," able to "associate and converse together like children of the same family" (I, 19).[2] Europe remained divided by linguistic confusion, a "[c]ontinent inhabited by nations, whose knowledge and intercourse are embarrassed by differences of language." Americans, exactly in sharing a single language would not "consider ourselves as inhabitants of a particular state only, but as Americans" (*OBA*, 23–24, 43–44).

The New World, in fact, had gathered into its midst a wide range of languages: German in Pennsylvania, Dutch in New York, French in Canada and Louisiana, Spanish in the South and West, as well as the variety of African tribal and Native American languages. In this light, what is remarkable is that neither a sectional polyglot nor a patois emerged as linguistic result.[3] As President John Witherspoon of Princeton, who coined the term "Americanism," was pleased to observe, "moving frequently from place to place, [Americans] are not so liable to local peculiarities either in accent or phraseology. There is a greater difference in dialect between one county and another in Britain, than there is between one state and another in America."[4] Noah Webster made these linguistic bonds a political issue—"Our political harmony is therefore concerned in a uniformity of language"—as well as one of class: distinctions against British speech that alarmingly "make[s] a difference between the language of the higher and the common ranks" (*Dissertation*, 20, 24). Webster's *Speller, Reader*, and *Dictionary* offered for language what the proliferating nineteenth-century etiquette books promised for manners and class. Alongside a multitude of grammars, guides to correct speech, and the spelling bee—instituted by Webster as a national rite of public education—Webster opened to the American middle class the standard of speech that in Europe had been reserved for aristocrats and was acquired not in schools or books but in elite social contexts.

Yet, defining an American English was in many ways a quixotic project.[5] Despite Webster's efforts in his Dictionary "to dissolve the charm of veneration for foreign authorities which fascinates the mind of men in this country and holds them in the chains of illusion" (*OBA* 136), the American lexicon he offered in the end was hard to tell apart from the contemporary British one. American English remained a child of Britain, closely resembling its parent. Webster's call to independence in his *Dissertations on the English Language* (1789) no less conceded just how dependent Americans remained to their mother language: "Great Britain, whose children we are, and whose language we speak, should no longer be our standard; for the taste of her writers is already corrupted, and her language on the decline" (20).

These tensions of independence and dependence, inheritance and invention, sorely try the work of Henry Wadsworth Longfellow, the poet closest to Noah Webster's project. Longfellow set out to create a foundational American poetry. But in doing so, he equally registered America's contradictory relations to its cultural past, at once disclaiming and yet requiring one, and also its ambivalent relation to a cultural future, not least regarding the place of poetry itself within the emerging American cultural economy.

Albeit differently from Webster, Longfellow had a genius for languages. Born in Portland, Maine in 1807, Longfellow attended (with Hawthorne) the newly founded Bowdoin College, rather than the Harvard of his father and grandfather. At the age of nineteen, he was offered to take up Bowdoin's new Professorship in Modern Languages on the condition that he go to Europe to learn some. Longfellow spent the next three years (1826–29) in Europe, successfully acquiring Spanish, Italian, French, and German. A second visit (1835–36) added Dutch, Danish, Icelandic, Swedish, and some Finnish. Invited at last to Harvard in 1835 to become Professor of Modern Languages and Literature, he spent the next nineteen years teaching Romance languages and writing scholarly articles, as well as most of the textbooks he taught from, in the hope of introducing his students to European culture. His significant body of translations, written both while at Harvard and after his retirement, was in many ways devoted to the same end.[6]

But America remained a poor linguistic resource compared to the polyglot Europe Longfellow had experienced. "Nobody in this part of the world pretends to speak anything but English," he complained to a friend on returning to Maine, "and some might dispute them even that prerogative."[7] Longfellow's task, then, was to found an American culture that would accomplish a *translatio studii* from Europe westward. To Webster, British English is "ancient and foreign languages" that he warns against as substituting for "the improvement of one's own language" (*OBA* 84). But Longfellow set out to transpose, indeed to translate, the Old World, making it uniquely New.

Some viewed Longfellow's efforts with skepticism. To Henry James, Longfellow presented a "large, quiet, pleasant, easy solution" in which "American consciousness...could feel nothing but continuity and congruity with his European."[8] Poe made Longfellow the very maelstrom of an ongoing literary "war" to which he devoted page after page of accusation and denounced European elegance as a form of plagiarism. A kind of boring conventionalism haunts Longfellow's reputation, but in his own day he was wildly popular. Masterful in his craft, Longfellow offered virtuoso variations in metrical, stanzaic, and generic forms that reflected a wide range of European resources while making them available to his American audience.[9] His poetry could fulfill his readers' expectations; remaining readily assimilable, while also extending and educating their literary experience.

But this attempt to assimilate English and Continental models also prevented Longfellow from breaking radical American ground, inscribing the tension between new invention and old inheritance that he hoped to overcome. He had committed himself to the use of American materials—landscape, climate, customs—as what would define an American literature. In "Our Native Writers," he urges an American writing that "hallows every scene, renders every spot classical," so that "every rock shall become a chronicle of storied allusion and the tomb of the Indian prophet be as hallowed as the sepulchres of ancient kings." But this is a problematic project. America does not have a history embedded in landscape such as England might, where every hillock, every scene has a communal memory—at least, not for English Americans.[10] The historical past evoked in Longfellow's "tomb of the Indian prophet" is neither his nor his ethnic compatriots' but that of the Native Americans the English were in the process of displacing. Claiming it as their own involves an appropriative sleight of hand, indeed a form of theft.

The Song of Hiawatha, embodying Longfellow's dream of a great American epic, in fact also exposes its questionable basis. Written in Finnish tetrameter, it puts into European metric a lexicon gleaned from notes on the Ojibwa Indian language made by Schoolcraft and Tanner as part of the project of Indian removal. Longfellow's translation of Indian words into English forms attests less to an authentic American language than the difficulty of achieving one. This is the case in much Longfellow poetry: drawing strongly on tradition, he exposes discontinuities as much as continuities between America and cultural pasts. *Hiawatha*, in fact, is not a living testament to Indian culture, but an elegy to it. Indian language is not reborn in white American language, but rather buried in it. The central canto on "Picture Writing" presents Hiawatha's gift of writing to his people as the ultimate, but also the final, act in his role as culture hero.

> In those days said Hiawatha,
> "Lo! how all things fade and perish! . . .
> Wise men speak; their words of wisdom
> Perish in the ears that hear them,

Do not reach the generations
That, as yet unborn, are waiting
In the great, mysterious darkness
Of the speechless days that shall be!
"On the grave-posts of our fathers
Are no signs, no figures painted;
Who are in those graves we know not...
And they painted on the grave-posts
On the graves yet unforgotten,
Each his own ancestral Totem...
That the chief who bore the symbol
Lay beneath in dust and ashes. (XIV)

Hiawatha introduces the picture writing lest the "words of wisdom" perish and be lost to "unborn generations." The painted signs are on graves "yet unforgotten," but, as Longfellow knows, are about to be through the encroachments of white Europeans. In fact what the verse inscribes is a future of "speechless days that shall be." The "dust and ashes" stand for Indian culture itself. This is the course traced by the poem, whose natives are shown to graciously vanish before the advance of the white man. Writing here commemorates a dead past rather than transmitting it. It is not initiation but epitaph. What it marks is not the continuation, but the passing away of a culture.

This image of dying language is surprisingly persistent for a poet supposedly enacting the birth of American literature. Indeed, dead language comes to be a Longfellow trope for American poetry itself. Longfellow's interest in *Hiawatha* is less in the actual plight of the Indians (although he did once meet one in Harvard Yard) than in Indian language and lore as an anxious figure for American culture itself. His equally popular "The Jewish Cemetery at Newport" (1858) similarly features Hebrew—not out of any interest in live Jews (although Newport was the site of an early Jewish community), but as an ambivalent figure for the survival of literary culture in America at all. Even the poem's homage to America as refuge for the persecuted is registered in the epitaphs of the cemetery as buried, not as part of and contributing to a live American culture. "These Hebrews in their graves" are "silent beside the never-silent waves"; their "rest" a striking contrast against the sea's "moving up and down"—a recurring image in Longfellow for restlessness ultimately idle rather than purposive. The image of "Exodus to America" becomes for the Hebrews a "long mysterious Exodus of Death." Yes, these people with "strange names" came to America to escape European "persecution, merciless and blind," but their journey was also to their own oblivion. The poem ends with a declared finality:

> But ah! what once has been shall be no more!
> The groaning earth in travail and in pain
> Brings forth its races, but does not restore,
> And the dead nations never rise again.

Emma Lazarus, in protest against this ending, tried later in the century to rewrite the poem as a persisting American-Jewish history. But Jews, like Indians, are present in Longfellow's poem not as an ethnic group but as another figure for cultural pasts that America, instead of transposing, buries. And just as in *Hiawatha*, where language is made into an image not of transmission but of cultural death, so here Hebrew is:

> No Psalms of David now the silence break,
> No Rabbi reads the ancient Decalogue
> In the grand dialect the Prophets spake...
>
> And thus forever with reverted look
> The mystic volume of the world they read,
> Spelling it backward, like a Hebrew book
> Till life became a Legend of the Dead.

The Hebrew language, written backwards, becomes an image of time erased, spelling poetry not as creative growth but as a "Legend of the Dead."

These poems on past languages become texts of cultural threat and cultural loss. But it is finally his own American culture and its future that concerns Longfellow. If these ancient cultures find place in poetry, this signals their removal from live circulation. Poetry itself emerges as a kind of cemetery and poetic dead language. The backward cast of Hebrew especially encapsulates Longfellow's anxiety about poetic language in his "Elegiac Verse," a group of poems that to an extent names Longfellow as lamenting, even as he creates an American poetic tradition:

> Wisely the Hebrews admit no Present tense in their language;
> While we are speaking the word, it is already Past.

Yet, not least in this cultural ambivalence, Longfellow sets the scene of major trends in attempting to define American poetry. Santayana had Longfellow in mind when he dismissed the genteel

poet as "grandmotherly in sedate spectacled wonder," an "intellect
without will," "female against male," and cut off from America's
"aggressive enterprise."[11] But Longfellow was aware of the contradictions of American initiative veering into restlessness and self-
consumption rather than imaginative venture, as De Tocqueville
had warned. Longfellow had become a poet against his father's
warning that "a literary life to one who has the means of support
may be very pleasant...but there is not wealth and munificence
enough in this country to afford...patronage to merely literary
men."[12] As Benjamin Franklin observed in 1763, "After the first
Cares for the Necessaries of Life are over we shall come to think
of the Embellishments."[13] Only Longfellow's unexpected professorship rescued him from becoming a lawyer. He attained further
financial success by cannily marketing his books across upper-,
middle-, and lower-class readerships, from leather-bound parlor
volumes to cheap paperbacks (as well as through marriage to a
wealthy wife).[14] Yet, the work he successfully marketed itself projects the bare place poetry holds in American society.[15] Poetry is a
kind of aside that is outside the real business of the day. Like "The
Children's Hour," poetry offers "a pause in the day's occupations."
In the poem "Night," poetry appears as a "palimpsest" that contrasts and erases "the dull commonplace book of our lives." The
very popular "The Tide Rises, the Tide Falls" describes "footprints
in the sands"—a figure for metric—that the endless, purposeless
motion of "little waves, with their soft white hands, efface." In
his first best-seller poem, "The Psalm of Life," Longfellow had
insisted that "life is not an empty dream," but he seems to have
been preaching to himself. In the "Fragments" that are appended
among his last verses, Longfellow almost sums up his whole poetic
work as a "neglected record of a mind neglected." Set apart from
actual "day with all its toils and occupations,"

> All I remember, feel, and hope at last,
> All shapes of joy and sorrow, as they pass,—
> Find but a dusty image in this glass.

The poetic page is no more than a "dusty image" in its own unreal
"glass." American culture had, as all the great mid-century writers
insisted, in its initial promise been dedicated to multiple realms of
possibility. What Longfellow records is the narrowing of American
culture to an enterprise foremostly material, so that at the very

moment its national birth, he laments the demise of literature as an active force in American life.

Divisions between revolutionary culture as against materialist interest rend not only literary but also political life in ante-bellum America. Longfellow takes his place among a group of "genteel" writers whose work is framed by the rise of industry, technology, and commerce, but also by the still more contradictory rupture of slavery. This is the case of poets in both the North and South, in whose work emerges not only political but also linguistic schisms. The contest here was within American English, over the language of the American Revolution. Both Northerners and Southerners, poets included, laid claim to revolutionary discourse, but they meant by it contrary and contesting things. Often sentimental in ways that link it with American women's verse, which similarly addressed social issues (notably slavery), genteel male poetry is particularly caught in the fractures opening in American self-definition and/as American public discourses. Besides sectional local-color idioms, within the basic lexical uniformity in American English the sectional strife opened differences and contesting directions in common words of the American heritage. Especially in the poetry around the Civil War, different sections of the country claimed the American language for their own interpretive interests, engendering variant forms of usage, emphasis, and intention.

In poetry, then, as in the country at large, the picture to emerge is continuity and mutual entanglement alongside increasing contention over the historical and ideological meanings of a shared lexicon. Writers in the South and North alike observed genteel conventions that muffled so much Victorian poetry in America. Both were further constrained by a mutual economic, intellectual, and political complicity. Northern publishers censored writing deemed too strident in order to protect commerce with the South. Southern writers reciprocally and ironically depended on the North for publishers, audience, market, and colleagues. Low literacy rates in the South among both whites and enslaved blacks, along with the scarcity of urban centers able to house and fund publishing initiatives, denied it the resources for either literary production or consumption. Henry Timrod complained about the necessary reliance on the North for literature, as indeed for most goods:

> We grew fat upon Yankee butter, we plied our daily avocations with Yankee tools, we taught our children in Yankee books on Yankee principles, we amused ourselves with Yankee magazines, and while turning a deaf ear to our own modest litterateurs, we went into ecstacies over Yankee poetry and Yankee romances.

Timrod went so far as to welcome "the very blockade that has cut off so completely our supply of Northern and English books," so that "forced to supply ourselves, we have, also, learned to criticize without regard to foreign models." But Timrod's hopes for a Southern national literature were defeated when *Russell's Magazine*, a journal that he and fellow poets Paul Hamilton Hayne and William Gilmore Simms had founded as a Southern equivalent to the North's *Atlantic Monthly*, failed to take hold. The South thus displayed its "scornful indifference" to native writers, demonstrating a "firm conviction that genius—literary genius at least—is an exotic that will not flower in southern soil."[16]

Mutual reliance between the Northern publishing industry and Southern markets form part of the shared conventions that also serve as backdrop to distinctive rhetorical fields, wherein common terms took on divergent and contradictory significance within differing ideological contexts. Myths central to American destiny and identity in particular take on different coloring in Southern and Northern poetic hands. In a poetry closely associated with political oratory and a ritualized poetry that was oratorical and occasional, South and North each laid claim to revolutionary inheritance, biblical sanction, and American mission, each according to its own ideologies.[17] The common American heritage became the material for competing usages. Yet conversely, even warring claims found strangely similar expression and overlapping visions.

Such ritualized, occasional poetry is prominent, for example, in the writings of both Henry Timrod and Oliver Wendell Holmes, Sr. Both wrote poems commemorating Washington's Birthday, capitalizing on the Washington cult that had rapidly spread to supply America with a ready-made hagiographic tradition, heroic exemplar, and historical unity. Each poet, moreover, casts his scene as a nativity, complete with sacred mother:

> Who guessed as that poor infant wept
> Upon a woman's knee,
> A nation from the centuries stept b
> As weak and frail as he? (Timrod)

> See the hero whom it gave us
> Slumbering on a mother's breast;
> For the arm he stretched to save us
> Be its morn forever blest (Holmes)

In both poets, a community of expression—the "founding infant" represented through religious iconography in a domestic setting—acts as common frame for quite different purposes. The nation had in fact inherited a split birthright. The revolution's rituals were enacted North and South through Fourth of July celebrations, Thanksgivings, and Washington's birthdays. But in the South, revolutionary "liberty" was seen to authorize self-determination and rebellion against a tyrannical centralized power now identified with the federal government; the constitutional protection of slavery as property; and a hierarchical social structure. For the North, revolutionary "liberty" meant the commitment to individual rights and equality; the constitutional protection of the Union; and resistance to despotism now identified with the South. To each section, then, liberty, revolution, and America had different resonances, references, and even plain meaning.

This bifurcated rhetoric penetrates Civil War poetry, even as it does the states at war. Popular songs, such as the "Battle Cry of Freedom," were sung both in the Union and the Confederacy, but with different lyrics and intentions: "And although he may be poor not a man shall be a slave" (North); "Their motto is resistance to tyrants we'll not yield" (South).[18] Poets more or less elite also contended over shared discourses. Henry Timrod in this way acted almost as official spokesman for the Southern position. Born in 1828 to a non-patrician family in Charleston, South Carolina, he received the irregular instruction characteristic of the Southern educational system, with the benefit of an additional year at the University of Georgia. He spent the years before the war as an itinerant tutor on various plantations. Due to his tubercular condition, he was unable to sustain action either as a soldier or a journalist during the Civil War. But, after publishing a first book of poems in 1859 (through Boston publishers Ticknor and Fields), he emerged as "The Laureate of the South" by writing war poems (including "Carolina," which was adopted in 1911 as the South Carolina State Hymn). These poems provide a showcase of American terms as deployed through Southern sectional rhetoric, as do Timrod's "Ethnogenesis," (the birth of the nation) written on the occasion of the first Confederate Congress, 1861; "The Cotton Boll," an ode to cotton with a fantasy of New York City destroyed; "Carmen Triumphale," which celebrates Southern victories; and "Ode," his most popular poem, commemorating the graves of the Confederate dead at Magnolia Cemetery, Charleston.

"Ethnogenesis" weaves together the American vision of special political mission with the religious rhetoric of biblical typology. "To

doubt the end were want of trust in God," he writes of the birth of
the Southern nation "under God":

> Who, if he has decreed
> That we must pass a redder sea
> Than that which rang to Miriam's holy glee,
> Will surely raise at need
> A Moses with his rod.

Red Sea, Miriam's song, Moses's rod, all here lead the South in triumph against the North's "evil throne" as it "warred with God."
Anti-slavery is unchristian and unbiblical, daring "to teach / what
Christ and Paul refrained to preach." The South emerges as millen-
nial "type," whereby "distant peoples we shall bless."

Timrod cannot entirely be summed up as a partisan Southern poet,
although his death in 1867 left him little time to commemorate other
occasions. Still, his rhetoric is largely linked to Southern senses of
identity. His "Dedication" introduces archaic forms concordant with
the South's self-representation as derived in "cavalier" courtly tradition—what Mark Twain called the South's "Sir Walter Scottism."
("we should never," he writes in *Life on the Mississippi*, "have had any
war but for Sir Walter"). Even Timrod's attempts to alter sectional
rhetoric often serve instead to entrench it. The poem "Christmas"
is launched as a prayer for "peace in the crowded town, / peace in
a thousand fields of waving grain...peace in our sheltered bays and
ample streams, / peace wheresoe'er our starry garland gleams." "Our"
is ambiguous, and could include the nation as a whole, except for:

> Shame to the foes that drown
> Our psalms of worship with their impious drum.

The rhetoric divides into a sacred "Our psalms" against "their impi-
ous" one. Even a poem dedicated to the "New Theatre at Richmond"
that attempts to demarcate some space for art free from politics, where
"sight and sound of pain / are banished," features "Liberty" as "the
dear rights for which we fight and pray"—that is, the defense of slave
property and the right of secession.[19]

Timrod's Southern rhetoric is matched and inverted by Oliver
Wendell Holmes Sr.'s Northern one. Holmes is the ultimate occasional poet. His father lost his post as minister to the First Church
of Cambridge in doctrinal battles between Orthodox and Unitarian

camps, leaving Holmes anti-Calvinist and, indeed, anti-creedal.[20] But even Holmes could not resist his country's rhetorical need. In a style matching Timrod's "Ethnogenesis," Holmes could pen a typological poem like "To Canaan: A Puritan War-Song," with the lyrics:

> We're marching South to Canaan
> to battle for the Lord!...
> The Mighty One of Israel,
> His name is Lord of Hosts!
> To Canaan, to Canaan
> The Lord has led us forth,
> To blow before the heathen walls
> The trumpets of the North.

Like Timrod, Holmes appeals to a "fair heritage spotless descended" that "the fathers made free and defended," but intends different fathers, different freedoms, and, despite the overlapping words, a different heritage. To Holmes, the "tyrant crew" is the South, which is trying to "tear down the 'banner of the free." Appeals to the same symbols, using the same words, bespeak different ideological Americas.

Holmes's war poetry is of a piece with his general body of occasional verse. A medical doctor by profession, he also practiced as a poet, but ultimately defined both through his most serious calling: that of Harvard Alumnus. He unswervingly produced verse for Harvard commencements and reunions, club meetings and official dinners, birthdays, centennials and July 4ths. Often the poems are addressed to dinner guests or fellow club members. The "Chambered Nautilus," Holmes's most anthologized poem, is one of his least characteristic. "At the Saturday Club" is far more characteristic, where he versifies contemporary literary history as his fellow guests at a private dinner party: Longfellow as "Poet, Laureate" with "ray serene;" Hawthorne "like the stern preacher of his sombre tale;" and Emerson the "Concord Delphi...prophet or poet, mystic, sage, or seer." The Revolution itself appears in Holmes as a family affair, conjured through the familiar Boston figure of Major Thomas Melville, uncle to Herman and among the last of the "Indians" of the Boston Tea-Party of 1774; or through Holmes' grandmother's account of "Bunker-Hill Battle" as witnessed from the Belfry.

Holmes' occasions represent language specifically as social identity. The dinner parties serve up the elite idioms spoken by a Boston society to which Holmes gave the name "Brahmin." Holmes' "Autocrat of the Breakfast Table," a series he contributed to the *Atlantic Monthly*, is a set of observations on language as on other habits. In "A Rhymed Lesson," the section on "Language" presents class difference as difference in idiolect, which inevitably gives the person away: "Words lead to things; a scale is more precise,—Coarse speech, bad grammar, swearing, drinking, vice...One stubborn word will prove this axiom true— / No quondam rustic can enunciate *view*." Yet American egalitarianism also gets its poetic due, when a poem given at a dinner for President Hayes mocks titles in accord with American linguistic-political principles:[21]

> How to address him? awkward, it is true:
> Call him "Great Father," as the Red Men do?
> Borrow some title? this is not the place
> That christens men Your Highness and Your Grace;
> We tried such names as these awhile, you know,
> But left them off a century ago.
>
> His Majesty? We've had enough of that:
> Besides, that needs a crown; he wears a hat.   (239)

Holmes' genteel language comes close to a regional idiom, at times breaking into full dialect. The "Deacon's Masterpiece, or the Wonderful One-Hoss Shay" is known for its attack on Calvinism, figured as the "one-hoss" carriage that breaks down. But its subject is the New England idiom no less than its religious heritage, from Brahmin to dialect:

> Now in building of Chaises, I tell you what,
> There is always somewhere a weakest spot,—...
> And that's the reason, beyond a doubt,
> That a chaise *breaks down* but doesn't *wear out*.
>
> But the Deacon swore (as Deacons do,
> With an "I dew vum," or an "I tell yeou"
> He would build one shay to beat the taown...
> It should be so built that it could 'n break daown.

In Holmes, genteel language proves to be the speech of his society and region. This includes the limitations of its decorum, where, as he puts it in "Over the Teacups," certain subjects were "banished by general consent from the conversation of well bred people and the pages of respectable literature."[22] Yet genteel language becomes less stultifying when presented as regional speech and approaches dialect, rather than posing as the norm and arbiter for poetic language thus made to match social class. Holmes' praise for James Russell Lowell as "New England's home-bred scholar," who well "knew / her soil, her speech, her people, through and through," applies rather more to himself.

James Russell Lowell's own writing tends to lack the comic, regionalizing energy Holmes gives to his. Rather, it breaks schizophrenically apart into official poetry, which is genteel as it comes, and dialect poetry, which is much more political. Lowell mainly continues to be included in literary history because as Harvard professor he was among the first to write such histories. His career includes the editorship for *The Atlantic Monthly* (1857–61) and *The North American Review* (1863–68); Smith Professorship of Modern Languages at Harvard (in which Lowell followed Longfellow); and Minister to Spain (1877–80) and England (1880–85).[23] Lowell's genteel verse, such as "The Vision of Sir Launfal" and "A Fable for Critics," offers a language galaxies away from the dialect that appears in his Civil War *Biglow Papers*. As for "Sir Launfal," the less said, the better. It pursues an excruciating metric through an incoherent structure, punctuated by intrusive moralisms. "A Fable for Critics" is meant to emulate Pope's "Essay on Criticism," but more resembles Holmes' "At the Saturday Club," making literary history into personal social roster of Lowell's own social/ literary circle, all patiently waiting for Lowell to fulfill his own literary promise. Emerson, known to Lowell from the days he had been "rusticated" to Concord (for wearing a brown coat to Harvard Sunday dinner instead of a black one), is not unwittily represented as

> A Greek head on right Yankee shoulders,
> In whose mind all creation is duly respected
> As parts of himself—just a little projected.

Outsiders are mentioned only to emphasize their exclusion: Poe, exiled from New England literary society for his plagiarism attacks on Longfellow, appears as "three fifths of him genius and two-fifths sheer fudge." Margaret Fuller, who had dared to say that Lowell "is absolutely wanting in the true spirit and tone of poesy...and posterity will not remember him," is mocked as "Miranda": "The whole of whose being's a capital 'I,'" putting "her infinite *me*" into everything she treats. The "Fable" includes some interesting observations, such as how, while Americans "brag of your New World, you don't half believe in it; / And as much of the Old as is possible weave in it." But at best it remains a form of society-verse like Holmes', only with far more pretension to act as arbiter of serious poetry such as Lowell himself claimed to write.

Lowell, however, does have a second voice, which he adopts not out of literary but rather political commitment. In *The Biglow Papers*, he drops his high poetic diction to write dialect representing and defending Northern politics. Lowell's marriage to Maria White, a strong anti-slavery poet before her early death from consumption, brought him into radical Garrisonian abolitionist circles, as well as helped give his poetic language political energy and focus. *The Biglow Papers*, first series, attacks the Mexican-American War as a ruse to extend slavery. The second series treats the Civil War through the characters of Hosea Biglow and Birdofredom Sawin, whose native idiom launches and reflects contemporary political rhetoric. Hosea Biglow rejects the nationalist call as Christian duty: "it's curus Christian dooty / This 'ere cuttin' folks's throats." *Biglow Paper* v, first series, contests Southern claims to the Revolution and to the Bible by putting a "Debate in the Sennit" into the words of H. Biglow:

> Freedom's Keystone is Slavery,
> thet ther's no doubt on,
> It's suttin' thet's—
> wha' d'ye call it?—divine.

The second series, Number III, includes a letter from Birdofredum Sawin, who has settled in the South, reporting its "pulpit ellerkence" on slavery, which claims:

> All things wuz gin to man for's use, his sarvice, an' delight;
> An' don't the Greek an' Hebrew words thet mean a Man mean
>   White?

Mutual counter-claims over Revolutionary heritage and rhetoric becomes a history of debate and distortion over Thomas Jefferson who

> prob'ly meant wal with his "born free an' ekle,"
> But it's turned out a real crooked stick in the sekle.
> It's taken full eighty-odd year—don't you see?—
> From the pop'lar belief to root out that idee."

"In choosing the Yankee dialect," Lowell writes in one of the many notes appended to the poems in *Biglow,*

> It had long seemed to me that the great vice of American writing and speaking was a studied want of simplicity, that we were in danger of coming to look on our mother-tongue as a dead language, to be

sought in the grammar and dictionary rather than in our heart, and that our only chance of escape was by seeking it at its living sources. (Introduction, Second Series)

Only in his dialect verse was Lowell able to make this escape from the dictionary into living language. In his role as poet, he rarely rises above rhymed speechmaking, such as his "Commemoration Ode" at Harvard, which unfortunately uses an English he mocks in *Biglow* as "ever more pedantic and foreign, till it becomes at last as unfitting a vehicle for living thought as monkish Latin."

When Holmes and Lowell spoke for their region, they considered themselves to be speaking for America. This was also the ambition of Southern poets, but theirs was a much more difficult project. Northern genteel norms set their standard, yet they also felt these were a threat to their indigenous culture. The need to defend slavery, which intensified through the ante-bellum period in response to abolitionist attacks, began to define Southern rhetoric, just as slavery itself defined not only Southern labor and land organization in plantations, but also its traditions, values, and modes of self-representation. Southern poetry took its shape in identification with the South's "peculiar institution" and then from its post-war cultural devastation.

After his unhappy experiment with Arthurian legend in "Sir Launfal," Lowell turned to his more successful figure of the Yankee farmer as archetypal New Englander in *Biglow*. But Arthurian lore remained a central element in the genteel Southern image of the "cavalier," who would safeguard social order by his grace, honor, and dominance over the lower and slave classes. Archaic language consequently enters the writings of both Timrod and Southern genteel writer Sidney Lanier. In Lanier, however, archaism aligns with other interests. The first is music. Lanier, whose ancestors had been court musicians to Queen Elizabeth, Charles I, and Charles II, was a musical prodigy and an accomplished flautist. He earned his living and prolonged his life against the tuberculosis he had contracted in prison during the Civil War, as first flutist in a Baltimore Symphony Orchestra. After years of vain attempts, he succeeded in gaining a teaching post at Johns Hopkins, a position, however, cut very short by his death from his disease. The treatise he wrote there, *The Science of English Verse*, sets out to find direct correlations between musical and poetic meters, a correlation he tried to create in his verse.[24]

Lanier at his best writes a language that is richly musical. At his worst, he overdoes his musical effects and becomes mired in his second interest, which looms on obsession: the demonic effect of trade, industry, and commerce on the South. This comes near to raving in dialect poems. Musical heavy handedness combined with commercial paranoia come to especially dire effect in Lanier's ambitious poem, "The Symphony," which opens: "'O Trade! O Trade! would thou wert dead! / The Time needs heart—'tis tired of head: / We're all for love,' the violins said." Lanier's archaic, melodic cadences jar against the direct social-economic commentary he tries to invest them with.

The Southern genteel romance with courtly forms shapes his early poem, "The Tournament," which clumsily allegorizes a joust opposing "Heart" against "Brain" and "Love" against "Hate." Later poems continue this chivalric interest in their imagery, style, and rhythm. Beautiful moments can result, but these are rarely sustained in Lanier's longer, ambitious odes. The most successful of these is perhaps "The Revenge of Hamisch." There the ballad form and archaic language seems also self-critical, as its story of a maddened servant turning terrible punishment back on his master almost inevitably implicates the South's feudal order, turned against itself.

Lanier's shorter songs are his most accomplished, perhaps because they are less distracted by topicality and inconsistency. Birds in the poem "In Absence" cross

> the windage of each other's wings
> But speeds them both upon their journeyings.

While Lanier's language here is quite remote from ordinary speech, it images the devotion that is his subject. Other poems offer concrete images drawn from the Southern landscape, flowers, and natural features. Lanier's description of Florida, "From the Flats," where he hoped to ease his tuberculosis, instead infects the landscape with it:

> Inexorable, vapid, vague and chill
> The drear sand-levels drain my spirit low.
> With one poor word they tell me all they know...
> Do drawl it o'er again and o'er again.
> They hurt my heart with griefs I cannot name:
> Always the same, the same.

This language is haunting and haunted. The Southern "drawl" repeats, entraps, and drains. But Lanier's poetic effort to construct a unitary system in which music, poetry, and social remedies correlate with each other ultimately dramatizes the impossibility of such a project. This failure is most apparent when Lanier is most grandiose, as in the "Centennial Cantata" he was commissioned to write through the patronage of Bayard Taylor:

> O Music, from this height of time my Word unfold:
> In thy large signals all men's hearts Man's heart behold:
> Mid-heaven unroll thy chords as friendly flags unfurled,
> And wave the world's best lover's welcome to the world.

Melody comes close to compulsion here, not least when coerced into public message. Lanier's more homely poems, however, can achieve a musical language, still essentially genteel but in closer contact with actual worlds. The sonnet form of "The Mocking Bird" allows Lanier a control and detachment that reflects his problem of disjunction between art and reality. The poem opens with a bird "superb and sole" whose song "summ'd the woods; or typic drew...Whate'er birds did or dreamed, this bird could say." But then the bird, and the verse, plunges:

> Then down he shot, bounced airily along
> The sward, twitched in a grasshopper, made song
> Midflight, perched, prinked, and to his art again.
> Sweet Science, this large riddle read me plain:
> How may the death of that dull insect be
> The life of yon trim Shakspere on the tree?

How, indeed, to reconcile eating an insect with making a poem remained to Lanier a perplexity. Lanier, like Timrod, worked under the desperate conditions of the Southern war devastation. But the problem posed by this sonnet, of reconciling poetry with a world of grasshoppers, is one that extends beyond the South and the immediate pressures of livelihood. Lanier, like most of the mid-century genteel writers, seems unable to balance the social, political, ideological, and cultural pressures and the rhetorics of their conduct, which become confused in their poetic language. A comparable confusion emerges in the much better known work of John Greenleaf Whittier (1807–1892), who, like Longfellow, was acclaimed, admired, and enjoyed by a wide-reading public, and like Timrod, was strongly associated with his section's cause. Living all his life in northern Massachusetts, he was a dedicated activist in the anti-slavery movement.[25] Up until emancipation, his poetry, like his journalism, is placed in the service of abolition, an expression of his

Quaker Inner Light theology. His is a theo-political verse, show-
casing Northern meanings of words such as freedom, justice, and
America. "The Yankee Girl" is courted by a planter whose promise
of "freedom" from daily labor she rejects as enslavement: "Yet know
that the Yankee girl sooner would be / in fetters with [slaves] than
in freedom with thee." Whittier repeatedly appeals to the Founding
Fathers as the basis for his vision of freedom: "is this the land our
father's loved, the freedom which they toiled to win." He closely
joins political freedom with the biblical message of the divine image
in all men and women, affirming the historical religious resources of
American democratic vision. Both this religious and political faith
in the absolute value of the person are betrayed when "God's own
image [is] bought and sold / Americans to market driven, and bar-
tered as the brute for gold." America has departed from its mission
of following the divine presence that "went before / Our fathers in
their weary way . . . The fire by night, the cloud by day."

Whittier's political verse can be ideologically programmatic. Yet
he still represents the predicament of American freedom inextricably
linked to American slavery with special force, implicating the North
no less than the South.[26] The Northerner must also "be told his
freedom stands / on Slavery's dark foundation." The very founding
words of the nation are compromised by contradictory meanings. As
the "Song of the Negro Boatman" observes in black dialect and point
of view:

> O, praise an' tanks! De Lord he come
> To set de people free;
> An' massa tink it day ob doom,
> An' we ob jubilee.

But Whittier's work finally insists on one, moral linguistic register
that needs to be restored to the nation. There is no confusion as to
which is the true meaning of freedom or sin in "Laus Deo," as it
celebrates emancipation: "Freer breathe the universe / As it rolls its
heavy curse / On the dead and buried sin."

After the war, Whittier turns to descriptive pieces, ballads, and
hymns deeply rooted in the local places and people in whose midst he
lived, representing their religious, economic, and linguistic culture.
These often serve moral functions, with poetic energy subordinated
to stylized, predictable verbal forms, whether social or pious. Yet he
can almost suddenly plunge into an idiom that is native, concrete, and
dramatic. In "The Prelude" to "Among the Hills," the New England

farm family emerges not as a static moral emblem, but as a living place
of moral struggle:

> Shrill, querulous women, sour and sullen men,
> Untidy, loveless, old before their time,
> With scarce a human interest save their own
> Monotonous round of small economies…
> Saving, as shrewd economists their souls
> And winter pork with the least possible outlay
> Of salt and sanctity.

Whittier's anti-apocalyptic "Abraham Davenport" is written in similarly rugged language; its speaker resists the cries of the people that
"it is the Lord's Great Day" with a "slow cleaving…steady voice"
and the very plain words: "Let God do his work, we will see to ours."
"Telling the Bees" has all the dignity and reticence of the mourning custom and personal tragedy it recounts. "The Preacher" features Jonathan Edwards, who remained a commanding presence in
Massachusetts, but against whom Whittier registers his own resistance
to the Calvinist view "that man was nothing since God was all."

In a poem such as "Snowbound," Whittier achieves a language of
quiet dignity and natural strength, consecrating imaginative power in
and of ordinary life. Rather than a nostalgic portrait of his past farm
life, as the poem is often taken to be, it celebrates poetic power as integral to the daily struggle to meet the world's exigencies.[27] Whittier
opposes the "art" of building the fire against the "shrieking of the
mindless wind." The farmhouse's hearth fire, as in Emerson's "Snow
Storm" that serves as the poem's epigraph, thus becomes an image
of poetic consciousness, confronting and contesting brute nature
through imaginative labor.

The poetry of the genteel writers, North and South, confronted
and addressed questions of culture taking shape and competing around them as they took linguistic form: the relation to past
European forms, the relation between different sections, economies,
and social structures within the United States themselves. They did
so in the straining contexts of economic transformation, political
division, and, finally, war. Their poetry, for all its decorum, registers
anxiety concerning poetry's audience and function. Far from assuming poetry's sacral or elite status, mid-century genteel poets remain
uncertain about their own role and position in American culture.[28]
F.O. Matthiessen criticizes nineteenth-century verse as weak precisely
in its inability "to distinguish between the nature of the two arts"

of poetry and rhetoric.[29] But the problem is not poetry's integrity as against rhetoric, but rather its failure to master the languages circulating around it. Poetry, far from being the pure, self-enclosed language demanded by formalist aesthetics, inevitably constructs its forms and its language out of the discourses of the cultural worlds it inhabits. Not poetry's inundation, but its remoteness from a living idiom, is what Mark Twain spoofed in his own ill-fated appearance at the *Atlantic Monthly* dinner for Whittier ("the expression of interest," he comments, "turned to a sort of black frost"). In the story of this speech, Twain pictures Emerson, Longfellow, and Holmes declaiming their poetic lines in a miner's cabin, and the miner's rebuke to them in the clarity and plainness of his own language: "Beg your pardon, Mr. Longfellow, if you'll be so kind as to hold your yawp for about five minutes and let me get this grub ready, you'll do me proud."[30] Lowell, among the first to introduce just such dialect idiom into verse, was generally unable to transcend the kind of linguistic restrictions that kept him from publishing Melville, Thoreau, and Whitman in *The Atlantic Monthly*.

Poetry's challenge, then, is not to dissociate itself from the discourses around it through some formal purity, but rather to command without being overwhelmed by the rhetoric it shares with the culture it represents and addresses. But most mid-nineteenth-century writers do not succeed in creating a language at once both rooted in their cultural world and giving it shape and order. They instead are either mastered by the rhetoric around them or divorced from its living idiom. Nonetheless, their work reflects the American languages emerging and contesting through the nineteenth century, even if not fully or often made into poetry.

CHAPTER 5

EDGAR ALLAN POE: METAPHYSICAL RUPTURE AND THE SIGN OF WOMAN

It is telltale that Edgar Allan Poe devoted more of his critical writing to his hatred of Longfellow than to any other purpose. This hatred has a complex structure. It marks a clash between North and South, wealth and poverty, privileged membership and marginality and disownment. It points, in effect, to broad gaps within antebellum American life. Poe has often been claimed as a French poet writing in the American language. Translated lavishly by Baudelaire, canonized by Mallarmé and Valéry, he has been adopted by the French poetic tradition much more than by the American.[1] Since recognized as a strong impetus to Modernism,[2] Poe remains a poet of his time. As William Carlos Williams was the first to claim, Poe's work is "the first great burst through to expression of a re-awakened genius of place."[3]

Yet Poe's historicism tends to be counter-worldly. His are reflected images of society and history in a severe mirror. Reflection, inversion, and imitation are themselves core problematics of Poe's aesthetic, expressed in the obsession with plagiarism that led him to publish hundreds of pages denouncing Longfellow, and also in his aesthetic theory that essentially rejects art as imitation. Poe, like and against Longfellow, was concerned about American literature as a mere echo of British, without its own originality. He was also concerned with the status of art in an American culture increasingly commercial, industrial, and material. If one great Romantic project is to recast experience through imagination, to infuse reality with poetic meaning, then Poe's poetry is a measure of its American impossibility. In Poe, this led to a particular repudiation of natural-ism. But Poe's work also exposes the intimate relationships between aesthetics and metaphysics so fundamental to, and also destabilizing within, American Romanticism itself. Religion emerges as a cru-cial context for Poe, as it is for, and situates him within, American cultural trends.

Poe's own biography suggests the American dream in reverse. At the age of two, Poe was twice abandoned: by his father through deser-tion and his mother through death from tuberculosis. He was then taken in but not legally adopted by Frances Allan and her ambivalent husband John. Poe's years spent with the Allans trace a complex and distressing course of ambition and betrayal. Frances and John, small slave owners who were financially precarious until a late inheritance from a wealthy uncle lifted John to the plantation life he had long desired, raised Poe as a Southern gentleman without ever establishing him as their heir. Educated partly in England and partly in Richmond, he enrolled at the University of Virginia in 1826 at age seventeen. During this time, he was also coming into increasing conflict with his foster-father over drinking, gambling, and debts. Following a quar-rel, Poe abandoned college to enlist in the army, which he abandoned in turn. John Allan's death in 1830 left Poe disinherited and penni-less but also released him from bourgeois expectations, enabling him to pursue the writing that had been, since his earliest precocity, his true calling. For the remainder of his life, he vainly attempted (like Melville) to support himself by his art, enduring grueling magazine work in both Northern and Southern cities—an effort to survive as a writer that equally spelled its defeat in distracting and secondary labor. Poetry, which he called in the preface to *The Raven and Other Poems* (1845) "the field of my choice," remained a luxury he could ill afford. His personal life was marked by a series of strangely cur-tailed relationships to women: an unconsummated marriage to his thirteen year-old cousin Virginia in 1836, and following her death from tuberculosis at the age of twenty-five, a series of duplicating and intercrossing courtships, none of which were brought to conclusion. In 1849, Poe was found unconscious on a Baltimore street, dressed in someone else's clothes apparently in order to cast, for payment, a bogus ballot at Ryan's fourth-ward polls on Election Day. He died four days later of alcohol poisoning. A headstone at his grave was erected only twenty-six years later; the placement attended by Walt Whitman alone among America's literary personalities but commem-orated by Mallermé's great sonnet on Poe. After his death, Poe's work fell into the hands of the indefatigable Rufus Griswold, who further darkened the writer's biography through falsification of his letters and accusations of immorality.[4]

Poe is not the only nineteenth-century American poet to be self-conscious about poetic form. Dickinson, Whitman, and Longfellow each come (differently) to mind. But Poe made form itself the direct and overwhelming topic of art:, the "poem written solely for the poem's sake," as he announced in "The Poetic Principle." In this, he vehemently turned his back on what he called (attacking Longfellow) "The Didactic," by which he intended not only a "moral sense" but "truth of description"—that is, mimetic art altogether: any art that imitates reality or makes direct reference to it. As Theodore Adorno later theorized about anti-bourgeois art, Poe's work is historical precisely by being anti-representational. Oscar Wilde is said to have remarked about art that it imitates reality, "who needs two of them?" Poe seems to wonder who needs even one.

T. S. Eliot and Aldous Huxley condescendingly suggested that the French were wild for Poe because their English wasn't very good. But this remark points to important aspects of Poe's anti-mimeticism. English readers can be distracted trying to refer Poe's words outside his texts. But Poe's language works the other way, toward dissolving reference. He seems to name and indicate, but his words instead block reference and point only back into his own text. Thus "Ulalume" makes landscape into wordscape:

> It was night in the lonesome October
> Of my most immemorial year;
> It was hard by the dim lake of Auber,
> In the misty mid region of Weir—

Early critics assumed "Auber" and "Weir" to be nonsense words. But research uncovered information: that Daniel Auber was a French composer and that there was an Awber river in England; that Robert Weir painted misty landscapes; and that "Mount Yaanek," in the next stanza, denotes Mt. Erebus, the one active volcano in Antartica. Erebus, of course, would not rhyme with "Titanic" and "volcanic" as "Yaanek" does, just as "Auber" echoes "October."[5] These locations are not so much red herrings as bait. The words, pointing outward, are then retracted inward. They hold their place as sounds and associations. The reference is conjured to be defeated and withdrawn.

Blocked reference is one of many techniques of Poe's anti-mimetic art. Poe wrote a string of dream poems (there are six versions of "A Dream within a Dream)" taking place in worlds "Out of Space—Out of Time." "The City in the Sea" presents a counter-world that "resemble[s] nothing that is ours." "The Valley of Unrest" is a place where "people did not dwell." One of the many provocative claims Poe makes in "The Philosophy of Composition" is that he came to "The Raven's" refrain of "Nevermore" out of liking the sound of the letters 'O' and 'R'. Here pure sound joins with the nostalgia for a lost past, another form of desire for what does not exist. The word's repetition sets up the sort of regressive reflections that Poe cultivates in his self-referential art: "the pleasure deduced solely from the sense of identity—of repetition."[6]

Poe's obsession with plagiarism is one form the question of repetition takes for him, as it engages with the question of creative originality as such. Originality haunted his generation of American poets. How was one to make English into an American language for poetry? The only originality, as Emerson put it in "Self-Reliance," is one without any derivation from outside the self. Tradition becomes suspect, the reliance on it a mode of repetition. But self-reliance takes the form in Poe of enclosed, self-reflective textuality. As Poe wrote in a long 1842 review essay on Longfellow (who he calls "the GREAT MOGUL of the imitators"), and then revised in "The Poetic Principle," the repetition of "the lily in the lake" may be "a duplicate source of delight," but "this repetition is not poetry." However "vivid a truth of imitation" the artist may provide, "of the sights and sounds, which greet him in common with all mankind—he, we say, has yet failed to prove his divine title"

The divine power of poetry inheres not in any representation of the world, "not [in] the mere appreciation of the beauty before us," but as "a wild effort to reach the beauty above":

It is the desire of the moth for the star... It is a passion to be satiated by no sublunary sights, or sounds, or sentiments, and the soul thus athirst strives to allay its fever in futile efforts at *creation*. Inspired with a prescient ecstasy of the beauty beyond the grave, it struggles by multiform novelty of combination among the things and thoughts of Time, to anticipate some portion of that loveliness whose very elements, perhaps, appertain solely to Eternity. (*E* 685–686; cf. 77).

Art should not repeat reality, but rather remove itself from nature as inferior to it. Yet art also is never fully perfect. It remains only a shadow of "the beauty beyond the grave." Art does not fulfill nature. Rather, like "the desire of the moth for the star," it is destructive to nature and indeed to the artist himself. Its purpose is not to point to "sublunary sights, or sounds, or sentiments" or anything in "creation" but only to a total unity of "eternity" beyond time, which it can at best "anticipate" but never achieve.

The image of the lake that Poe here invokes is one that recurs throughout his work as a core image of just such reflection: not of reality, but of the mind reflecting on itself. In the early poem "To the River," the poet, his beloved, and the river join together in mutual reflection. But such harmony is unusual in Poe. Most often the reflective lake acts to cut off the poet from the world he looks at. In "The Sleeper," the poet stands beside a lake "like Lethe" in "a conscious slumber," while the "Sleeper" herself is a frozen consciousness, death–like and silent: "Some tomb from out whose sounding door / She ne'er shall force an echo more." The scene represents interiority as poetic visionary power, but not as mimetic or even transformative of any exterior world with which it corresponds or which it illuminates. The poem is situated in the break between interiority and exteriority, mind and world—not the mutual imaging of them. It is as if Poe were caught within Romanticism's moment of negation, when the imagination is freed to effect its changes on the world, but then characteristically returns to restore the world in reconciliation with the imagination's design.[7] Here there is no restoration. Rather than being directed towards reality, imagination is released by blocking it out. As Poe writes in an 1849 *Marginalia* entry, "Art is not the mere imitation, however accurate, of what is in Nature," but rather "the reproduction of what the Senses perceive in Nature through the veil of the soul." The "veil of the soul," not "Nature," becomes the subject of representation (*E* (1458). Thus the poem "The Lake—To" concludes in "lone imagining / Whose solitary soul" makes "an Eden of the dim lake."

One of Poe's legacies to Modernist symbolist poetry is this interior reflection as poetic site. The poems are deeply self-reflective, the exterior world the image of an interior mind. Such self-reflection as poetic process especially impressed Valéry, who focused on the poet's mind as it acts in poetic (and its own) construction.[8] Yet Mallarmé seems truer to Poe when he declares the poem should, in being about itself, be essentially about nothing. The interior process Poe pursues in representing poetic process itself emerges as empty mirror reflecting empty mirror. His "The Haunted Palace," the poem interpolated into "The Fall of the House of Usher," is emblematic. The poem is a self-reflection of the story's protagonist, but also of the narrator, the twin sister, and Poe himself as the writer, as in a hall of mirrors. It constructs, stanza by stanza, the person as a house: inhabited by reason ("thought's dominion"), with a roof of "banners yellow, glorious golden" as hair, "two luminous windows" as eyes, and the "pearl and ruby glowing" teeth in the "fair palace door" of the mouth. This exteriorized interiority, this architecture of the mind, is then dramatically overturned, carrying with it the reader who has, step by step, taken up his or her own habitation in the house as well. In an overthrow of reason and disintegration of selfhood (with imagery again of water—"like a ghastly rapid river"), the eyes become "red-litten windows." Language itself breaks down as the "pale door" mouth lets forth "a hideous throng" of demented utterance and hysteria.

Yet this poetry of the mind in self-reflection—Poe's major legacy to symbolism—does not fully suggest an autonomy of art and independence of aesthetic experience as it would later do. Poe is not really French.[9] Art remains in Poe radically incomplete, pointing not merely to itself but also beyond, toward a realm it can never fully grasp. As he writes in "The Poetic Principle," there is "still a something in the distance which he has been unable to attain." "We weep," he continues, not

> through excess of pleasure, but through a certain, petulant, impatient sorrow at our inability to grasp now, wholly, here on earth, at once and for ever, those divine and rapturous joys, of which, through the poem, or through the music, we attain to but brief and indeterminate glimpses.

Art here emerges as metaphysical break. Later symbolism might make art for the sake of art a substitution for metaphysical experience, with the poem itself the ultimate object. Poe does not. What he instead registers is a disturbed relationship with older metaphysical frameworks, a haunting of its borders as it recedes, leaving behind voided but still impelling spaces. Like Emily Dickinson, he strains to peer over the edge of the world into an afterworld no longer certainly believed in.[10] These are the territories of his stories about the afterlife, or rather, about postapocalyptic destruction: "Mesmeric Revelation," "The Colloquy of Monos and Una," "The Conversation of Eiros and Charmion," "The Power of Words." Situated after death (with the last three situated after the utter apocalypse of the world), they attempt to imagine reports from the other side.

What these stories, and Poe's poetry, show is a disturbed relation between the worlds that takes on a peculiarly American character and format. Poe was baptized and confirmed into the Southern Episcopal Church. His background, however, is also Calvinist, through his

Scotch foster-father; and it spans the Second Great Awakening.[11] Poe's school in England, located in a dissenting community (home to Daniel Defoe, Isaac Watts, and Mary Wollstonecraft), required attendance at morning and evening services and copious Scripture reading.[12] In an 1836 review, Poe defends the South and its Episcopal Church against "political prejudices" that are being "enlisted against the religion we cherish" (*E* 560). In his own writings, Poe's references to the Bible are many and learned, such as his comments on Hebrew grammar in the *Marginalia* and the list of Hebrew words in his review of John L. Stephens. Allen Tate remarks that "in spite of an early classical education and a Christian upbringing, [Poe] wrote as if the experience of these traditions had been lost." But this is so only in the sense that Poe is addressing exactly that loss—in the guise, Tate continues, of "a religious man whose Christianity, for reasons that nobody knows anything about, had got short-circuited."[13]

Poe in fact illuminates perhaps too brilliantly two specific modes of American religious imagination: the utopian "Kingdom of God" and antinomianism. Indeed, Poe shows how these two are interconnected, for, as his work dramatizes, an absolute Kingdom turns out to stand in negative relation to the world as it exists. Attempting to achieve the absolute almost necessitates repudiating earthly norms and conditions—an antinomian identification with an ultimate reality whose main attribute is the abnegation of this earthly one. It is this negative implication of the apocalyptic that Poe underscores—an apocalypse that for him is further disjunctive, in being destructive but without rebirth. In Poe, after apocalypse there is no transformation, no new heaven and new earth.[14] At most there is repetition. The drive toward annihilation, expressly announced at the opening of *Eureka*, Poe's cosmological fantasy, repeats in endless recurrence: "In the original unity of the first thing lies the secondary cause of all things, with the germ of their inevitable annihilation."

Rather than seeing the world as a sign or signifier of a higher signified, as in sacramental symbolization; or the world as a chain of signifiers without further signified reference, as in a secular one; for Poe the world's signifiers are so extremely opposed against a signified higher reality that only their destruction can symbolize that higher world. The relation between the two is then utterly negative, with all earthly norms suspended and repudiated—a Gnostic tendency that emerges in the American tradition as antinomianism.

Poe's imagination falls into this last category. What he depicts in his poetry is a battle between worlds, an opposition so utter as to make it impossible for this world to positively symbolize a higher one. This is the force of Poe's anti-mimetic theory of art. Any "deter-minate" concrete specification would deprive art of its "ethereal, its ideal, its intrinsic and essential character," reducing it to "a tangible and easy appreciable idea—a thing of the earth, earthy" (1331; cf 1435). The things of the earth cannot represent the absolute he yearns for; nothing in the present world can image or conduct to it. It must instead be figured as against worldly experience; not rooted in, but defiant of it. His is a "Romance" (1831) that opposes rather than completing, elevating, or transfiguring reality:

> Romance, who loves to nod and sing
> With drowsy head and folded wing,
> Among the green leaves as they shake
> Far down within some shadowy lake,
> To me a painted paroquet
> Hath been—a most familiar bird—
> Taught me my alphabet to say—
> To lisp my very earliest word
> While in the wild wood I did lie,
> A child—with a most knowing eye.
>
> Of late, eternal Condor years
> So shake the very Heaven on high
> With tumult as they thunder by,
> I have no time for idle cares
> Through gazing on the unquiet sky.
> And when an hour with calmer wings
> Its down upon my spirit flings—
> That little time with lyre and rhyme
> To while away—forbidden things!
> My heart would feel to be a crime
> Unless it trembled with the strings.

The poem opens in an apparently Blakean mode of personifying nature as a potent figure. But this proves not to be the case. The "green leaves" turn out not to be in nature, but "far down within some shadowy lake" of the reflective mind. Creativity is imaged not in response to a natural bird, but rather as a fake one. It is from a "painted paroquet" that the poet has learned his "alphabet." The "child" here, similarly, is not a figure in innocent bond with nature, but almost a Gnostic figure, as Harold Bloom describes, born outside of the world and whose "knowing eye" knows an other, alien knowledge altogether.[15] As to the world itself and its time, this is figured as a bird of a different feather, a living condor who threatens "the very Heaven on high" and whose prey is ultimately the poet himself. Under its threat he can barely escape the tumultuous triumph of time, as it assaults what he describes as "forbidden things": the "lyre and rhyme" that oppose a world that in turn forbids and opposes them.

This is not a redemptive art, but an oppositional one. As in the poem "Israfel," true song inheres in a realm utterly removed from our own. "Imbued with all the beauty / Which we worship in a star," far different from this our world, so inverse that our "sunshine" is the other world's "shadow," which penetrates and betrays our human poetry. Only removal from this world would elevate poetry to its true fulfillment.

The most brutal poem in this vein is "The Conqueror Worm," inserted into the story "Ligea." This is set up as a stage performance of earthly life to an "angel throng" witnessing a copy of a copy. The height of the drama is reached when they

> see amid the mimic rout
> A crawling shape intrude! . . .
> It writhes!—It writhes!—with mortal pangs
> The mimes becomes its food,
> And seraphs sob at vermin fangs
> In human gore imbued.

The corruption of the body becomes the central fact of human life. The body, as in the oldest traditions of dualism, is essentially nothing but corruption. "The play is the tragedy, 'Man,' / And its hero the Conqueror Worm." There is a confrontation with suffering, "the tragedy 'Man'," which haunts Poe but for which he has no access to traditional solutions.

Poe, in repudiating "our" world, does not truly gain entry into a higher realm, either. Instead, he presents a war between worlds, draining both of reality. It is as if Poe's loss of metaphysical reality equally undermines his belief in this immediate one. In general, the boundaries between reality and unreality, fiction and fact blur in Poe, most blatantly in his hoaxes and science fictions—but no less in his poetry. Life becomes a "dream land," a Kingdom "with forms that no man can discover,"

> Mountains toppling evermore
> Into seas without a shore; . .
> Lakes that endlessly outspread
> Their lone waters—lone and dead.

This is the imploding Kingdom of "The City in Sea," where "Death has reared himself a throne." There the shrines and palaces that "resemble nothing that is ours" finally topple until

> amid no earthly moans,
> Down, down that town shall settle hence,
> Hell, rising from a thousand thrones,
> Shall do it reverence.

This last image seems a reference to Isaiah 14:9: "Hell stirreth up the dead for thee; it hath raised up from their thrones all the kings of the nations." The towers recall Babel, while the poem's reflective sea recalls the Dead Sea, a name Poe surely loved. But here there is no Judgment, nor the particular wickedness of Sodom and Gomorrah. Spatio-temporal reality is itself condemned.

Both D. H. Lawrence and Allen Tate describe Poe's as a rejection of limitations (what Tate calls an "angelic imagination") in its attempt toward "unmediated knowledge of essences."[16] What Poe's work discloses is how such revolt against limitation marks a crossing between the antinomian and the utopian, the radical desire for the ultimate as a condemnation of the earthly. This comes out most explicitly in Poe's cosmological fantasy *Eureka*, where a utopian-aesthetic principle of unity renders the cosmos into an all-encompassing artwork, an "Original Unity" which, however, results in "inevitable annihilation." That is, the reduction to nothingness is revealed as a consequence of the pursuit of unity.

But this vision of unity as nothingness is not only metaphysical. It is in Poe also social, or rather, at once metaphysical and social. These two dimensions intersect in Poe through women's bodies, especially dead ones, which is one way to be absolute "The trouble about man," D. H. Lawrence said in discussing Poe, "is that...he insists on *oneness*...and by this means he acquires an ecstasy of vision, he finds himself in glowing unison with all the universe." But this impulse, as Lawrence goes on to observe, is a deadly one. Poe in particular applies it to women, in a vision of love as unity that also makes love deadly: "Carry this too far...and a form of death sets in."[17] Allen Tate in turn suggests a social context for Poe's figures of woman as idealized, metaphysicized to death, in the Southern lady: Poe's "exalted idealization of Woman [is] only a little more humorless, because more intense, than the standard cult of Female Purity in the Old South."[18]

Poe, of course, famously declared in "The Philosophy of Composition" that the most "poetical topic in the world" is "the death of a beautiful woman." There are those who weirdly speak of Poe's figures of women as homage to an "ideal," at least in the poems (it is a harder to make this claim for the tales, where the women tend to be luridly murdered, ghoulish, entombed, and/or mutilated).[19] Yet Poe's mainly dead poetic women are ideal figures in ways that are consistent with his ideal in general, as negating and repudiating human experience. "The Philosophy of Composition" establishes dead women as the sign of a particular aesthetic of unity such that, first, all points in a text must be directed to a single intention, determined backwards by the end and second, that there should be a complete "unity of impression." Yet Poe is far from the only writer to idealize dead women. In fact, in reading Poe, one becomes first aware of how pervasive this topos is. The sonnet tradition is full of women removed from earthly life. Platonism, starting with the "Symposium," establishes love of beauty as a ladder from which to ascend beyond this life to a higher realm. "The Poetic Principle" may be called Poe's "Symposium." There, too, he speaks of "a sense of the Beautiful" as "an immortal instinct, deep within the spirit of man," insisting that what we seek is not "appreciation of the Beauty before us—but a wild effort to reach the Beauty above." The "multiform combinations among the things and thoughts of Time" impel us only in order "to attain a portion of that Loveliness whose very elements, perhaps, appertain to eternity alone." In this sense art moves us, not to pleasure in the world but to

> a certain, petulant, impatient sorrow at our inability to grasp now, wholly, here on earth, at once and forever, those divine and rapturous joys, of which, through the poem . . . we attain to but brief and indeterminate glances . . .
>
> The Poetic Principle itself is, strictly and simply, the Human Aspiration for the Supernal Beauty.

In Platonic tradition, as redirected through troubadour courtly love, the ideal woman is a conduit from the earthly to the heavenly world. In Poe, she is rather the sign of their disjunction and discontinuity. The inaccessible beautiful woman is Poe's focal figure for displacing present forms with an unreachable "Supernal Beauty." The poem "To Helen" is exemplary in this regard. The voyage that the Helen figure inspires is not to a loved woman, nor even to an historical Greece or Rome, but rather into the speaker's own interiority—the "native shore" of himself via a self-reflexive water-journey "oe'r a perfumed sea." The last stanza, as H.D.'s later rewriting of the poem makes

explicit, annihilates the woman, subsuming her into a statue that ultimately signifies the aesthetic space inside the poet's own head:

> Lo! In yon brilliant window-niche
> How statue-like I see thee stand,
> The agate lamp within thy hand!
> Ah, Psyche from the regions which
>   Are Holy Land!

Helen here is made into an art object frozen in place, as good as
dead.[20] Ultimately she represents not desire as *eros* but as Poe's own
creative mind. The lamp is his reflective consciousness, the Psyche,
his own soul, the Holy Land, his art.

This reification of woman and the artist's union into it takes shape
in Poe most often as necrophilia. The poet does not rise to higher
experience through his lady but instead becomes fixated with her in
a death-vision. "The Sleeper" turns out to be not a lady dreaming,
but a corpse, whose "closed and fringed lid" is both eye and coffin,
whose hair has continued to grow after death ("Strange, above all,
thy length of tress"), and who is now reduced to pure body, vulnerable to decay as "the worms about her creep." In "To One in
Paradise" (which William Carlos Williams named Poe's best poem),
desire is shown to be desire for total possession ("and all the flowers
were mine"), doomed and voided by the lady's death ("No more—no
more—no more—"). "The Raven," of course, remains transfixed on
the lost, dead Lenore, who may be "within the distant Aidenn," but
leaves the poem's speaker in eternal shadow. One extreme instance of
Poe's necrophilic love is "Annabel Lee." This widely sung ballad is
among Poe's creepiest. His absolute realm, at once ultimate and self-
reflective in the mirror of water, is here "a kingdom by the sea." His
unity of love is here an absolute possession: "This maiden lived with
no other thought than to love and be loved by me." Here we find his
Gnostic child, alien rather than innocent to the world. Here we find
the dire opposition between the higher world and the human one, as
child and child love "with a love that the wingèd seraphs of heaven /
Coveted her and me." But

> Neither the angels in heaven above,
> Nor the demons down under the sea,
> Can ever dissever my soul from the soul
> Of the beautiful Annabel Lee.

The children's antinomian love clashes with human society, as heaven clashes with earth, the other world with this one. Yet it is as a kind of other world, reified, rigid, frozen, that the love is concretized, in an unending embrace of living turned dead, of dead inhabiting the living. Total unity of soul to soul is oddly imaged in a word of bodily violence ("dissever"). The final stanza announces love-bed as crypt, wedded love as necrophilic possession, all in watery self-reflection:

> All the night-tide, I lie down by the side
> Of my darling—my darling—my life and my bride,
> In the sepulchre there by the sea.

The world is turned into a grave. Afterlife becomes eternal death. Love is the gateway not to a higher or redemptive experience, but to a macabre reification on earth.

Poe's "idealized" woman turned into death-effigy may be a hyperbolic exaggeration of a feminine idealization that is unnervingly enduring. Poe's intentions in pursuing this topos may be ironic, as an attempt to expose such gendered types rather than adopting them.[21] Yet even if irony is intended (and surely behind Poe's dead women hover his actual ones: his mother, his foster-mother, his wife all dying lingering tubercular deaths), his is no merely personal imp of the perverse. What Poe shows are the implications of the tradition itself: the place of women in imagining ideals and the sorts of ideals then imagined. Poe's interest is not in the woman as natural. On the contrary, he sets out to repudiate this notion in an exaggerated spiritualization, especially in his courtship letters that explicitly deny any sexual interest. His woman is unnatural body, reified as art that points only to itself, disjoined from any ladder of ascent. Whether in commitment or counter-commitment, idealized women lead Poe to a dead end: a failure to provide him either with a viable avenue of ascent or a redemptive imagined desire.

In his pursuit of women—which is to say, his reduction of them—to emblems of the absolute, Poe converts them into pure sign, one without reference to any signified. Poe was famous as a code-breaker. As editor of *The Southern Literary Messenger*, he challenged any comer to send in a code he could not solve. His invention of detective fiction likewise turns on such decodings. As a poet, he wrote encoded verses to a number of the women who emblemized for him true love. "An Enigma" and "A Valentine" each spell out the name of his different beloveds: as he explains in a note, "the first letter in the first line, the second in the second, and so on." Could "Annabel Lee" also be an anagram or cryptogram? Poe likes "ana" words. A favorite is "analytically." In one *Marginalia* (1846), he comments on "Anastasis" as the Doctrine of the Resurrection of the Body. Elsewhere he praises an "Anacreontic" verse, and in another *Marginalia* (of 1849, the same year as "Annabel Lee"), he commends Anacreon as a poetic model for whom "verse has been found most strictly married to music" as "the spirit of antique song." Perhaps Annabel Lee is an anagram, combining the prefix "ana-," meaning, "up," "back," or "through," the French pun "belle," and the suffix "-ly" to yield 'ana-belle-ly': 'anabeautily,' or 'ascent-through- beauty.' This would uncannily recall the opening lines of the very early "Al Aaraaf": "O! Nothing earthly save the ray (Thrown back from flowers) of Beauty's eye." The direction is away and up, out of the world to some other realm. "In every glimpse of beauty presented, we catch, through long and wild vistas, dim bewildering visions of a far more ethereal beauty beyond" (*E* 337). And yet in "Annabel Lee," the conduct is obstructed, the ascent turned in on itself in a reified death-in-life.

Poe's work has been described as marking a turn to the linguistic "signifier" so important to much contemporary theory.[22] Yet this turn remains tied in Poe to an older metaphysic, as a yearning for a lost signified rather than a secular celebration of open signifying play that dispenses with a signified no longer available. Poe's are blocked signifiers, not free or independent ones. His words seem to point outward or upward, but then they recoil back to pointing to themselves. They are not freed signifiers but rather defeated ones. His verse seems caught between a pull toward an absolute signified that seems to escape signifiers and the signifiers that impossibly try to attain it. This ambivalent linguistic course shapes the enigmatic "Sonnet—Silence," where Poe speaks of "things / that have a double life," caught between "matter and light," "solid and shade," "sea and shore—/ body and soul." This poem is explicitly dualist, but just what its dual sides are is not clear. The first set of dualisms is rather standard, between material and spiritual worlds. But the poem moves on to a dualism within the spiritual world itself, to a "two-fold silence" that on the one side signifies loss (Poe's ever-present "No More") but on the other erases language itself: "Nameless elf / that haunteth the lone regions where hath trod / No foot of man." Here Poe's linguistic path ends in the utter immolation of signifying altogether. In similar vein, the "Sonnet—to Science" contrasts science as a materialist and consuming vulture, "whose wings are dull realities" against a poetry that is also unreal and impotent, banishing

Naiad and elf, and leaving the poet in his own ideal "summer dream beneath the tamarind tree."

In entering realms that ultimately seem to repudiate language itself, Poe seems as remote as possible from history. But his repudiations remain historical. In Poe's "Fifty Questions" (cited by Baudelaire and wherein Poe uses the term "belles"), he distinguishes the Parisian lady's purse from the American lady's, which "must be large enough to carry both her money and the soul of its owner."[23] Calling the American dollar "one-tenth" a Roman Eagle, still, "we make all even by adoring it with ten-fold devotion" (*Marginalia* of 1849: E 1455). Poe's imagery of dream must surely be in tension with the increasingly material American Dream, just as his kingdoms stand in macabre reflection against the American utopian impulse. At issue seems to be Poe's own horribly uncertain social standing: his dispossession from coveted Southern gentlemanhood and continued ambivalence about it, his distrust of the crowds that also fascinated him.[24] As recent discussion has begun to probe, the Allan household where Poe grew up had slaves, one of whom may have served as Edgar's "mammy," yet another possible dark/light lady. Poe thus lived in a society where the very notions of gentleman and lady were founded on the reductions of humans to property, the very idea of liberty founded on subjection.[25] This is the case for the North as well as the South. Longfellow, among his other sins, is an image of hypocritical Northern materialism, a professor sitting "at ease in his library chair, and [writing] verses instructing the southerners how to give up their all with a good grace, and abusing them if they will not"—a privilege the professor himself would not "be willing to surrender" (*E* 763). Poe's turning away from the material world and yet his inability to embrace a metaphysical one, his dispossession and skepticism of a Southern inheritance and yet his barred entry into and disdain for Northern society; these polarities leave him in a gap between, with art as its image. Apocalyptic antinomianism seems not only a consequence, but also an image of the American state. What is glimpsed in Poe is the destructive drive of a particular society: a South given over to self-defeating, ruinous "ideals" and a North whose soul was increasingly reified in the image of money. Poe's dislocation thus extends to both North and South, to both this world and the next, to both history and utopia, to both speech and silence. His is not an autonomous language displacing reality, but rather a language reflecting the reality of his own displacement.

CHAPTER 6

CLAIMING THE BIBLE:
SLAVE SPIRITUALS AND
AFRICAN-AMERICAN TYPOLOGY

The origins of the slave songs reach far back into slave history. But the Civil War is the scene of their emergence into national consciousness, with the publication of "Go Down Moses" by the *National Anti-Slavery Standard* (1861) as the "Song of the Contrabands"— the terms for escaped black slaves—who fled to Northern soldiers stationed at Fort Monroe.[1] This spiritual is strongly marked by many of the features that define the slave songs: their hybrid forms, intercrossing and mutually transforming African and American religious and expressive modes; their specific combination of the sacred and secular, of theology and politics; and the contest, as well as confluence, between American visions and claims of which the Civil War itself is the most palpable and violent expression.

Discussions of the slave spirituals have largely centered on their music.[2] Their antiphonal and improvisational character ties them more closely to West African than to Euro-American musical styles.[3] Their textual composition, which has attracted much less discussion, is likewise highly syncretist. Discredited views deriving the spirituals in gospel songs have given way to recognition of the biracial revivalist contexts, in which black and white forms of worship mutually influenced each other. Here, song is the particular medium bringing white confessions to blacks and making the experience of worship more emotional and improvisational for whites.[4] The songs are, then, an intense scene of what W.E.B. Du Bois describes as African, African-American, and American encounters in hybrid cultural performances.[5]

Much remains unknown about the history of the spirituals' formations. Slave owners were not given to ethnographic interests in the cultural life of slaves, whose very status as human they were bent on repressing.[6] The transmission and recording of the slave songs is in itself a complex enterprise, facing obstacles and challenges in their collection from oral histories of former slaves and in notating their highly improvisational structures and the variant forms integral to their aesthetic, social, and political project. Here, such pivotal undertakings as the arrangements and performances of spirituals by the Fiske Jubilee Singers during the 1870s have heroic importance in the preservation and dissemination of the spiritual traditions.[7]

Within the frame of American poetry and poetics, the slave spirituals stand as a major monument of American culture and literature that has yet to be fully brought into the official canon. Indeed, far less attention has been given to the spirituals' texts than to their music. To the extent that texts have been discussed, they have been treated as secondary—"dictated," as one commentator puts it, "more by a logic of rhythm and sound than of verbal meaning."[8] Many features seen as strengths in the music are judged weaknesses in the texts, with the choral exchanges and repetitions regarded as "patchwork" lacking in "logical coherence" and with little "continuity of thought between the various lines of a stanza, between stanza and refrain, or between the various stanzas."[9] The biblical materials that make up one of the spirituals' major engagements similarly tend to be treated in desultory terms. As Thomas Wentworth Higginson was among the first to state, the spirituals appear to present a "a vast bewildered chaos of Jewish history and biography," in which "most of the great events of the past, down to the period of the American Revolution, they instinctively attribute to Moses."[10] Generally privileging Old Testament texts over New (except for Revelations), the spirituals have been described as drawing "without regard for biblical chronology or even accuracy on the whole Bible story, conflating the New Testament with the Old, and the Old with the New." Even James Weldon Johnson speaks of the "misconstruction or misapprehension of the facts of [the] source of material, generally the Bible."[11]

Far from being an accidental, derivative, or random assemblage of biblical citations, however, the spirituals offer a powerful reading of biblical textual traditions within exegetical practices that are fundamental to the formation and conduct of American identity. Sacvan Bercovitch has explored and emphasized ways in which biblical narratives emerged as American Puritan ones, as if biblical history and American history were in fact the same.[12] Werner Sollors traces how this peculiarly Puritan identity formation as biblical narrative was then adopted and transformed by subsequent and varied groups who, however remote from this specific cultural practice, made their own claims to it as part of their Americanization—thereby transforming America as well.[13] In the case of African-American slaves, this process was particularly violent. The only group to come to American not by choice but by coercion (the other systematically violated group, Native Americans, were already here), the African-American encounter with Christianity was highly fraught. Christian mission to the slaves was complicated by white planters reluctant to concede that their slaves had souls. Fear that slaves, once baptized, could claim the legal right to emancipation had been hurriedly settled with legislation explicitly denying that conversion required manumission.[14] But resistance against religious expression by the slaves remained. Slaveholders suspected religious activity would undermine slave servitude. The fundamental conditions of slavery itself, including the destabilization of family life through sexual assault and slave markets, obviously opposed the basic tenets of Christianity. A general religious indifference on the part of the slaveholders, the dispersion of the slave community across large plantations, and the lack of clergy in the South compounded the obstacles to Christian mission, which was generally tied in the South to slave politics.[15]

The problem of literacy further complicates the slaves' reception of the Bible. Frederick Douglass tells the story of the class leaders of the church "who ferociously rushed in upon my Sabbath School" and "forbade our meeting again, on pain of having our backs made bloody by the lash" (for, "if the slaves learned to read, they would learn something else, and something worse.").[16] This is no mere anecdote. It finds its place in the coercive record of slave owners enforcing illiteracy by code and deed, as against African-American resistance to these measures. On the side of repression, a comprehensive legal system against literacy was in place in the South, beginning with the 1654 and 1723 ordinances forbidding assembly, through the 1740 Slave Act forbidding teaching slaves to read, through the South Carolina law of 1800 forbidding blacks to assemble from sunset to sunrise "for the purpose of mental instruction or religious worship." As one North Carolina law declared, it is a "crime to teach, or attempt to teach any slave to read or write . . . [which] has a tendency to excite dissatisfaction in their minds and to produce insurrection and rebellion."[17] Slave accounts report punishments such as having the "forefinger cut from his right hand" for any slave caught writing.[18]

These prohibitions have implications beyond literacy, extending into symbolic and political claims regarding the African and his or her very status as a full human being.[19] Just how successful repressive measures were remains a subject of investigation, with exact rates of literacy among slaves difficult to determine. A considerable body of slave testimony portrays not only the difficulty of learning letters, but also the success, despite all, of doing so. Assessments range from 5 to 10 percent; W.E.B. DuBois speaks of 5 percent.[20] Legal restrictions, however brutal, were never uniformly instituted or applied, and the achievement of literacy is impressive in the face of dangers and difficulties.[21]

What all accounts do attest to is the religious context in which the drive to literacy took place. Both the pursuit of literacy, and to some extent the opposition against it, centered in the Bible. Slave owners attempted to edit the Bible, with emphasis on texts that promoted what John Blassingame has called the "slave beatitudes": "Blessed are the patient, the faithful, the cheerful, submissive, hardworking, and above all, the obedient."[22] Howard Thurman describes his ex-slave grandmother's enduring antipathy to selected Pauline texts such as "let every man abide in the same calling," "servants, be subject to your masters with all fear," or servants, obey in all things your masters according to the flesh."[23] Other slave testimonials report typical sermon texts: "Servants obey our masters."[24] Against such attempts to control Scripture, African-Americans themselves considered learning to read almost a religious act, and those who succeeded often assumed roles of religious leadership, providing a core of preachers able to communicate the biblical message to their communities.[25]

Against this campaign of prevention, how did African-Americans gain access not only to the biblical narrative texts, but also to the particular exegetical traditions of American interpretive historicity? One major link is the hymnal. Widespread Christianization of slaves took place within the contexts of the Great Awakenings, when dependence on literacy was displaced by other modes of conversion. Catechetical instruction gave way to evangelical preaching, increasingly democratized, which focused on the drama of sin and salvation with a spontaneity and participation familiar to African religious modes (which in turn transformed American Christianity itself). Preaching was the central religious event of the Awakenings, but alongside it in both black and white communities, song commands a central place, linking African-American Christianity to Euro-American religious traditions.[26] New methods of oral instruction ("religion without letters") were adopted, relying heavily on simplified catechisms and repetition of question and answer.[27] Of greatest significance for the spirituals, hymn singing was conducted through "lining-out," where the preacher would sing and the congregation would respond line by line.

The hymns offered more than access to biblical verses and stories. They also provided exposure to specific exegetical methods, creating a link between the slave community and sophisticated structures of biblical interpretation through which the slaves then constructed their own scriptural American history and identity.[28] The Watts hymnal has particular place in this process. Records show Watts' *Psalms, Hymns, and Spiritual Songs* was the preferred and most widely disseminated hymnal.[29] Mission records repeatedly refer to the hymnal, and specifically Watt's hymnal, as one of the earliest and most effective means of reaching a population who could not read, but could sing.[30] This widespread importance of Watts holds throughout the Great Awakening for both blacks and whites as one of the many modes of their mutual interpenetration of culture.[31]

The Watts hymnal has a special exegetical status as well. It connects the African-American experience directly to the New England heritage, reaching not only back to the Puritans, but also laterally to other contemporary uses. Watts had for generations reigned in New England churches as the primary song liturgy. It is this very Watts hymnal that Emily Dickinson took as a basis for her prosody, tropes, images, and even texts, with her own strong twists and improvisations.[32] And, Watts provides a concrete basis for studying the transmission of biblical history to the slaves and their reworking of it in the spirituals. For, unlike the Wesley Methodist hymns, which tend to dramatize the inward call to salvation, Watts centrally focuses on biblical history. Watts offers a large group of verse translations of Psalms alongside many Bible-based hymns. Moreover, the exegetical form he explicitly follows and at times explains is that of typology: a mode especially potent within American religious cultures. Far more than an interpretive method of texts, typology offers a comprehensive historical vision, with far-reaching social and political implications. Its reading of biblical history served foundationally in the shaping of American identity. The Puritans had cast their Errand into the Wilderness as an Exodus bringing them, the New Israel, across the Atlantic Ocean/Red Sea, delivering them from the bondage of Egypt/ England to found the New Jerusalem in the New World. These parallels extend beyond analogy or metaphor to historical scheme and claim. They comprise a highly structured correlation of prediction and fulfillment between events of the Old Testament and the New, and then, through a peculiarly Puritan extension of earlier Catholic traditions, to current (i.e., American) history and its meanings. In each of these timeframes—ancient Israel, the life of Christ, the inward Christian life, and contemporary American history—events correspond, extend, and ultimately fulfill each other. Catholic tradition emphasized how biblical patterns had interior and personal eschatological meanings, focusing on the spiritual life of each individual Christian and his/her final judgment. The medieval tradition, that is, generally turned the force of the biblical model inward and upward, away from historical events to the inner life or to the heavenly afterworld. The Protestant Puritans rework typology, radicalizing its historicist dimension. Not just the inner life of the individual, but also the social life of the community comes to be read in light of biblical patterns. Puritanism thus restored an external and communal historical dimension to biblical pattern.[33] The biblical types apply not only to the interior self, but also to the historical world, whose ultimate drama they identified with their own American venture as present fulfillment announcing the ultimate and final ends of history.

This American typology finds its own unique expressions in the slave spirituals, in what can be called an African-American typology.[34] This can be witnessed in "Go Down Moses." This spiritual goes well beyond a general parallel between African-American and Israelite slavery, with the Israelite redemption from Egypt an image and promise for African-American freedom. The spiritual offers a full and highly structured elaboration of biblical texts with very concrete historical claims. The song's imagined release from bondage, including claims on the Southern wealth they had produced as "Egypt's spoil," has immediate historical reference in terms of the hopes and aims of the Civil War. But it continues into a future, at once historical and prophetic, of spiritual guidance, providential intervention, Christian salvation, and finally triumphant judgment. Its terms move through quite exact biblical reference of Moses crossing the Red Sea (and duly drowning "Pharoah and his host") into the sojourn in the wilderness, and then onward through Old Testament history, across Jordan, to Joshua before the walls of Jericho:

> Jordan shall stand up like a wall (Let my people go)
> And the walls of Jericho shall fall (Let my people go)

The entry and possession of "fair Canaan's land" then opens into visions of Christian salvation, significantly figured as apocalyptic:

> O let us all from bondage flee (Let my people go)
> And let us all in Christ be free (Let my people go)

What a beautiful morning that will be! (Let my people go)
When time breaks up in eternity (Let my people go)

What emerges here are the specific and elaborated typological relationships such as can be found in the Watts hymnal. As occurs no
less in the spirituals, multiple historical and textual references appear
together in single texts. But this is not due to confusion. Rather,
it projects the intimate union between these different moments
within a divine, eternal pattern. In Watts, Christ is linked to Moses
as "redeemer" (I:56, 188); to the first Adam as his anti-type antidote
(I:57, 124); to Aaron as "priest" (I:145); to the Passover lamb as sacrifice (II:155). Watts's *Hymns* and *Psalms* even offer notes at the foot of
pages expressly declaring Old Testament figures to be "Shadow[s] of
[Christ the] Son" (Watts I: 89). Within hymns as well, Watts directly
employs such terms as "types" or "shadows." Christ appears (II: 12)
as "the true Messiah" before whom "the types are all withdrawn,"
just as "fly the shadows and the stars / Before the rising dawn." The
"types and figures" of the Old Testament in Watts Select Hymn 7 are
the "glass" for viewing Jesus as the "paschal sacrifice," the priestly
"lamb and dove," the "scape-goat"—each a "type, well understood."
Multiple figures are incorporated, placed in careful parallels and
asserting together a unity of divine purpose and divine will.

A text such as "Go Down Moses" projects a vision of history
stretching from biblical through present times into a promised future.
And yet there are significant shifts in focus and structure, even while
there are important continuities that shed light on central aspects
of the spirituals. Arguments over the spirituals' unique combination
and balances between the secular and the sacred, the political and
theological, this-worldliness and next-worldliness, take on further
resonance in the context of typological practices. African religious
sensibility has often been associated with the spirituals' deep sense
of continuity between sacred and secular realms, earthly experience
and divine presence between past, present, and future experience.[35]
But these are also characteristic of typology, and find ready form in
typological correlations. The mundane becomes an arena for divine
concern and manifestation in both the spirituals and early Puritan
typologies of events. The divine hand is seen in the most ordinary
circumstances, as when the railroad becomes a "Gospel Train."
Spirituals characteristically cross immediate conditions with ultimate
concerns, attempting, as does typology, to negotiate the distance
between them. Meanings sweep from present life into sacred realms.
This is reflected not only within the texts of individual spirituals,

but also in the fluid transitions between songs of work and songs of worship—a distinction apparently more assignable to song collectors than to song singers.

To connect daily activity with eternal reality through biblical patterning does more than deepen the spirituality of everyday existence. Establishing ties that reach from this world into the next is also a political action, claiming theological sanction and power for current undertakings. The Bible offers an appeal to the past in order to validate the present and empower the future. This is the case with the Puritan venture, and also within the African-American one. Its most dramatic instance is slave rebellion. White fears of slave literacy and the access to the Bible it provided were essentially affirmed by slave revolts: the Stono Rebellion of 1739, Gabriel's Rebellion of 1800, and the rebellions led by Denmark Vesey and Nat Turner. In each case, the leaders claimed to be realizing biblical paradigms and figures. Nat Turner identified himself with Moses, Zachariah, and Joshua, declaring "behold the day of the Lord cometh."[36] Gabriel claimed that his people, like the Israelites, shall conquer "five on hundred."[37] Anti-literacy laws were strengthened in the wake of these very rebellions.[38]

But the political context, and hence also structure, of the spirituals mark serious distinctions from other American typologies, even while they underscore the strong political implications in biblical hermeneutic. The adoption of typology by the black community introduced fundamental shifts in the structure of interpretation, in the relationships operating between past, present, and future, and in the function of the paradigms within the communal life of the spiritual singers. The difference is, above all, power. Seventeenth-century Puritans, at least in New England, early established themselves as the ruling group. It was the Puritans who defined the terms of settlement, both economically and religiously, to which other groups conformed. Within the rhetoric of typology, even within Jeremiad warnings of divine chastisement, there was an underlying sense of continuity between present conditions and future fulfillments. In general, prophetic promises were already, at least to some extent, felt and evident in present providences.

The slave community, in contrast, was without political control of economic, religious, or even personal circumstances. This difference in situation significantly shifts the balance between the poles that typology mediates. The Puritan extension of typology to their own immediate history entailed a greater correlation and integration between individual and community to follow in the paths of redemption. The carefully distinguished territories of inner and final spiritual experience as against outer history and politics—Augustine's City of God as against his City of Man—drew, for the Puritans, closer together. The pattern of conformation to divine plan is now visibly revealed in the history and politics of the Puritan colonies. This shift to history did not eliminate the eschatological level pointing beyond it. Rather, the one was in a sense incorporated into the other. Puritan politics can claim to realize biblical pattern exactly because God's Plan, in them, was approaching its final fulfillment. The Puritan "City on the Hill" is not only an event within history; it is also the final fulfillment of the divine plan as history's end.

African-American typology asserts a still more radical turn to history, where history is experienced in far more disjunctive ways. There is first an emphatic sense of the "literal" level of historical events, often recognized as an unusually immediate "identification," "parallel," "correspondence," or "literalization" in the spirituals between present and biblical history (although this identification is generally seen as based in "obvious parallels" in experience rather than a biblical hermeneutic).[39] The biblical past is more immediate. It is felt not only as interpretive paradigm, but also as present, lived experience. Slavery is both image and reality.

What occurs, then, is a collapse of the typological present and past. At the same time, a stark discontinuity looms between immediate conditions and dreams of redemption structured through biblical promise. The distinction is not so much white identification with the "new Israel" against black identification with the "old Israel;"[40] new Israel and old are, in typological terms, aspects of each other. What is different is the severity of strain in negotiating from one to the other. The past is more immediately present, and yet its relation to the overarching pattern is more problematic. Present history appeals to, but also challenges, a redemptive pattern not yet manifest. The different typological levels are in this sense discontinuous. The immediate present in slavery asserts itself in all its tragic power, against a future deliverance that penetrates in faith. But its promise has not yet been fulfilled, and the present has not been visibly incorporated into redemptive pattern. That is, such future promise is not actually evident in present circumstances, but is rather severely remote from and contradictory to them. It is this strain that serves to confirm the reality of history and its present conditions, even while passionately committed to a divine plan that remains, for now, tragically remote. History is read in light of future fulfillment and, despite faith in the triumphant outcome, retains its immediate and terrible present. What emerges, rather than a continuous world reaching from present to future by way of the past,[41] is instead an explosive and ultimately apocalyptic appeal to the future in the name of the past, not only to shape the present but also to abolish it.

There are many spirituals, even under the constraints of incomplete renderings of all the verses in variant versions, which exhibit a quite systematic and complex typological architecture. "Didn't Old Pharoah Get Los'," for example, directly juxtaposes Isaac, infant Moses, Joseph, and Samuel:

> Isaac a ransom while he lay upon an alter bound;
> Moses an infant cast away, By Pharoah's daughter found.
> Joseph by his false brethren sold, God raised above them all;
> To Hannah's child the Lord foretold How Eli's house should fall.
> (Johnson I: 60).

Each of these Old Testament figures are, of course, a type of Christ, each reenacting (before the event) Christ's passion of suffering and his glorious redemption. The parallels are, however, remarkably articulated not only through this general correlation but also in terms of the range of roles finally gathered into the Christic antitype. Isaac evokes sacrifice. Moses represents both priesthood and kingship, as does Joseph (but here, each is cast in his most vulnerable moment—as infant and sold slave—such that miraculous rescue is underscored, a type of Christian salvation). Samuel, Hannah's child, specifically invokes prophecy. The song then pursues a fuller course, through added verses, focused on Moses' confrontation with Pharaoh—including again a very specified type of "hidden manna," making the biblical bread also the spiritual body of Christ—and concluding, as the spirituals' title and refrain promises, with how "Old Pharoah an' his host/ Got los' in de Red Sea."

But historical disjunctions often haunt and undermine historical corollaries, as in "He's Jus' De Same Today":

> When Moses an' his soldiers, f'om Egypt's lan did flee,
> His enemies were behin' him, an' in front of him de sea.
> God raised de waters like a wall, And opened up de way,
> An de God dat lived in Moses' time is jus de same today.
>
> When Daniel faithful to his God, would not bow down to men,
> An' by God's enemies he was hurled into de lion's den,
> God locked de lion's jaw we read An' robbed him of his prey,
> An de God dat lived in Daniel's time is jus de same today.   (Johnson I:80)

The immeasurable odds against Moses and Daniel give way to the miraculous deliverance that overturns those in power against them. Each of these biblical events thus reflects the other, revealing an eternal pattern at work through all time and hence also "today." But when exactly is "today?" It is not, alas, the here and now of the spiritual's creation, which remains instead caught between enemies and the sea. Indeed, although "today" remains a reenactment of past sorrows, it is not yet a participation in future redemption. It is promise, but very far from fulfillment. In the spiritual "Who'll Be a Witness for My Lord," a series of biblical witnesses are cited, from Methuselah through Samson and Daniel—each as a model and image of the present-day soul (Johnson I: 130). But the deliverance they were witness to remains undisclosed in present history. Such spirituals, on the one hand, bring the promise of rescue into the present as its true paradigm. But on the other hand, redemption remains quite remote from the continued actual enslavement that has not yet met its end.

Typology as practiced here verges on apocalyptic. It is striking how many spirituals introduce scenes of judgment and trumpets, of falling stars and world immolation, when, as in the conclusion of "Didn't my Lord Deliver Daniel," the pattern is carried forward from Daniel and Jonah to "King Jesus." Jesus appears when the "moon run down in a purple stream, de sun forbear to shine, and every star disappear" and the historical world enters its final throes (Johnson I: 150). "My Lord What a Mornin' " celebrates that dawn "when de stars begin to fall...when ye hear de trumbet sound...to wake de nations under ground" (Johnson I:162). "O Rocks Don't Fall On Me," bids rocks and mountains to fall, as with "Jericho's walls," only on sinners, as "de trumpet shall soun' and de dead shall rise" (Johnson I: 164).

In such songs, the focus of energy fastens on past and future, with the present of slavery elided. And yet slavery remains the painful, defining term in all its historical force. Immediate present history is both absent and unmentioned, but still the controlling center of the asserted pattern. In this way, the slaves' political condition generates an interpretive mode. Vulnerability in political position makes the biblical past less a set paradigm for the slaves than a crisis and drama as yet unresolved. History, though interpreted in light of an encompassing pattern, is nevertheless reaffirmed in all its painfully discontinuous process. Slavery and redemption point as much away from as toward each other, requiring less fulfillment than erasure of the present by the future. This tension multiplies the relationships between parallel events cited within the spiritual texts. It calls for more radical acts of interpretation, with stark tensions and jumps, implying not only a claim to a chosen redemption, but also a counter-claim, especially against their immediate biblical/historical/political competitors, the slaveholders.

It is ultimately this immediate political context that shapes slave adaptations of typological tradition, requiring sharp transfers of meaning and discontinuities of language in a truly dynamic, communal production. Their differences in interpretation pose participants and audience against, and often in contrast with, other competing interpretive communities, as well as differently situating each interpretive community relative to the prophetic histories it claims. It is a defining feature of American culture that the Bible became a model for all who would be American. Exodus served as a central American theme: Benjamin Franklin even proposed the division of the Red Sea for the country's Official Seal. Each ethnic group came in turn to claim its own ordination as God's chosen ones. On the one hand, adopting the exodus theme signals the assimilation of diverse groups into a central American mythology. On the other, it gives rise to divergent and even conflicting usages, shifts in emphasis and in the basic structure of interpretation, as each group makes its claim against others. That is, different groups lay claim to biblical authority in order to assert their own special place in an unfolding American society. The exegetical practices for construing the Bible and applying its lessons to oneself is a form of cultural politics with profound resonance and ramification.

What this makes possible is the Bible as a common discourse between divergent American groups, but also as a scene of conflicting claims and visions. This potential for biblical conflict unsurprisingly intensifies through the ante-bellum period, as America becomes increasingly riven by competing ideological positions. Divergent readings of Scripture pose one denomination against the other, North against South both outside and within church institutions, finally culminating in church schisms that prefigure the greater national crisis.[42] Not least among these competing biblical engagements stand black against white, with the drama of evolving biblical claims and counterclaims especially charged in the emergence of the slave songs. The spirituals themselves represent a powerful vehicle of counter-claim for an African-American biblical authorization against white interpretations in all their political-economic implications. Slaves enter into the battle for the Bible, reflected in the reception, selection, and re-presentation of biblical material among African-Americans. The spirituals thus register both difference and continuity within an American culture where biblical interpretation constitutes a major dynamic of political identity.

It is of course no accident that Pharaoh's defeat should emerge on central stage. Of all the biblical histories, the story of Hebrew slavery and deliverance would have deepest resonance. Nevertheless, even this almost self-evident point of connection projects specific differences in the African-American treatment of shared symbols, as well as distinctive historical structures and the African-American relationship to them. The sharpest contrast lies in the dramatic fact that the roles of the types have been thoroughly reversed. This has, first, historical force. As against the Puritan tradition claiming America as the promised land, a tradition inherited (with differences) by both North and South, in the spirituals the South is not the New Israel, but rather Egypt. America is the land of the pharaohs, its white population the Egyptians, while African-Americans are the chosen Israelites. There is thus a stark and systematic reassignment of typological roles, which shape the choice and treatment of favorite figures and events claimed by the slaves.

It may be too much to claim, as some African-American theologians have done, that such differences amount to a "reversal of meanings of terms" and even a separate Christianity.[43] Yet there are genuine distinctions in the Bible as it is received, interpreted, and projected through the specific interests of the African-American community. As in the African-American literary practice Henry Louis Gates calls "signifyin'," within black typology the direction of the signifier/signified relationship is destabilized.[44] The correlations between present histories and eternal patterns become uncertain and contested, as do the relationships between African-American and other American typological versions. The slave songs above all directly contravene the versions of the Bible propagated by white masters. In doing so, they make distinctive and competitive claims to the Bible as a potent center of authority and power. The spirituals mark the battle between the slave community and their masters over which biblical texts should be cited as models—those preaching obedience as against those preaching deliverance; what theological interpretation should be given to them—a purely inward and otherworldly one, or an assertion of redemption reaching from past to future but with immediate historical reference; and ultimately, which community can look forward to divine reward, and which to punishment and damnation.

The slave spirituals have repeatedly been described as using codes, as when, for example, Frederick Douglass glosses: "the north was our Canaan."[45] But all typology is in some sense a code, a complex interaction and intervention between and among the signs that compose it. Each exegetical level always points beyond itself to another, with the balance between them kept in relational play. In the most fundamental sense, the whole business of typology is to mediate between an immediate history and a pattern encompassing and directing it. In its multiple structures, typology is devoted to asserting connections between secular venture and sacred vision, communal destiny and individual salvation, history and eternity, the present and an eternal plan extending into past and future. This it continues to do in the spirituals, whose "codes" remain mutually referring. They can finally be resolved neither into a purely political and this worldly meaning (with Africa an ultimate site of redemption), nor into an exclusively otherworldly longing.[46] Rather, multivalent meanings operate throughout, in ways that typology helps to illuminate.

Typology thus emerges not as a fixed set of practices but as a dynamic, interactive, and multiple political-textual mode. A founding form for both American historical consciousness and American literary practices, it comes to reflect the changing conditions and stages in an American society undergoing rapid transformation. Rather than functioning as a stable reference generating clear or unitary prophecies, typology moves back and forth between groups in mutual reflection and competition in a highly syncretist fashion, as each group seeks its own reflection in the magic mirror of the Bible, trying to project the future in the image of its chosen past.

CHAPTER 7

WOMEN'S BIBLES

In 1895, Elizabeth Cady Stanton compiled a *Woman's Bible*, collecting verses and commentary exposing "women's subordination [as] reiterated times without number from Genesis to Revelations" (II. 8).[1] Stanton's *Woman's Bible* was too radical even for the progressive National American Woman's Suffrage Association, which repudiated it. But it was nonetheless widely read, and stands as a culmination of a century of biblical controversy in religion, scholarship, and politics. Such biblical controversy extends well beyond women's issues into much of America's political and cultural life. But Stanton's feminist understanding of the Bible as an authority implicating political, legal, and social powers particularly illuminates American women's poetry, in which biblical revision constitutes a distinctive sub-genre. Albeit from a wide variety of religious and ideological positions, many women poets display an acute awareness of the Bible's power to define models, morals, and social strictures.[2]

Women poets are pious or skeptical, conservative or radical, with varying combinations of these impulses, and pursue a variety of methods in their biblical interpretation. Commonly cited stories and persons can be read with different emphases, from a specifically female point of view. Or, attention can focus on neglected texts, especially those involving female figures generally passed over in official church culture (Elizabeth Cady Stanton complained, "We never hear sermons pointing women to the heroic virtues of Deborah as worthy of their imitation." II. 19). But which texts are chosen already implies particular values and interests, across intentions that may be actively feminist and religiously liberal, or they may remain conservative and devout, with feminized viewpoints sometimes overt, sometimes hidden; or perhaps asserting themselves against and despite a conservative framework.

The very entry of women into the field of exegesis, however, already carries with it implications for their rights as women, both with regard to the constitution of religious authority and in terms of the political roles these carried in nineteenth-century America. Such a politics of exegesis is implicit in women's literary strategies and extends beyond the content of any particular reading. Specific textual explication represents only one element in a complex series of decisions and commitments. Interpretation itself is framed, first by the texts selected for exegetical attention: which actors, which events, which images will receive interpretive energy. But, second, this selection implies a prior decision as to what is significant: which figures and events are exemplary, to be taken as models for behavior, proof texts for argument, or illustrations of principles. That is, the selection of texts already privileges specific values and behaviors as exemplary. These, however, themselves derive from fundamental understandings of what the Bible teaches—a vision of the Bible's central message that the preferred passages are then adduced to demonstrate. Finally, inseparably linked to these broad principles of understanding, is the question of who has the power to do the interpreting.

These last two points are closely linked. Broadly speaking, there emerged, particularly around the issues of both slavery and women's rights, two opposing understandings as to the Bible's central and fundamental teaching. On the one hand, a "subordinationist" reading regarded the Bible as a book of hierarchical authority, extending from the text to the church and urging patient acceptance of one's lot as ordained by God within a fixed order. Such a reading asserted the divine sovereignty of God, ruling over the world through his church institutions, and authorizing hierarchical structures in which, for example, men governed women and masters governed slaves. In contrast stood what may be generally called a liberal egalitarian interpretation, which defined the Bible's central teaching as the principles of freedom, liberation, individual conscience, and the sacred integrity of every soul created equally by God.

The principles of subordination or liberality implicated not only the biblical message but also the right to interpret it.[3] If the Bible declares both sexes equal, then Scripture itself allows women, and not only the established male, white clergy (such as those who denounced Stanton's Bible as "the work of women and the devil" [II, 7]) the power of exegesis. The issues of biblical exegesis thus extended from the content of a given interpretation to questions regarding which

biblical texts should be emphasized, which figures should be adopted
as exemplary models, which criteria should guide interpretation, and
who possessed the right to do the interpreting.[4]

Contests over women's right to interpret the Bible take their place
within a proliferation of competing claims and approaches to the
Bible, in an America increasingly pluralist—or at least increasingly
divergent—in its religious groupings and their modes of organization.
America from the outset had presented difficulties for centralized
religion. Its spatial extent and multiple colonies made it logistically
impossible for any one authority to establish extensive control. But the
theological principles inherent to Puritanism itself guarded, implicitly or explicitly, against too tight a central authority. Inner voice,
"calling," and conversion all grounded religion in individual experience, even if this was then disciplined into church organization. And
churches themselves increasingly varied as the dearth of ministers
opened church leadership to itinerant lay preachers, untrained in the
niceties of divinity and outside any formal church structure.[5] As to
the Bible, Protestant traditions emphasizing personal encounter with
Scripture had from the start democratized access to the text. New
exegetical methods, introduced through the higher criticism, further splintered biblical modes of reading and understanding, including fundamental questions of truth and authority. Its historicist,
Wissenschaft orientation approached the Bible not as an ahistorical
revelation, but rather as a set of documents written, transcribed, and
redacted under varying historical circumstances by divergent authors
and groups.[6]

Within such contexts of multiplying biblical access and authorities, women too took their place as interpreters.[7] Such participation
enacted disparate if not outright contradictory impulses. On the one
hand, the Bible remained a key point of reference and authority. On
the other, the Bible was seen to sanction conflicting positions, which
in turn called into question traditional notions of authority itself.
These two poles frame the Bible's cultural power: it provided a common discourse in America, even for warring camps.[8] Whatever the
disagreements of purpose and dissent of opinions, they were conducted in terms of a shared biblical discourse as fundamental to both
personal identity and American cultural community. Both disagreement and consensus inform women's uses of the Bible. In it intercross trends traditional and radical, conservative and reforming, with
the Bible as a common language in which opposing ideologies could
clash. Yet through it, these divergent voices could also participate in a
joint American community.

Lydia Sigourney's uses of the Bible, as with her other discourses, exemplify how conservative affiliations are altered by the very fact of a woman's disseminating them. Sigourney's conformity in her piety and deployment of feminine roles made her as immensely popular in her own day as she has since been dismissed for sentimental "hack work." But hers are resolutely female voices, which structure her work in determined ways. Her poem "The Ark and Dove," for example, is set as a scene of female domestic instruction, in which a mother tells her daughter a biblical story. But the retelling of Noah and the Flood as "The Ark and the Dove" domesticizes the tale and gives to it a female heroine. It is on the "meek dove" that the fate of all depends. This dove is "gentle," but she is also adventurous and courageous, setting out on her own initiative rather than being sent by Noah, in a solitary, heroic venture that leaves her mate behind, who "with sad moans wondered at her absence."

The dove thus emerges as a figure of heroic devotion, and she is not the only hero(ine). The mother who recounts the story concludes by encouraging her daughter to adopt the dove as model, to "dare the billows of the world...like that exploring dove." But the mother is heroic in her own turn. The poem's conclusion in many ways proposes the mother as corresponding to Noah himself, placing her into a chain of biblical types that ultimately refer to Christ, and also the poet. The mother's "heart's eloquence" forms a "prayer [that] goes up / From a sealed lip," telling a "voiceless wish" that when her daughter, that "timid soul," should at some time

> ...find no rest,
> A pierced, a pitying, a redeeming hand
> May gently guide it to the ark of peace.

Christ is the ultimate redeemer. Yet, as a pitying, gentle guide, he appears more as mother than male, with the mother/poet made in his/her image, not least in the modesty of her "sealed lip," which however speaks, and "voiceless wish," which, however, she voices.[9]

In Sigourney's text, female nature continues to be described as "timid," just as the dove herself is "meek." But this becomes a basis for action, at least in the interest of protecting domestic arks—and also of writing about them. Despite, and indeed through, these conservative images, Sigourney takes the Bible into her own interpretive hands and speaks for female experience and redemptive power.

Thus, even texts committed to conservative Christian and social values introduce progressive features in the very fact of new, women interpreters speaking in their own voices and from their own experiences. Often texts represent volatile combinations of these conflicting impulses. Such is the case in the writing of Frances Harper. Harper is as radical as Sigourney is conservative. Yet she too is a devout Christian, and makes clear the progressive potential in the American religious traditions. For her, the Bible becomes the ground for defense of women and attacks on slavery, as indeed was the case throughout ante-bellum discourses of abolition and pro-slavery forces, as well as temperance, moral reform, and even suffrage. In these debates, the Bible was a central weapon, with proof texts blandished on both sides. To slave owners, it provided God-given sanction for their own legitimacy and a means of attack against their opponents as rebels against God. To abolitionists and women's rights groups, the Bible taught personal dignity, responsibility, and equality.[10] As Lydia Child observed, "sects called evangelical were the first agitators of the woman question" (*Liberator*, July 23, 1841), even if their activities went against the intention of a more conservative clergy who was losing control of their female crusaders.[11] Thus Angelina Grimke's *Appeal to the Christian Women of the South*, urges Southern women to "read the Bible" so as to "judge for yourselves whether he sanctioned such a system of oppression and crime" as slavery. Sarah Grimke's *Letters on the Equality of the Sexes and the Condition of Woman* makes this case concerning women's rights: "I shall depend solely on the Bible to designate the sphere of woman," against "the perverted interpretation of Holy Writ" invoked to defend corrupt institutions. The Bible is a text not of hierarchical oppression but of deliverance. It mandates not "anti-Christian traditions of men," but "the commandments of God: Men and women were CREATED EQUAL: they are both moral and accountable beings, and whatever is right for man to do, is right for women."[12]

Frances Harper's Christian piety is characteristic of the African-American community, whose radical religious energy is visible in the emergence of black women preachers and activists.[13] Calling, conversion, and conscience all summoned women to preach the Lord's message, even, as they themselves vehemently insisted, against any intention to assert themselves. Jarena Lee, Zilpha Elaw, Julia Foote, who emerged as African-American women preachers, all modestly cite divine authority as impelling them to transgress gender roles. Maria Stewart, the first woman to speak publicly in mixed gender settings, makes the same modest claims.[14] They enact an egalitarianism revealed in God's power to call them, and preach a committed liberal reading of religious equality.[15]

Frances Harper self-consciously addresses Bible interpretation as a scene of competing power. Her "Bible Defense of Slavery," responding to a pro-slavery tract of that title, attacks such biblical appeal as a false "mockery of praise" by the white church, through a steady course of rhetorical inversion:

> A "reverend" man, whose light should be
> The guide of age and youth,
> Brings to the shrine of Slavery
> The sacrifice of Truth.
>
> For the direst wrong by man imposed,
> Since Sodom's fearful cry,
> The word of life has been unclosed
> To give your God the lie.

"Light" is made darkness by a falsely "reverend" man, who, instead of upholding "Truth" sacrifices it, making it serve the "lie" of slave interest. At the poem's end, white Christians themselves are shown to be the true "heathens."

Harper here, unlike Stanton and against the trends of Higher Criticism, does not doubt biblical inerrancy.[16] Nor do opposite claims and interpretations make her doubt the existence of biblical truth. To Harper, the Word of God remains "unique and pre-eminent, wonderful in its construction, admirable in its adaptation, [containing] truths that a child may comprehend," as she writes in her epilogue to *Poems on Miscellaneous Subjects* (1891). The Bible is abused in defenses of slavery. Its true message remains "the word of life," which has been "unclosed" to give God "the lie," as she writes in "Bible Defense." Harper's own duty is instead to disclose the true word against distortions and misappropriation.

Harper's work has close ties to the spiritual tradition. In her poem "Deliverance," she effectively writes a spiritual of her own, tracing the Exodus story through its historical and typological unfolding, from the Hebrews to Christ as sacrificial lamb to the still awaited Jubilee of full deliverance to come. The Exodus story is still more fully elaborated in her long narrative poem, "Moses, a Story of the Nile." Like her novel *Iola Leroy*, it is a story of passing and resistance against it. Moses abandons his Egyptian identity to rejoin his enslaved people, suggestively placed in Southern slave cabins, harvesting Southern crops.

In such poems as "Bible Defense of Slavery" and "Deliverance," Harper's racial identity takes precedence over gender. "Moses" introduces interesting gendered elements, making Moses' mother and

Pharaoh's daughter central figures, who initiate Moses into his own history and whose viewpoints mediate Moses' experience and decision. Miriam, Moses' sister, also is featured in her Song of Triumph on crossing the Red Sea. But even if gender is not underscored, Harper takes on herself a prophetic voice and role. In this she enacts egalitarian readings of the Bible, which she also explicitly announces in "Moses" when she makes the Revelation at Sinai declare: "the one universal principle, the unity of God," as this "link[s] us with our fellow man [in] peace and freedom...instead of bondage, whips and chains." In other poems, Harper features biblical women who have been traditionally neglected or cast as negative figures. Hagar, Abraham's disinherited concubine, becomes the type of divine mercy and redemption from despair in Harper's "Dedication Poem." Vashti, too, emerges as a defining figure. The first wife of the Persian King Ahasveros as told in the Scroll of Esther, Vashti is generally viewed as the rebellious woman as against Esther, who takes her place as queen after Vashti refuses to appear unveiled before the drunken courtiers at the king's feast. But Harper presents Vashti's defiance as not only heroic, but also womanly. In response to the king's summons to "unveil her lovely face" amid the lordly (and drunken) men at his feast, Vashti "proudly" answers:

> I'll take the crown from off my head
> And tread it 'neath my feet,
> Before their rude and careless gaze
> My shrinking eyes shall meet.

What is striking here is that Vashti's rebellious disobedience is based in her womanly modesty. Hers are "shrinking eyes," but this is the ground for her rejecting the men's "rude and careless" sexual "gaze." Modesty is thereby reversed from a marker of submission to one of self-defense and self-definition. Vashti defies the king's decree that would bring her "shame," exposing the king as the one who is shameful. The political implications of these gender displacements are recognized in the *Scroll of Esther* itself, where the king's advisors warn that Vashti will make all "husbands contemptible" and therefore must be removed to safeguard the order of home and kingdom (1:17). Harper inscribes this in her poem: "The women, restive 'neath our rule, / Would learn to scorn our name." But "Vashti" does just that, with "name" itself a vital scene of contest. As queen, Vashti's name was not in fact her own. In the poem Vashti reclaims it: "A queen unveil'd before the crowd! / Upon each lip my name!" At the last,

Vashti claims for herself an independent social status in her own name as woman rather than queen:

> And left the palace of the King,
> Proud of her spotless name—
> A woman who could bend to grief
> But would not bow to shame.

Harper does not contest the Bible's claim to authority. On the contrary, she appeals to it. Nevertheless, by offering her own versions of biblical events, she takes part in a proliferation of exegetical practices that implicitly challenged biblical authority. Her work displays an ambivalence that seems deeply embedded through the entire evolution of women's self-representation in the nineteenth century. She remains, on the one hand, traditional regarding Scripture's sacred status, and even appears genteel in some of her assumptions about Christianity and women's sphere. In a prose epilogue, for example, she reaffirms the Christian faith as a "system uniform, exalted and pure," which "has nerved the frail and shrinking heart of woman for high and holy deeds." Nevertheless, in practice, her commitment to the rights of African-Americans and women led her to untraditional emphases with potentially liberal implications.

Vashti, as a figure bringing together these various and contesting elements, is not only evident in Harper, but also in a whole series of poems by nineteenth-century women. Elizabeth Cady Stanton had singled Vashti out (along with Miriam, Deborah and Huldah, and against Sarah, Rebecca, and Rachel. I, 13) for special commendation: "Huldah and Vashti added new glory to their day and generation— one by her learning and the other by her disobedience" (II, 83). Anna Howard Shaw similarly praises Vashti in an article entitled "God's Women" (*Woman's Journal*, March 7, 1891),[17] as does Lucinda Chandler, for whom Vashti is the symbol of "that point in human development when womanliness asserts itself and begins to revolt and throw off the yoke of sensualism and of tyranny" (II, 87). What is striking about Vashti is that her rebellion is made in the name of modesty, which in many ways made up the heart of the cult of domesticity and of female definition. Vashti is womanly, upholding specifically female virtues, but also defiant, making those virtues the basis of self-assertion.

Vashti emerges as this combination of submission and assertion in a Helen Hunt Jackson sonnet. Jackson's Vashti is "pure and loyal-souled as fair." But she is "bold to dare / Refuse the shame which madmen would compel," exactly in the name of her womanly "love." Underscoring that Vashti in fact was royal on her own account and not just through her marriage ("I am his queen; I come of king's descent"), Jackson's poem makes Vashti the figure worthy of royal standing. Jackson in fact prefers Vashti to Esther, who she depicts in a companion sonnet as too self-sacrificing. Of Esther, Jackson writes:

> Thou heldest thy race too dear, thyself too cheap;
> Honor no second place for truth can keep.

This poem criticizes Esther's sacrifice of "truth" to herself, in subordination to the "honor" of her people. In these figures, the difficulty of negotiating between self and service strongly emerges. Stanton had written: "Our motto is: self-development is a higher duty than self-sacrifice" (II, 131). Yet even Stanton, while making Vashti a type of rebellion, imagines her response to the chamberlains to be: "Go tell the king I will not come; dignity and modesty alike forbid" (II, 85). Modesty and defiance, restriction and rebellion, remain contesting forces difficult to reconcile.

Another extended treatment, called "The Revolt of Vashti," was undertaken by Ella Wheeler Wilcox. Wilcox's Vashti openly challenges gender assignments, insisting she will not only "loose my veil" but also "loose my tongue!" Modesty is exposed as an economic, social, and sexual status, tied above all to the power of speech itself:

> I am no more than yonder dancing girl
> Who struts and smirks before a royal court!
> But I will loose my veil and loose my tongue!
> Now listen, sire—my master and my king:
> And let thy princes and the court give ear!
> 'Tis time all heard how Vashti feels her shame.

Vashti's "shame" here is not her rejection of modesty, but her reduction to being the king's concubine and possession. This she brings to public notice in the name of true, self-chosen modesty, in what amounts to a political speech delivered before the court. She goes on to claim her own selfhood outside the hierarchical gendered order— that is, to name herself:

> I was a princess ere I was a queen.
> And worthy of a better fate than this!
> There lies the crown that made me queen in name!

Here stands the woman—wife in name alone!
Now, no more queen—nor wife—but woman still—
Aye, and a woman strong enough to be
Her own avenger.

Imagery of the "name" emerges as central to this and other women's poetry. Here, naming herself and exchanging the dependant titles of "queen" and "wife" for "woman," mark Vashti's accession to her own self-identity and strength.

Vashti is a figure of particular interest in the way she combines modesty and assertion as contradictory impulses being renegotiated. She, however, is only one of a number of figures from the Bible, each of whom represents different combinations of feminine attributes undergoing reassessment and transformation. Maria Gowen Brooks' narrative poem, *Zophiel* (1833), rewrites the Book of Tobit. Here Brooks introduces her own characters and events in what is in many ways an erotic fantasy. Rufus Griswold nevertheless includes portions of it in his 1848 *Female Poets of America* anthology—an essentially conservative collection with little verse dedicated to biblical topics. Brooks had also published an earlier work, *Judith, Esther, and Other Poems* (1820), which reworks biblical material in quite traditional ways. Modesty remains the central, defining attribute, but it is also a mode of heroic strength and courage. Thus, although Esther is "gentle, meek, and mild," the poems also investigate Esther's fears and ambivalence, exploring a female interiority and projecting a female heroism. Brooks is critical of the treatment Vashti receives, who despite "all her beauty" was dishonored "for one slight offense." Brooks' Judith is similarly presented as "proudly meek." But she is also wily and courageous, with a heavy emphasis on erotic power that becomes, in the end, communal leadership, as Judith calls to the "weeping Judea: arm thee in his might / Arise, Arise, the enemy is thine."

In some writers, then, conventional heroines are treated, but their traditional virtues are given new interpretations. In other writers, figures traditionally disapproved of are reinterpreted in positive and often surprising terms. Wilcox wrote a poem on "Delilah," a figure even Stanton saw as wicked. Adah Isaacs Menken, like Maria Brooks, retells the story of "Judith." But she quite thoroughly redefines what makes her heroic. Menken was notorious in her day for scandalous love affairs and marriages (she claimed there were six), changes of identity (probably born in New Orleans in 1839 to free African-American parents, she converted to Judaism on marrying Alexander Isaac Menken, and claimed Jewish ancestry), many places of residence in both America and Europe, and a sensational professional career as an actress. After reading her poem on Judith, what comes to seem strange is how the iconographic tradition could ever have represented this dauntless and deceptive woman as embodying the victory of chastity and humility over lust and pride. Menken's Judith is a wild warrior and contentious prophet, aggressive both in flesh and spirit. Menken is selective, even fragmentary, in her presentation of story elements. Instead of the narrative of Judith as attracting, fêting, and then decapitating Holofernes, the general who has laid siege to Bethulia in the wars of Nebuchadnezzar, the poem shows Judith primarily engaged in acts of prophetic speech. Menken is one of the few nineteenth-century women poets to break free of traditional metric and stanzaic form, writing in a verse clearly influenced by Whitman. Judith speaks in the poem in the loose, rhythmic cries of the Psalms, calling on the "God of Battles" as her guide and claiming the visionary "sword of the mouth" of Revelations (II.16). Her theme, indeed, is "the advent of power" of both word and sword in apocalyptic intensity ("Power that will unseal the thunders! Power that will give voice to graves!"). The poem's final section glorifies Judith herself in self-proclaimed identity and self-naming: "I am Judith! ... Oh forget not that I am Judith!"

Judith is somewhat gruesome in her blood lust, with Holofernes's murder a frenzy of sensual passion. Menken seems intent on making the point, as Judith puts it, "I am no Magdalene waiting to kiss the hem of your garment." In an almost inverse typology, Old Testament figures consistently displace New Testament ones in women's writing, with submission replaced by anger. Judith is become a woman of desires, not of sorrows. Above all, what emerges as central is the imagery of voice itself: the dead Holofernes's "great mouth" opens vainly "in search of voice," but Judith calls to speech the living and the dead, "each as their voices shall be loosed." In Menken's "Judith," both battle and prophecy are ultimately those of poetic power and identity.

This central place of voice and its assertion, of self-naming and identity, is evident throughout women's treatments of biblical materials, with all that this implies concerning public roles and political definition. Beyond specific interpretations, the role of biblical interpreter, especially within American cultural politics, itself entails emergence from the strictly private into the public sphere, in ways that cast both in new light. Religion in many ways crosses these divisions. Private conscience grounds public action and authority. For women, this could impel to public involvement and address, exactly as based on religious principles in many ways conservative, yet also themselves inextricably communal and public.

This is the case even for so private a poet as Emily Dickinson. On this, as on other topics, Dickinson's poetry is, unsurprisingly, more complex than most other women poets of the period. Her handling of biblical material must be placed in the broader contexts of her religious stances, as well as her poetic practices. Emily Dickinson's religious position is particularly fraught. Despite her powerful critique of dogma and institutional religion, Dickinson is not merely secular. Although she largely abandons church life, she never loses her sense of urgency over religious questions. She painfully appeals repeatedly to a God who she could not understand and who she blames for the world's suffering. But without Him, the world stood even more inexplicable and terrifying. Her poetry traces the intense confrontation between two impossibilities: neither faith, nor the complete abandonment of it, was acceptable to her. Each continued in her work in ongoing struggle and mutual contest.

Dickinson's poems on the Bible take their place within this ongoing religious disputation, with the further resonance the Bible had in the cultural and, indeed, political American world surrounding her. While there are relatively few poems that overtly rework biblical figures, many Dickinson poems cite Scripture and incorporate allusions to it. And while there are no women biblical figures in her work, Dickinson's uses of the Bible remain framed by the fact that she is a woman.[18] In the poem "I took my Power in my Hand," for example, the speaker compares her attempt to "go against the World" to David's. But her sense of being "against the World" already situates her differently from him, who acted for a people, even if against an enemy. Moreover, her attempt, unlike David's, does not succeed. "I aimed my Pebble—but Myself / Was all the one that fell" (J 540). The very effort to assert herself also works against her, who remains torn between her desire to act and speak with authority and the male authorizing figures and texts that she would need to call on to do so. David thus proves a problematic model for her as a woman. Indeed, Dickinson's writing on and to God registers issues of how her gender counts in and structures a woman's relationship to the divine. She can never simply say, "Title Divine Is Mine" as, for example, Emerson might, but must always add "The Wife without the Sign." Her title remains derivative, and depends, in a pun, on being "bridalled"—at once made bride and reined in, indeed silenced. Here and elsewhere, Dickinson's relation to the Bible and to God remains divided against itself. Like Jacob in the poem "A little East of Jordan," she wrestles with and against apparent biblical claims and indeed against Divinity itself, to find that "s/he had worsted God!" (J 59). But this is not the same as to abandon Him.

Even more pervasive through Dickinson's work than the Bible is the hymnal, in which she based her poetic meters and formal patterns.

Her model, significantly, is *Psalms, Hymns, and Spiritual Songs* of Isaac Watts, which provides her with more than prosody. Careful examination of her and his texts shows Dickinson to have reworked not only his hymnal forms but also his language: imagery, rhetorical figures, and tropes, even rewriting specific hymns. More than irony is at work here.[19] As in other areas of her religious sensibility, parody and sincere performance presuppose and penetrate each other. Dickinson's subversions of the hymnal also assert her tie to them, making them another arena of religious conflict, and ultimately raising general questions about the powers and claims of imagery and rhetoric as such.

Dickinson's rewritings of the hymnal include her poem "Go slow, my soul, to feed thyself / Upon his rare approach (J 1297 / Fr 1322), which reworks Watts', "Stand up my soul, shake off thy fears, / And gird thy gospel armour on" (2:77). "Heaven is so far of the Mind" (J 370 / Fr 413), echoes Watts', "In secret silence of the mind, / My heaven—and there my God, I find" (2:122). "The Road to Paradise is plain / And holds scarce one" (J 1491 / Fr 1525) takes for its text Watts' "broad is the road that leads to death" (2: 158), which Austin Dickinson called "sufficiently depressing in plain print" and "appalling" when sung.[20] Typically, Dickinson twists and complicates Watts' intentions, and yet at the same time continues to operate in their frame, often subverting her own subversions and attesting their continued claim on her. For example, Watts'

> Faith is the brightest evidence
> Of things beyond our sight;
> Breaks through the clouds of flesh and sense,
> And dwells in heavenly light   (1:120)

becomes in Dickinson equivocal. His "Faith" as "brightest evidence" becomes in her "Faith as "Pierless Bridge," a pun on peerless that revokes its meaning to imply a denial of proper support (J 915 / Fr 978). Dickinson's text, like Watts', is based in Hebrews 11. But for Watts, the bridge of faith conducts from the visible world to the invisible one: "breaks through clouds of flesh and sense." For Dickinson it betokens a "scene that we do not" see, that is "too slender for the eye." This could denote the invisible spiritual world, or it can occlude it. Yet Dickinson's ambiguous counter-hymn in the end does not simply repudiate faith, but rather retraces its own "vacillating feet." We remain "behind the Veil" of this world and do not see beyond it. Dickinson here may be distinguishing faith as against knowledge: to believe is not to know; or, she may be challenging belief as such. In Dickinsonian usage, the "Veil" is often a sign of the body, specifically the female one, covered and covering. Here, this is a sign of both limitation and the hope of reaching beyond it, a hope, however, that turns back on itself. Dickinson finally does not renounce the "Bridge" that is faith, but instead pronounces it to be a "Necessity" to "Feet," that remain "vacillating."

Dickinson wrote over half of her verse during the Civil War, a time when Scripture was as torn apart as the country, with each side, as Lincoln said, praying to the same God and reading the same Bible: "The prayers of both could not be answered." This political use of Scripture frames Dickinson's own uses of it.[21] But she refuses to invoke the Bible as proof text for her own positions. She instead opens the biblical text to skeptical warning against any such clear cut claims fully to possess its meanings. To her, the war was an intensification of the suffering she felt to be inherent in human experience. The Bible at once invokes justifications and becomes a vehicle for expressing doubts about them. It becomes an authority against itself. "Moses wasn't fairly used," Dickinson writes in one poem (J 1201). "It always felt to me—a wrong," she writes in another, "To that Old Moses—done—/ To let him see—the Canaan—/ Without the entering" (J 597 / Fr 521). God's punishment to Moses seems excessive, an exercise of (male) power, like an older "boy" to a "lesser" one. This failure, or barrier, to entering the Promised Land may have an American resonance in terms of failed or impossible political mission. The poem in any case sides with the human Moses against the divine: "My justice bleeds—for Thee! (J 597) Here the voice of judgment is earthly and female, claiming its own authority.

Dickinson's poetry remains oblique regarding historical and political matters, including her biblical engagements. But the Bible's cultural position and resonance in America makes any reference to it communal and not merely private, while using it in explicitly public ways was an especially powerful rhetoric. The Bible marks in fact the two most public, and also most circulated, poems by nineteenth-century women: Julia Ward Howe's "Battle Hymn of the Republic" and Emma Lazarus's "New Colossus." Howe herself had begun as a genteel female poet, whose early poetry is perhaps especially marked by the uncertainties of modesty as a basis for poetic venture. Much of her early verse enacts apologies for its own existence. It was in turning to more public issues beyond herself that Howe also found a strengthened poetic voice. Her *Later Lyrics* features poetry addressed to the conflicts of American culture, and ultimately the Civil War. Her tour de force is the "Battle Hymn," which she claimed came to her from a higher power—as indeed it may be said to have done, that is, the power of biblical rhetoric itself. In the poem, Howe displays an almost technical virtuosity in her patterning of biblical correlations and typologies, assembling and compounding a series of apocalyptic texts from Daniel, Joel, Isaiah, Ezekiel, and Revelations—texts that are mutually referring already in the Bible itself. Particularly American is Howe's extension of them to the immediate historical scene around her, making America itself a biblical type and fulfillment of sacred history. Thus the harvest of wrath (Joel 3:1 / Revelation 14:19) becomes the lightning of the Second Coming (Revelation 19:15), seen as now present and revealed in the military "watch-fires" and "dews and damps" of the Civil War camps.

As in all exegetical undertakings, interpretation here is not neutral, either in its assignment of roles or in its working principles. As a white, Northern, Unitarian, Julia Ward Howe unhesitatingly identifies the North with God's army and the South with his "contemners." In a conflict at once immediate and cosmic, the "burnished rows of steel" of historical guns write a "fiery gospel" in which the hero (North) crushes the serpent (South) in present and eternal time. The text as a whole powerfully joins liberal with religious faith:

> In the beauty of the lilies Christ was born across the sea,
> With a glory in his bosom that transfigures you and me.
> As he died to make men holy, let us die to make men free,
> While God is marching on.

The "Battle Hymn" offers a creed of the American civil religion equating the sacred integrity of every individual soul transfigured in Christ with freedom, itself the image of holiness. This individual actor is asserted above all in the poem's own speaker, who is "swift my soul to answer" and calls each soul to such response. Howe's call is not only to a specific interpretation, but also to the right for each self to interpret, yet within the language and ethos of communal values and toward a social redemption beyond individual salvations. The characteristic mix of conservative and progressive is strong here: the poem's patriotic apocalypticism is highly nationalistic, but its individual call is liberal.[22]

Not least, the voice of this call is a woman's. There is little overt gendering in the "Battle Hymn." The hero "born of woman" reminds us, perhaps, that the sex said to have brought sin into the world also brought its redemption. But the poem repeatedly dramatizes the status of the speaker, who is a woman, by repeatedly underscoring her visionary stance and prophetic action of witness: "Mine eyes have seen," "I have seen," "I can read his righteous sentence by the dim and flaring lamps," "I have read a fiery gospel writ in burnished rows of steel." Howe underscores her own visionary powers. The text finally proclaims not only the divine power unfolding before her, but also her own power to see into the world's events and unveil their ultimate and eternal meanings. Without direct reference to her gender, she nevertheless asserts her power to read history in all its political force.

Women's uses of the Bible focus many paradoxes, not only for them but within American ideologies and the Bible's role in shaping and conducting them. Accepted by all as foundational to American self-understanding, the Bible nonetheless could be enlisted to defending slavery and hierarchy, as well as to attacking them in the name of individual conscience and the equal value of all before God. This power of biblical discourse within the public and political arena had been recognized by radical and conservative women alike. Already at the 1837 Anti-Slavery Convention of American Women, a resolution had passed explicitly associating biblical interpretation with women's access to power: "Woman has too long rested satisfied in the circumscribed customs that a perverted application of the Scriptures have marked out for her, and that it is time she should move in the enlarged sphere which her great Creator has assigned her."[23] Even Frances Willard, president of the essentially conservative Women's Christian Temperance Union, called in *Woman in the Pulpit* for "women commentators to bring out the women's side of the Bible."[24]

How far America's shared biblical discourses could contain the competing claims conducted within it is a question dramatized by the Civil War itself. From the viewpoint of the history of women's poetry, what is especially striking is the poems' decidedly and self-evidently public concern, and not least in their biblical engagement. The poems, simply in engaging in exegesis, already contest restrictions against women's participation in public and indeed political activity. In an America relatively naked of institutions, the Bible remained a central reference for any attempt at self-definition: religious, political, or social. Women poets, by taking part in biblical discourse, are not only exploring their personal or religious identities, but also their place within the American political community. At stake in this poetry is their very right to speak, which itself becomes a central poetic subject, and which in turn implicates their right to participate within the American polity.

CHAPTER 8

FRAGMENTED RHETORIC IN
BATTLE-PIECES

Melville's *Battle-Pieces* is an intractable work, but this is part of his purpose. Melville had been driven to poetry after a decade that began with the dazzling success of his novels of South Sea adventures, but traced his course of increasing failure as a writer, in exact ratio as his novels became more serious and artful.[1] By the time of the Civil War, Melville had retreated into the custom house office job (no. 75), whose bureaucratic enclosure he had dreaded all his life. The urgencies of the war pressed him to write what he hoped would become part of the common discourse of Civil War verse, which was at the time wildly popular. Nevertheless, what he wrote was a poetry he generally called "eminently adapted to unpopularity."[2] His "Battle Pieces" not only refused the side-taking partisanship that enlisted other writers and readers, but also unraveled the very grounds for doing so. Their outstanding feature is their resistance to interpretation. As a fierce encounter with contemporary culture, the poems are centered on not only history, but also the effort to construe it. Interpretation is at the crux: the compulsion toward it, and beyond even its impossibility, its endless pitfalls.

It has long been known that Melville took as his source for "Battle Pieces" a compilation of newspaper accounts of Civil War events called the *Rebellion Record*, a project already begun during the war years themselves. Melville scrupulously marks each of his poems with the place and date of the events he ties them to, as reported in the *Record*. But the outstanding feature of the poems, as of the *Record* itself, is not the events detailed, but the wildly antagonistic points of view represented in the different accounts of them. It is a mistake to assume, as is often done, that Melville intends his poems to cover the Civil War events, but in verse forms inadequate to the task. Edmund Wilson's view of *Battle-Pieces* as "a chronicle of patriotic feelings of an anxious middle-aged non-combatant as, day by day, he reads the bulletins from the front," already condemns it as "versified journalism" and "some of the emptiest verse that exists."[3]

Yet it is also unhelpful to try to reduce the poems to "themes" seen to structure Melville's prose writings: his philosophical, moral, and political concerns. The poems certainly raise these concerns, along lines that have been described as posing order against anarchy, law against empire, problems of evil and other moral and metaphysical challenges, or the tragic need for action in a world of ambiguity.[4] They are, additionally, political, based in Melville's thoughts on slavery, democracy, union, and America. But the poems cannot be made into a systematic account of any of these concerns, as has been repeatedly attempted.[5] What the poems render, instead, is neither event nor political judgment nor moral dilemma, but rhetoric itself: how the language in which both events and politics are represented has its own force, its own structure, its own impact, energy, and power. *Battle-Pieces* provides less an historical or philosophical record than a rhetorical one. It does not record events so much as examine and rework the role of rhetoric in shaping the meaning of the war and of America itself. This proves to be an explosive field in which differing accounts contest with one another. Melville shows both the importance of rhetoric in shaping national self-understanding and how even shared rhetorical modes become, in the Civil War, arenas of contention and competing claims.

Battle-Pieces, then, offers an experience of rhetorical contest and division (and the title surely puns on fragmentation). The contest is ultimately over interpretative patterns and their power to shape the meaning of events. This was made vivid to Melville in the juxtaposed accounts provided by the *Rebellion Record*, which make visible the ways in which historical positioning directs how events are construed rather than forming mere background, framework, or material of reportage. Articles from *New York World*, *New York Times*, *Boston Transcript*, and *Philadelphia Enquirer* appear alongside those from *Richmond Enquirer*, *Charleston Courier*, *Baltimore Sun*, and *Louisville Democrat*, to name a few.[6] Not only battles but political speeches (Abraham Lincoln's alongside Jefferson Davis') and sermons are included, each registering severely different points of view.[7] Sermon and speech, religion and politics follow each other, with national fasts called for in the service of each different cause and political division penetrating denominations as ministers in churches recently split through the sectional strife invoke Bible and Christ each against the other. Each volume of the *Record* then concludes with patriotic verse, Northern and Southern, with a wide selection of battle hymns, the genres Melville's *Battle-Pieces* presumably are to join.

But Melville's work deviates from both the politics and the roles of Civil War verse. He renders not historical sources, but contemporary rhetoric and interpretive paradigms as these shape and impel experience, and as these are ultimately distorted and unreliable. The poems represent not Melville's own viewpoints, but the force of viewpoint itself and its modes of presentation. This is dramatized in the long poem "Donelson (February, 1862)," whose sections are organized (pre-James Joyce) through headlines and news bulletins: "IMPORTANT," "LATER FROM THE FRONT," "GLORIOUS VICTORY OF THE FLEET!" "WE SILENCED EVERY GUN." Opening with a scene of "anxious people" crowding around a "bulletin-board," newspaper formatting and its effects are as much the poem's subject as any of the events it announces. As the poem slyly remarks: "(Our own reporter a dispatch compiles/ As best he may, from varied sources)". Its subject is how presentation interprets its material, a comment on the modes of newspaper reporting as much as on what is reported.

Melville is particularly fascinated by the way patterns of interpretation are interwoven in time. Interpretation relies on some sense of prediction and memory, linking the two together. But Melville is adamantly suspicious of the possibility of knowing outcomes, of using end points to judge or organize the order of events presumably leading up to them. Instead, he sees forecast to be negated by event, and interpretation refracted by the contradictory interests of the competing sides. In his poems, young men march as soldiers to dooms they do not foresee or suspect. *Battle-Pieces* is strewn with words that project but also undermine foreknowledge—*doom, forebode, forecast, decree.* "The March into Virginia," for example, shows "youth" marching forth in "ignorant impulse," (mis)led by "The champions and enthusiasts of the state." These enthusiasms prove to be mere "expectancy, and glad surmise / Of battle's unknown mysteries." For, as the poem asks, "who here forecasteth the event?" Event confutes forecast, expectancy dissolves into unknown mystery. Melville's rhetoric follows a pattern of self-undoing, deploying oxymoron, contradiction, negation, and contorted syntax to overcome any clear course either in his sentences or what they seem to claim.

"The March into Virginia: Ending the First Manassas (July, 1861),"
commemorates one of the first Northern invasions into Virginia.
Seen in the South as the "desecration" of "the sacred soil of Virginia"
(*The Richmond Enquirer RR* Vol I: Doc. 195), it was first celebrated
in the North in "total confidence," resembling "a picnic more than
a military operation" with sightseers and politicians in tow to enjoy
the spectacle of victory.[8] Instead, after intense confusion, the battle
proved a complete rout for the North, with soldiers and spectators
fleeing back toward Washington, DC in disarray. Melville's textual
confutations thus register historical ones. *Battle-Pieces* repeatedly features battles marked by indecision, confusion, reversal, or accident.
Civil War battles were, through the first years at least, notorious for
their lack of planning or strategic conduct, their failure to respond to
opportunities, and their ambiguous outcomes. In Melville, accord-
ingly, victory and defeat confound each other. Thus, in the gnomic
verse memorials that conclude the volume, the war dead are said to
have "built retreat," ("On the Home Guard.") "The Fortitude of the
North" is shown "through retreat."

Battle-Pieces confutations are not only military, strategic, and
political. They also carry, as did the war, religious meaning. For
Melville, as for the nation, the Bible stands as the central guide to
interpretive design. As throughout Mellville's writings, the Bible has
a privileged place in *Battle-Pieces'* attempts to construe events, and a
privileged place in the defeat of these attempts. Raised in the Calvinist
Orthodoxy of the Dutch Reformed Church, Melville had lived since
childhood under the Bible's prophetic shadow. The typologies of history undertaken by the Puritans and echoing through the diverse
forms of American literature and ethnic refractions equally inform
Melville's writing. In *Battle-Pieces*, these patterns are brought to bear
on the Civil War, where indeed they took on immediate and violent
urgency as the scene of ultimate cosmic battle and divine judgment.
In the war, textual and historical pattern came into vivid conjunction
and consequence. Biblical exegesis emerged as key to historical understanding, purpose, and venture, issuing finally in pervasive, compel-
ling, and contradictory national rhetorics.

Melville's response is to see the contexts of slavery and war as
challenging the Bible's power to reveal the patterns and meanings
of history, not least because it was open to such divided rhetorical
purposes.[9] The contrary uses of biblical prophecy itself become his
subject as they contest each other, thereby undermining the possibility of prophetic knowledge. "The Portent (1859)," the opening
poem of the collection, stands as an ominous warning of the ultimate

inscrutability of signs and patterns. There the executed John Brown appears Christlike, "hanging from the beam." But rather than disclosing a revelation, this vision reveals only shadow:

> Hidden in the cap
> Is the anguish none can draw;
> So your future veils its face,
> Shenandoah!

The poem turns out to be addressed to "Shenandoah," devastated by Sherman's campaign. Whatever seemed promised in John Brown's "martyrdom" (as many, including Emerson, called it), turned out to be another veil concealing the future rather than revealing it. What the Shenandoah Valley shows is a "shadow on your green," which, unlike the 23rd Psalm's green pastures against the valley of the shadow of death, shows no security in faith or significance in any broader scheme. All that has been let loose is an ominous "meteor of the war," an unreadable and frightening "portent."

This poem is at once deeply typological and anti-prophetic. Invoking a language of signs, it denies any possibility of prediction by reference to them. As is true for all of *Battle-Pieces*, the careful dating of the text places it at a historical moment that is different from the time of its composition. Melville, always writing by hindsight, purposely refuses to use this later frame to help place and interpret events as they earlier happened. As against usual typological practices of interpretation, Melville's poems do not place historical events into retrospective prophetic patterns, but trace the collapse of prophecy into brute history. With regard to prediction and fulfillment, time future proves the ultimate irony.

Throughout the volume, as in this opening text, biblical paradigms are invoked, but in a way that reminds of the implicit shape events are meant to take, but don't; using at cross purposes language that wishes to assert such prophetic claims. Comparisons to biblical types in Melville in no way mitigate historical havoc. "The Battle for the Mississippi (1862)" is likened to "Israel camping by Midgol hoar" in witness to "Pharoah's crew" drowning in the Nile. But in historical fact, that battle consumed both sides. "The Armies of the Wilderness (1863–4)" compare the site where the battle of the "wilderness" took place, a large forest south of the Rapidan River in Spotsylvania County, Virginia, to the wildernesses at "Paran." But this historical "Pillar of Smoke" oversaw a prolonged, bitter, and inconclusive battle. "Gettysburg (1863)" combines the two encounters at Gettysburg, and inevitably Lincoln's dedication of the site as a "warrior-monument." But in its victory the Union lost more than one-quarter of its army, while more than a third of Lee's army was killed, wounded, or missing: 28,000 men. Nor did the victory prove decisive, with Northern generals repeatedly failing to pursue and destroy Lee's retreating army.[10] Melville's much noted imagery making land into ocean as storm, gale, and sea registers these vicissitudes. Here, as elsewhere in Melville, the sea is an antithetical image to the biblical wilderness, defying its typological notion of errand. In "Gettysberg," "three waves" of ocean-like troops "in flashed advance / Surged, but were met, and back they set." Tides and tempests confuse any final directional turn or resolution. The battle-scene is become

> a beach
> Which wild September gales have strown
> With havoc on wreck, and dashed therewith
> Pale crews unknown—

This oceanic "havoc on wreck" is not rescued by the subsequent biblical comparison of the North to "the ark of our holy cause" before which the South falls, "Dagon foredoomed."

At work here is a suggestion of typological connections that would join Old Testament to New, and both to the Civil War, with hints to a coming conclusive apocalypse. But in Melville the references work at cross-purposes. Analogies prove false in *Battle-Pieces*, with the falsest analogy history itself. Melville represents history at an impasse, set against prophetic paradigms and defeating them. Melvillean typology works like an historical short circuit. It is circular in every sense. Its only confirmation are the fulfillments to prognostications it itself sets into play. Historical time is not a progressive line. Neither is it an advancing spiral, with each event at once repetition and further fulfillment, confirming the pattern's validity and direction. The sacral-secular faith that had grown popular in the century's sense of destiny and onward march becomes in Melville military marches that dissolve into self-negating tropes.

Self-defeating tropes themselves emerge as the peculiar field of Melville's poetic genius. *Battle-Pieces* is an exercise in linguistic self-retraction, not only inapt to appeal to wide audiences but also, in fact, rendering them almost impossible to read. In a sustained procedure of linguistic unraveling, *Battle-Pieces* pursues a language of self-undoing through strained diction, abrupt meter, discordant rhyme, and tortuous syntax. Tautology, negation, and oxymoron are its central rhetorical figures. Melville converts analogical figures such as allusion, simile, and metaphor—indeed, any rhetoric of connection—into tropes of impasse. He perversely attempts to build rhymes out of what are often metrically impossible Hebrew and Indian words ("Shiloh," "Shenandoah") or surnames (McClellan, Lyon). On almost every level, analogies prove delusive, with typology as temporal analogy the falsest of all. The "Battle of Stone River, Tennessee (1863)" casts the Civil War into the patterns of Christ's life, each side battling with "Passion," "sacred fervor," under a "broidered cross." Yet here, the "crossing blades profaned the sign." "Apathy and Enthusiasm" likens the War of Secession with Milton's War in Heaven (itself biblical commentary on Milton's own civil war) come down to American soil.[11] The winter of 1860–1861 is marked through the Christian calendar from Lent to Easter, but this sacral pattern projects the "foreboding" of defeat. The question posed by the "Armies of the Wilderness" is finally, "has time gone back?"

Into this fearsome circle of collapsed analogy as reverse doom falls the figure of Lincoln. Poems on Lincoln's martyrdom in fact inundated the pages of America, with Christlike comparisons reinforced by the assassination taking place on Good Friday. In Julia Ward Howe's poem "Requital," for example, Lincoln is "Sweet Christ, with flagellations brought/ To thine immortal martyrdom." Melville calls his own poem on Lincoln "The Martyr," adding as subtitle: "Indicative of the Passion of the People on the 15th Day of April, 1865." But although Lincoln himself represents the "Forgiver" in Melville's poem, his redemptive power is cut off, rather than realized, through his death. Nor is his death the work of a single assassin, but rather of an encompassing "they" who kill him "from behind." This corporate body destroys the possibility for "clemency and calm" that Lincoln had promised, substituting for it "the iron hand." Thus, the very people who mourn Lincoln with "passion" have betrayed his Christic promise of redemptive history.

The collection of poems presents a dizzying array of positions. Which of these voices are Melville's? Not least among *Battle-Pieces* tremendous challenges is the problem of locating Melville's own viewpoint within the disintegrative rhetoric he deploys. Point of view shifts from poem to poem, including verses that seem to affirm American mission, as in "Lee at the Capitol," which declares, "faith in America never dies" and "Heaven shall the end ordained fulfill." The poem "A Canticle" is particularly troubling, putting into verse the overblown language of American prophetic confidence:

> Thou Lord of hosts victorious,
>   Fulfill the end designed;

By a wondrous way and glorious
  A passage Thou dost find—
  A passage Thou dost find;
Hosanna to the Lord of Hosts,
  The hosts of human kind.

Does this war-hymn represent Melville's personal sentiments? Melville's intractable language, where each word is nearly crushed under ambiguity, comes closest here to masquerading as the transparent, topical nineteenth-century verse in which guise he hoped to market it. This is a verse that might fit into the appendices of the *Rebellion Record* devoted to war verse. Volume III features "Hymn for our Country," by Elizabeth Oakes Smith: "God bless our country /...She standeth like a bride / Upheld by God's almighty hand/ How fair art thou, O Native land" (p. 59). Volume II includes "A Psalm of Freedom": "It is our nation's judgment Day / That makes her stars to fall, / And all the dead start from their graves / at freedom's trumpet call" (p. 78); also, a "Battle Hymn" by Rev. Woodbury Fernall:

Thine is the battle, mighty Lord
  The skill, the wisdom all are thine
The fire that lit the sacred Word
  Shall flash from out our battle line.

Rebellion Record Volume IV (p. 2) includes "A Thanksgiving Hymn" by Park Benjamin, of the Atlantic Monthly circle, who had written a negative review of *Mardi* stating that, "Every page fairly reeks with the smoke of the lamp":[12]

O God of Battles! By whose hand
Uplifted to protect the Right
Are led the armies of our land
To be triumphant in the fight...

But there is every reason, in the context of the collection, to doubt that "A Canticle" represents anything like Melville's own position. The poem's full subtitle makes clear its rhetorical framework: "Significant of the National Exaltation of Enthusiasm at the Close of the War." That is, Melville offers the poem as a representation of enthusiasm, not as an expression of his own. Melville, moreover, would be aware that enthusiasm was not single, but divided. The *Rebellion Record*, Volume II (p. 38) included, for example, a "Southern's War Song" by

J.A. Wagener, representing the South as David against the North as Goliath, and calling on the Confederates to

> Arise! Arise! With rain and might
> Sons of the Sunny clime
> Gird on the sword; the sacred fight
> The holy hour doth chime.

In "A Canticle," as throughout *Battle-Pieces*, Melville intends not to take up positions but to expose the rhetoric such positions deploy and that can commandeer them. None of the poems' voices are necessarily Melville's. When Melville, in a poem such as "Donelson," italicizes: "Our troops have retrieved the day...t he spirit that urged them was divine," the line must be placed within the poem's frame of newspaper bulletins, headlines, and reporting. It reiterates a claim made to divine guidance, but does not itself privilege this claim among others the poem also incorporates. The poem indeed concludes on a quite different note of a "death-list" flowing "like a river...down the pale sheet." Similar inconsistencies emerge between poems, as they do within them. *Battle-Pieces* represents Southern alongside Northern viewpoints, with both sharing similar rhetoric in very disturbing ways. "The Battle for the Mississippi," written from the Union side, claims God to "appear in apt events...the Lord is a man-of-war." "The Frenzy in the Wake," which describes "Sherman's Advance through the Carolinas, (February, 1865)" presents the Southern point of view. Yet it too claims the joy "which Israel thrilled when Sisera's brow/ Showed gaunt and showed the clot." This poem is followed in turn by "The Fall of Richmond," as its "tidings" are "received in the Northern Metropolis (April, 1865)." Bells peal and cannon celebrate Richmond's defeat as the fall of "Babylon," the defeat of "Lucifer." But the Southern-voiced poem matches even as it reverses rhetoric and claims, cursing "Northern faces," the "flag we hate," and the "African—the imp."

The poem called "The Conflict of Convictions" focuses, and in a way thematizes, the rhetorical complexities of Melville's simultaneous invocations and retractions. This poem almost encapsulates the volume as a whole, juxtaposing and confronting multiple and discordant understandings of the events it addresses. Although it has often been read as a coherent debate between viewpoints that oppose but also address each other in a dialectic, this is a temptation that should be resisted. Its dizzying variety of assertions makes any schematized assignments impossible. Nor can Melville's "true" philosophical or political "position" be deduced from the text. The poem is more productively seen as an ingathering of rhetorical moments, a display of the ways in which the formulae and figures for describing events already shape the expectations we have of them:

> On starry heights
>   A bugle wails the long recall;
> Derision stirs the deep abyss,
>   Heaven's ominous silence over all.
> Return, return O eager Hope
> And face man's latter fall.
> Events, they make the dreamers quail;
> Satan's old age is strong and hale,
> A disciplined captain, gray in skill,
> And Raphael, a white enthusiast still;
> Dashed aims, whereat Christ's martyrs pale,
> Shall Mammon's slaves fulfill?

Starry heights and deep abyss situate this as a landscape that is cosmic and apocalyptic. But "man's latter fall," while typological in its reference, is also immediate and historical. By it, Melville means both the fall into slavery and into war. This is the fall of the American promise of equality and order—Lincoln's vision, so powerfully wrought in the Gettysberg Address, of democratic government that yet could withstand anarchy and schism. As with all typological images, the temporal markers multiply. Thus the "bugle" points at once to Jericho and to apocalyptic judgment, as well as to the current calls to war. But these "events...make the dreamers quail," and not least those who would see Satan and Raphael in the contest before them. Almost every word here swallows itself like a Chinese box. "Heaven" is felt only as "ominous silence," a phrase which, like "dashed aims," verges on oxymoron. Ezekial's call to "return, return" summons here not forward through penitence but truly backwards from "eager hope." History becomes an iron circle—the "Iron Dome" cited later in the poem as an ironic image of the Capitol, revoking American democratic hopes: "The Founders dream shall flee." America, instead of representing Christ as type and history, has become a nation where "Christ's martyrs pale" before "Mammon's slaves."

"The Conflict of Convictions" seems to conclude the back and forth of the poem's arguments by offering two interpretations of American destiny. In the face of an ultimate historical doom, of endless repetition and without any advance or resolution ("Age after age shall be / As age after age has been"), Melville sums up:

> YEA and NAY,—Each hath his say;
> But God He keeps the MIDDLE WAY."
> None was by when He spread the sky;
> Wisdom is vain, and prophesy."

God's "middle way" seems to open an avenue of synthesis between the endless "yea and nay" of historical bewilderment and disagreement. Yet the poem's final appeals to biblical revelation of divine will are to two of the Bible's most recalcitrant and pessimistic texts: Job, whose questions are answered by a whirlwind realization that Job himself was not "by when He spread the sky" at the moment of creation, and Ecclesiastes, who declares wisdom a vanity, to which Melville adds prophesy.

The disintegrating voices of *Battle-Pieces* recall Melville's last prose works before he abandoned fiction for verse writing. Melville's early novels such as *Typee*, *Omoo*, and *White-Jacket* had already contained rhetorical set pieces reflecting contemporary American politics.[13] *Mardi*, Melville's first achievement of failure, multiplies dialogues representing varying positions of its contemporary politics. *Redburn* features a guidebook that does not guide. *Pierre* dissolves plot, retracts promises, and offers a parody of earthly time against heavenly paradigm. In *The Confidence Man*, written immediately before *Battle-Pieces*, character and plot further dissolve into serial masquerades, where no identity is certain and no confidence is possible. In *Battle-Pieces*, neither character nor plot any longer serves as framework for the rhetorical fragments, piecemeal and discordant, that it assembles. Nor does the subsequent move into lyric involve Melville's taking up the speaking voices as his own. Instead, he acts as spokesman for diverse and competing claims staged by war and its surrounding cultures.

The poems of *Battle-Pieces* are set between a "preface" and "prose supplement," in which Melville commits himself and his book to a "merciful and healing reconstruction" requiring "little but common sense and Christian charity." This political stance has been questioned as being more committed to union than to the abolition or punishment of slavery. But for Melville union is a positive hope. Still, this politics of reconciliation does not make the poems of *Battle-Pieces* into the united or cohesive voice that many of its readers have tried to see in it.[14] Melville comes closest to the book when he suggests reading it as "manifold as the moods of involuntary meditation—moods variable and at times widely at variance." As such, *Pieces* is, as he puts it, the dramatic "poetic record [of] the passions and epithets of civil war," a record of the way in which "unfraternal denunciations at last inflamed to deeds that ended in bloodshed." What it presents, then, is the way words themselves inflame: how American rhetoric failed to bind the nation into a common discourse, and instead contributed to national breakdown.[15]

But this is not to say that Melville repudiates America and its promise. What he does suspect, and warn against, is a rhetoric of American destiny grown intolerant, excessive, and absolute in its claims. This includes uses of the Bible as political design. Against the backdrop of a war of competing claims, with the Bible providing strategy and weapon, Melville's *Battle-Pieces* displays rhetoric set against itself. Melville in this sense remains the outcast figure he recognized himself to be. Most poetry of the war participated in its contests over interpretation, caught up in a rhetoric that takes sides and defines meaning. Melville instead exposes both rhetoric and interpretive claims. Melville, against visionary transport, urges and enacts prophetic restraint as the proper moral stance for humans who ultimately neither possess nor command ultimate visions and designs.

CHAPTER 9

PLURAL IDENTITIES AND
LOCAL COLOR

From the outset, the grammar of American identity has been a matter of dispute: is it singular or is it plural? Ethnic diversity characterized the American population since colonial times. The early settlers included not only English, but also Scotch, Scotch-Irish, German, Dutch, and Swedish peoples, in addition to the Africans brought by force and alongside the populations native to America, with Spanish and French groupings across shifting borders. This plural population took shape alongside and in complex alignment with regional distributions. Immigrant arrivals tended to congregate in broad geographic areas: the English in New England and Virginia, Dutch and Swedes in the Hudson and Delaware river valleys, Germans in Pennsylvania, Norwegians in Wisconsin and Minnesota, Africans in the South, etc.[1] But there was a range of options and tensions as to how these various groups would come to be defined in relation to each other, according to a number of models of cultural identity. Among these, unitary notions of American identity tended to prevail.[2] Yet even these take several forms, in response to a variety of historical conditions, including, in the nineteenth century, successive waves of immigration, democratization of electoral politics, westward expansion, urbanization, feminism, and emancipation.[3]

The first form, or model, for a unitary American identity might be called inclusive singularity. In this model, America is willing to accept diverse populations, but they are expected to assimilate to a dominant English culture in language, law, and religious and social structures.[4] John Jay speaks for this English norm when he describes Americans in

Federalist 2 as, "one united people, a people descended from the same ancestors, speaking the same language, professing the same religion, attached to the same principles of government, very similar in their manners and customs." John Quincy Adams similarly implies this singular view in his 1818 letter to a German Baron, saying that immigrants are welcome to "accommodate themselves to the character, moral, political, and physical, of this country," which means "cast[ing] off the European skin, never to resume it." This singular inclusive model also seems the position of George Washington, who claimed that "the more homogeneous our citizens....the greater our prospect of permanent union," and of Jefferson, who praised "manners, morals, and habits [that] are perfectly homogeneous."[5] Differences as they emerged in various geographical sections represent, in this model, less the possibility of genuine diversity than competing claims by each area as to which represents the true American heritage.

A second form of singular identity may be called exclusive singularity, which views America as English in culture, but rejects the idea that other groups could or should be absorbed and assimilated into it. This exclusive singularity found expression in the Know-Nothing nativist movements of the 1850s and 1890s, responding to a shift in the kinds of immigrants arriving on American shores to non-Protestant, non-Northern European peoples, and to new economic conditions. As land became less available, arrivals clustered in cities, providing needed industrial labor but also alien customs, new social organizations, and competition for resources. Exclusive singularity finally culminated in the laws restricting immigration of the 1920s.[6]

Yet a third form of singularity is implied in the notion of amalgamation, or "melting pot." Here, the diversity of American population is embraced, but instead of conformity to an English norm, a synthesis is imagined: the "New American" Crevecoeur famously named in his *Letters*, in whom "individuals of all nations are melted into a new race of men." Emerson, railing in an 1845 Journal entry against the Native American Party, likewise prophesies that "in this continent, asylum of all nations, the energy of...all the European tribes,—of the Africans, and of the Polynesians,—will construct a new state, a new literature." The boundary between composite and English singularity, however, remains blurry. The melting pot New Americans tend to be hard to tell apart from the original English ones.[7]

Finally, there is the model of plural identities, whose very diversity is seen as defining the American character. America in this vision is a place of toleration and, indeed, assertion of difference. Multiplicity contributes to individual freedom and expression, which are seen to define the essential American promise and polity. Such a vision of plural identities is implicit from the beginnings of the American political tradition, and even unitary or singular conceptions of America presume, if they also resist, pluralist forces present from the outset of the American venture.[8] Madison implies this multiplicity in *Federalist 10*, when he makes the counter-balance between interest groups the basis for republican freedom in America. Benjamin Franklin similarly defends party interests as integral to democratic government: "Such will exist wherever there is liberty; perhaps they help to preserve it. By the collision of different sentiments, sparks of truth are struck out, and political light is obtained."[9] America from this perspective is a complex pluralism, composed of different populations, interest factions, and sectional areas, all shifting through continued waves of new arrivals.[10] The historiography of Frederick Jackson Turner at the turn of the century is best known for its theories of the American frontier, but the frontier was also part of Turner's larger, sectional theorizing of American diversity, as a "variety which is essential to vital growth and originality."[11]

Within the nineteenth century, the vision of pluralism as an essential element in American social, cultural, and political life emerges in the philosophies of Josiah Royce and William James at Harvard. Their student, Horace Kallen, coined the term "cultural pluralism" to mean "a multiplicity in a unity, an orchestration of mankind." Kallen's vision, however, remains impressionistic, and tends to assume groups to be defined through ethnic descent, so that he imagines America as a "democracy of nationalities."[12] But this is to underestimate the voluntarist nature of affiliation in America (with the emphatic exception of the color line), including movements across permeable ethnic boundaries.[13] Congress itself had rejected identification between regional and ethnic identity in 1818, when it denied a petition by the Irish for a piece of land in the West and similar territorial identities among the German communities.[14] Mobility remains, as De Tocqueville declared (calling it "restlessness"), fundamental to American forms of association.

Especially after the Civil War, new senses of regional, ethnic, racial, and gendered identities emerged in a new confirmation of America's plural make up. This sense of multiplicity is registered in the rise of local-color writing. Traditionally referred to as "regionalism," geography is only one aspect of the literatures of diversity that emerged towards the nineteenth century's end. Yet characterizing this literary diversity is in some sense as challenging as characterizing American diversity. The term "region" was itself undergoing a dynamic change of meaning in the post–Civil War era within a newly reconceived nationhood.[15] And diversity is felt not only geographically, but through emerging senses of diverse language inflections and dialects, of religious, racial, and ethnic affiliations, both in terms of new immigrations and the newly emerging status of the African-American freedmen, as well as a new self-consciousness regarding gender definitions.

One context for local-color writing is the momentum towards consolidation that emerged out of the Civil War.[16] This can be traced as a complex of interrelated movements: demographically, from the country to the city; politically, from the section to a reconstituted and centralized federal government; economically, from agriculture to industry; alongside the revolution in technology permitting new communications and transport across far flung areas; and the experience of the Civil War itself, as it brought diverse groups into contact as well as conflict. The overall pattern may be read as a drive to greater and greater integration in American life; one which, however, also entailed a fragmentation and dissolution of earlier forms of community.[17] "Regional" literature in this way is paradoxically linked to an America emerging from the Civil War into more centralized national organization. Such centralization assaulted earlier senses of community while failing to provide a new communal cohesion for those being displaced.[18] The rise of regional writing thus involves new freedom to explore differences, but just as these are becoming minor and irrelevant, no longer politically or socially defining, and no longer nationally threatening.[19] It also seems closely allied to a sense of loss for an American world that is vanishing. Regional writing in this aspect is highly nostalgic; whether with backward-looking regret or in critique of the emerging social forms that it records.[20]

Yet local-color writing also represents a genuine moment in which plural identity emerges as a peculiarly American event. It was already thought of by its practitioners as a kind of literary pluralism, even if the specific balance, or direction, between diversity and unity remained unclear. William Dean Howells, in his essay on "American Literary Centers," praises the opening of multiple literary centers in a "decentralized literature" that gives "its fidelity to our decentralized life." But Howells also seems ambivalent about whether he approves diversity or only sees it as a fuller expression of a single national consciousness. As he also writes, "as soon as the country began to feel its life in every limb with the coming of peace, it began to speak in the varying accents of all the different sections."[21]

A similar ambivalence can be felt in Edward Eggleston's 1892 preface to *The Hoosier Schoolmaster*: "The taking up of life in this regional way has made our literature really national by the only process possible."[22] In these discussions, diversity continues to be thought of mainly in geographic terms, as regional. The question remains: is the regional a means towards constructing a national sense, or does it make its own claims, redefining the very sense of the national? This question is posed, but not answered, by Hamlin Garland as well. In "Local Color in Art" (a paper first delivered at the 1893 Chicago Exposition), he observes that "the similarities do not please, do not forever stimulate and feed as do the differences." Yet his plea for difference remains in the service of an American literature that "must be national, [although] to be national it must deal with conditions peculiar to our own land and climate."[23] These early discussions do less to affirm diversity as a positive value than to show that notions of it are undergoing transformation.

Most writing on local color has been concerned with prose. The genre of poetry in itself moves representation away from the realism strongly associated with regionalism.[24] What finds expression in prose as concrete, detailed description and psychologized portraiture is pushed in poetry toward stylization in character and setting, and a balladic treatment of narrative—with or without dialogue, represented speech, and dialect. But this generic difference allows impulses and issues to become visible in poetry, which are perhaps obscured in features specific to fiction and discussions of them. The very definition of the 'local' and its meanings within post-bellum American culture takes on a distinctive color when approached through its poetic representations.

Among poets, it is James Whitcomb Riley (1849–1916) who perhaps best incarnates local color in its aspect as a regional poetry of nostalgic loss. Riley is the most obvious poetic correlative to such prose writers as Thomas Nelson Page and Joel Chandler Harris in the South, with their dialect impersonations of happy slaves on happy plantations so cruelly disrupted by that inexplicable Civil War. Riley's writing has been collected into eleven volumes of more or less formulaic versification, all wildly popular within his lifetime. Born in 1849 in the village of Greenfield, Indiana, Riley came to verse writing after a motley career as sign painter, house painter, Bible salesman, traveling medicine salesman, and lawyer. In 1875, he became the local editor for his hometown paper, moving onto a journalistic career in which poetry proved to be his best ticket to fortune and fame.[25]

Riley addresses himself to the common man, saying: "It is my office to interpret him."[26] As such, his verse is peculiarly if not impersonal, unindividuated. He speaks for, and indeed as, the communal person. As Harriet Monroe observes in her obituary piece in *Poetry* magazine, he tells "the tale of the tribe."[27] This is reflected in Riley's incorporation of folklore elements and superstitions of the popular imagination, most famously in his poem "Little Orphant Annie," with its "gobble-uns 'at gits you / Ef you don't watch out." The poem asserts a general conformity and obedience to social norms of piety (the "gobble-uns git" the little boy for failing to say his prayers) or of family authority (a little girl is "git" for mocking her "ole folks").

As is fitting for a nostalgic poetry, the figure of the child pervades Riley's work. A sizable portion of it was marketed as children's literature, while the remainder offers adult memories of childhood—a "lament of my own lost youth," as Mark Twain put it, "as no words of mine can do."[28] But the child can be seen as a more generalized figure for an aging America bidding farewell to its earlier worlds. Riley's revisited places are not sites for solitary, Wordsworthian personal reconstitutions through recollection. They are instead crowded social gathering-places. At "The Old Swimmin' Hole," a Riley favorite, "tracks of our bare feet" merge together and the poet speaks as a collective "we." The pool is a mirror, not for individual consciousness but composite identity—a whole society's joint reflection and regret.

"But the lost joys is past!" What is Riley nostalgic for? There is, first, the threat to rural life by new technology, transport, and communications. At the ole swimmin' hole, "the bridge of the railroad now crosses the spot / Where the old divin'-log lays sunk and fergot." But Riley also generally responds to a new sense of region within a new national structure. At its inception, the country's regional divisions seemed to threaten national unity. Each section even had a separate judicial system from colonial times.[29] The greatest danger to the new Union, Washington had said in his "Farewell Address" (1796), lay in "geographical discriminations: Northern and Southern; Atlantic and Western; whence designing men may endeavor to excite a belief that there is a real difference of local interests and views." Individual sections were referred to as though separate nations: Benjamin Franklin called Philadelphia his "new country" in the *Autobiography*, while Hawthorne a century later observed: "We have so much country that we have no country at all...everything falls away except one's native State."[30]

But if ante-bellum regional divisions asserted America's sectional nature, they alternatively projected a national vision, where each section claimed to represent the entire nation. Each region regarded itself as a synecdoche representing the American whole.[31] This sense of universality and priority in the nation weakened with the Civil War. One scene for this shift is a new status and use of dialect. James Russell Lowell's *Biglow Papers* presents its Yankee dialect as representing the American Revolutionary discourse of freedom. But in Riley, as also in Twain, dialect is meant to mark an eccentric regionality, as a failure of synecdochic claim in which no region commands or embodies the country as a whole. Yet Riley also has a close relationship to genteel writing. Riley repeatedly said he modeled his work on the New England poets, particularly Longfellow, whose purpose in writing he took to be to make "worlds listen, lulled and solaced at the spell / That folds and holds us." To Riley too, poetry lulls and solaces, whether as dialect or genteel, although no longer for a New England audience. As he advised a younger poet, "Keep 'em all sunny and sweet and wholesome clean to the core; or, if ever tragic, with sound hopes ultimate, if pathetic."[32] Riley's dialect is little more than genteel verse spelled funny. It never establishes itself as a truly distinctive identity; neither does it attempt to create a nationally normative poetic language.

Local-color writing by women marks a bolder confrontation with the complexities of identity than Riley's does. Recent discussions have emphasized the tie between regional and women's writing, noting that a good deal of local-color work was in fact produced by women. But the attempt to define local-color as specifically a women's tradition of writing is weakened by the broad range of local-color writing by men. Edward Arlington Robinson's work fulfills many of the criteria claimed for a specifically female regional tradition, including both geographic and social marginalization and viewpoints.[33] Robinson's Tilbury Town, with its eccentric inhabitants abruptly illuminated, also features economic, social, and psychological displacement. Robinson, with other local-color writers, men and women, moves in directions Riley fails to, of exploring localized places and persons as complex figures.

What women's local-color writing does dramatize is a dawning sense of plural as opposed to unitary self-definition. Identity comes to be seen not as single and representative, but rather as containing or negotiating multiple elements, including gender. The point is not to subordinate the "regional" element in gender, but to see how the two are mutually negotiated. Region becomes one factor among others

in an ongoing work of defining a self complicated by a consciousness of gender, which emerges into prominence, often alongside a
further dimension related to social-economic placement as another
element in identity. The question of economic status, in fact, frames
local-color work in several directions. The subjects it depicts often are
drawn from the social margin—whether in country, village, or city.
At the same time, the genre's audience and market often consisted of
an upper-class, urban, spectator public wanting to consume its vanishing locations.[34] Local color tends to handle its economic contexts,
however, less as a self-conscious critique of class structure than in
terms of a more traditional criticism of materialism's dominance in
American culture.

Local color as a complex juncture between regional, gender, and
economic identities can be seen in the work of women poets such
as Lucy Larcom, Alice and Phoebe Cary, Rose Terry Cooke (who is
known more for her fiction). Emma Lazarus adds a religious dimension to definitions of identity that too often overlook or merely absorb
religion into other categories. Frances Harper adds both religion and
race. Lucy Larcom is especially noteworthy as herself belonging to the
working class (although, as she remarked, in those days "the term was
not working class or working people—everybody worked with their
hands."). At the age of eleven she began to work at the newly founded
Lowell Mills, one of the original textile factories in America, established specifically, as Larcom describes in her memoir, *A New England
Girl* (1889), for girls to be able to work in a homelike and benevolent
environment.[35] Larcom first wrote for the *Lowell Offering* newsletter
supported by the mills, and continued to do so through difficult years
trying to support herself as a teacher, first out West and then back East.
She eventually was freed from onerous teaching by working as an editor in Boston, collaborating extensively with Whittier in anti-slavery
work and compiling anthologies, which had become an increasingly
popular form during this period of literary diversification.

Larcom's poetry centers on the sea, land, and townscapes of
Massachusetts. These often are cast through feminized figures. The
poem "The Light-Houses (Baker's Island, off Beverly, Massachusetts)"
presents the light houses as "two pale sisters, all alone." Their "long
hopeless gleams" anticipate the grief of as yet "unconscious wid-
ows" over lost sailors. They also represent a steadfast, domestic hope,
keeping alive "Fireside joys for men." Larcom's most famous poem,
"Hannah Binding Shoes," recounts the faithful devotion of a New
England woman as she waits twenty years for her husband to come
back from the sea.

Larcom's strongest terrain is the representation of women's voices, especially those with little access to their own expression. In "An Idyll of Work," she explores new notions of what constitutes a "lady," as working mill girls discuss what are the values of womanhood and its truest definition, rejecting the idle woman of leisure, family, and fashion. Yet "Prudence" critiques a working world that reduces everything to "sweeping floors" and "baking pies." Constriction and conformity to women's roles is traced in the apparently unconscious irony of the woman speaking in "Getting Along," where a wife's claim to get along with her husband disguises, and is at the expense of, all the things she does not say about the problems in their marriage but that the poem indirectly tells. But "A Loyal Woman's No" is outright in rejecting a suitor on the ideological grounds of his failure to identify with the anti-slavery cause.

The poems of Alice and Phoebe Cary similarly move between geographic, gendered, and economic viewpoints. Born very poor in Cincinnati, Ohio, the Cary sisters moved to New York City in 1850, where they lived together, writing poetry and prose, and presiding over a weekly literary salon.[36] Both sisters wrote poems that present the historical experience of the country's westward expansion from the points of view of women. This includes deidealizations of Western adventure as the women experience their lives in terms of an uprooted domesticity. In Alice Cary's "The West Country," cabins lie "like birds nests in / The wild green prairie grass," but images of the "tired hands" of women with "fingers worn and thin" compromise that promise of freedom. In "Growing Rich," husband and wife lead separate lives; the man accumulates wealth on the farm while the woman mourns the family she has left behind, and who are still caught in the coal-pit and mill. "The Washerwoman" depicts the life of toil of a poor woman in a poor village.

While Alice Cary's work suggests a local-color extension of the conventions of female verse writing, Phoebe Cary more unusually ventures into sharper, satirical domains (although she is also an accomplished hymn writer). Her work brings into special relief the contiguities and transformations between local-color and genteel writing by way of satire. Poe, Wordsworth, and Goldsmith ("When Lovely Women") are all satirized, with Longfellow something of a specialty. Phoebe Cary's parodies characteristically work through gender shifts. "Annabel Lee" becomes "Samuel Brown," remaking Poe's erotics of beautiful, dead women into calculated wars between sexes and classes: the poem's speaker loses her "beautiful Samuel Brown" not to death but when "a girl came out of her carriage," courted him, and then "shut him up in a dwelling-house / In a street quite up in town." Wordsworth's "Lucy" becomes "Jacob":

> A boulder, by a larger stone
> Half hidden in the mud,
> Fair as a man when only one
> Is in the neighborhood.

As to Longfellow, his melancholy poetry about poetry is translated into workaday discourses of food and the politics of marriage. "The Psalm to Life" becomes a raucous psalm to wife:

> Tell me not in idle jingle
>   Marriage is an empty dream
> For the girl is dead that's single
>   And things are not what they seem...

In these women poets, region claims neither to represent the whole or core of American tradition, nor to determine individual identity. As Howells observes of local color, even New England ceases "to be a nation unto itself" and has become only another region.[37] If genteel poetry is generalizing, presenting itself as speaking for the American whole (which is then also narrowly defined), then local-color women's writing speaks from particular positions grouped in various combinations. Regional identity, recognized as partial, takes its place beside a newly self-conscious identity of gender, while both carry further social and economic implications.

Local-color writing emerges in an America increasingly complex in cultural, ethnic, and social composition. No single local-color poet attains the scope and stature of a Mark Twain, whose fiction, with its intersections between region, dialect, and race, retains close ties to regional literature. But a complex conjunction of multiple identities is apparent in a poet such as Frances Harper. In her work, ethnic and racial, gendered, economic, and regional self-definitions intersect. Their meeting is often contentious and painful, as she confronts an America whose institutions and attitudes often cause these identities to collide against or exclude one another. Harper's sequence of "Aunt Chloe" poems, which takes on the voice and viewpoint of a black freedwoman, presents such combinations and confrontations. Situated firmly in the South and tracing an historical progression from before the Civil War into Reconstruction, the poem-sequence matches, but also inverts, the nostalgic post-war plantation literature from the point of view of both a freed slave and a woman.

The first poem, "Aunt Chloe," records the slave's vulnerability, pain, and also fury at the betrayal and violence of white masters who sell children and destroy families. It does so in an idiom that approaches dialect, limiting sentiment through the craft of a controlled viewpoint and homely language. "The Deliverance" is a long account of the war and emancipation, orchestrated through contrasting viewpoints of master and slave as each oppositely witnesses the Yankee advance. At the poem's center is the clash of black and white responses to emancipation:

> But when old Mistus heard it,
> She groaned and hardly spoke;
> When she had to lose her servants,
> Her heart was almost broke.

> 'Twas a sight to see our people
> Going out, the troops to meet...
> After years of pain and parting,
> Our chains was broke in two.

Here the identity of each figure as a woman is ruptured by their opposition in color, class, and moral vision.

"Aunt Chloe's Politics" and "Learning to Read" are situated after the war. The first is a critique of political corruption in buying voters, spoken consciously by a woman who is herself excluded from the franchise. The second reflects on the political and cultural meanings of literacy for the African-American slave and then freedman/woman. Against ongoing efforts to prevent African-Americans from "book learning" and knowledge, and despite her age, Aunt Chloe learns to read—notably in the religious context of Bible and church:

> ...I got a pair of glasses,
> And straight to work I went,
> And never stopped till I could read
> The hymns and Testament.

In "The Reunion," the final "Aunt Chloe" text, Chloe is reunited with the sons who had been sold away from her in the first poem of the sequence (the son of the white mistress has been killed in the Civil War).

In these texts, refracted through Aunt Chloe's voice, American English moves towards African-American dialect. But dialect is not presented here as eccentric display, as in Riley. Nor yet is it intended as universal and representative. It stands instead as one of many diverse expressions worthy to take its place among other American languages. Harper's is an appeal to an American discourse that accommodates diverse voices. The complexity of Harper's languages, and the tensions of her position between conflicting communities, becomes central to the poetry of Paul Laurence Dunbar.

Local color is no doubt an inadequate term for the literary emergence of diverse American identities, as composed not only of region, but of ethnicity, gender, and new senses of economic status in American life. And local-color poems often remained partial, hesitant and limited in their realization. Nevertheless, late nineteenth-century local-color poetry can be seen to offer one emerging expression of pluralism in American identity, not only between groups but also as located—and contested—within each individual. It points to pluralist culture as one in which each identity affiliation takes its place beside other resources available to Americans for self-definition and social location. Regional, ethnic, gendered, religious, even racial identity in nineteenth-century local color is not exclusive or determining, and there are no fixed correlations between these various group identities.[38] Instead, local color suggests a notion of pluralist individuality such as has reemerged in late twentieth-century discussions. A number of affiliations contribute to identity, shifting the conception of pluralism away from group definitions and towards one in which multiplicity is experienced within each individual, who then negotiates among them. As one theorist of ethnicity writes:

> Each individual is, by right and by opportunity, responsible for choosing his or her own identity from among the many materials presented by the contingencies of human life...An individual participates in the cultural life of more than one social group...everybody participates in more than one social group and carries multiple associational identities."[39]

Religion and ethnicity, along with geographic, racial, and gendered identities each provides associations in which individuals can participate, even as they also acculturate into American patterns. The manner and balance between participations in such multiple affiliations remains, at least to some extent, voluntary in ways that suggest a specifically American cultural form, as suggested in the notion of "pluralist individualism."[40] William James's discussion of "pluralism as the intersection of independent loyalties" suggests a nineteenth-century formulation of such a heterogeneous and fluid notion of plural identities.[41]

Thus, within local color's representation, pluralism is not only a relationship between diverse social units. It also is situated within each individual's experience and self-constitution. What local color's literary diversities suggest is a structure of pluralism that resides not only between groups, but also penetrates into each individual's multiple identity. Construction of the self comes to involve the multiple participation in plural associations, with the literary text a site in which crossing, competing, conflicting, and coordinating identities confront each other. These are not only regional, but also ethnic, racial, religious, social-economic, and gendered elements, in complex relation to each other. None of these identities serves as necessarily prior to the others, nor is any one absolutely defining and exclusive. As against efforts to define the self essentially and fundamentally through one, overriding definition, these texts—often in a tentative, indirect, and incomplete fashion—explore and assert a number of different modes of self-definition, with identity represented as the intercrossing negotiation between multiple affiliations. The issue is not only (or exactly) a new assertion of marginal figures as against central ones, but rather a challenge to the whole notion of both the margin and the center. Pluralism itself comes to extend beyond the ante-bellum emphasis on region, while individual identity becomes an arena of pluralist multiplicity, conflict, and negotiation.

CHAPTER 10

EMMA LAZARUS' AMERICAN-JEWISH PROPHETICS

Emma Lazarus was among the first poets specifically to assert ethnic voice in America, and indeed ethnic voice itself as American. In doing so, Lazarus appeals to a biblical rhetoric that had from the time of the Puritan landing served as a founding ritual of American national identity. Written in the 1880s and 1890s, Lazarus' works mark a conjuncture between trends in women's writing and pluralist and ethnic post–Civil War literature, and the ways these reissue traditions of religious and biblical rhetoric in America. But Lazarus' identity as an American-Jew gives special characteristics to her rendering of this foundational rhetoric, altering the structure of its basic terms and their distribution while at the same time reconstructing and redirecting her distinctive Jewish commitments in their relation to America. In Lazarus, the biblical typology elaborated by women poets, African-Americans, Melville, and many others becomes a scene of mutual transmutation between her American and Jewish identities, one made possible by their convergences, but necessary by their disjunctions. This complex interchange comes to focus in the strange, and in many ways volatile, Christ figure that emerges as a center of Lazarus' poetic vision.

Lazarus' best known and most powerful text is the sonnet "The New Colossus," written to raise funds for the pedestal of the Statue of Liberty and then, much later, inscribed on it.[1] In this sonnet, Lazarus interweaves her multiple identities in an especially intricate representation. The poem's female gendering finds antecedents in Lazarus' earlier work.[2] Her poem "Critic and Poet" opposes a male critic against a poet-nightingale, a feminized trope that is also Emersonian in its defiance of mere classification for an "untaught strain." "Venus of the Louvre" proposes this female goddess, "the foam-born mother of Love," as a figure at once constrained in broken stone, "yet none the less immortal." Here a Jewish motif also appears. Heine, who Lazarus had been translating since childhood, is imagined as a "pale, death-stricken Jew" at the Venus statue's feet, mourning "for vanished Hellas and Hebraic pain." Greek and Jew, types that Heine, like Matthew Arnold, had taken as emblematic, are joined here to the figure of woman in a triple mirroring. In the poem "Echoes," Lazarus explicitly announces her voice to be a feminine one. Like Anne Bradstreet, she concedes that she is barred from epic and public topics of "the world's strong-armed warriors and...the dangers, wounds, and triumphs of the fight." "Late-born and woman-souled," she is instead confined to echoes heard in nature, figured in a cave that is a private, almost domestic space. Here modesty and claim are ambiguously joined. Even while affirming imaginative power, the poet does so with apologetic rhetoric and restriction to the private realms considered proper for American female poets: "Misprize thou not these echoes that belong / To one in love with solitude and song."

"The New Colossus," however, breaks out of this traditional feminine enclosure into emphatic public space while at the same time feminizing that public realm itself. This colossus, unlike the Greek one, is female: a mighty woman with a torch, serving not only as a powerful trope for national identity but also defining that identity according to a specifically feminized vision:

The poem proceeds through a sequence of oxymorons:

> Not like the brazen giant of Greek fame,
> With conquering limbs astride from land to land.
> Here at our sea-washed, sunset gates shall stand
> A mighty woman with a torch, whose flame
> Is the imprisoned lightning, and her name
> Mother of Exiles. From her beacon-hand
> Glows worldwide welcome; her mild eyes command
> The air-bridged harbor that twin cities frame.
> "Keep, ancient lands, your storied pomp!" cries she
> With silent lips. "Give me your tired, your poor,
> Your huddled masses yearning to breathe free,
> The wretched refuse of your teeming shore.
> Send these, the homeless, tempest-tost to me,
> I lift my lamp beside the golden door."[3]

Mighty/ woman, imprisoned/ lightning, Mother / of Exiles, mild eyes/ command, cries/ with silent lips: each oxymoron joins a feminine with an assertive power. This is a radical reworking of the modesty topos. On the one hand there is constraint, imprisonment, exile, mildness, and silence. But this mother is also mighty and commanding, crying out not only a welcome to the homeless but also a vision of America as a hostess, a place of care and community, as a monumental culmination and affirmation of a century's efforts by women in benevolent work, to cultivate and protect common life.

This intricate figure of a feminized, naturalizing America is then further interwoven with specific commitments of Lazarus' Jewish identity. The images for the statue uncannily recast the biblical text of Deborah (a preferred figure for many nineteenth-century women writers), who is not "Mother of Exiles," but "Mother in Israel"; whose prophetic presence empowers the army of *Barak*, the Hebrew word for 'lightning', and who is named *eshet lapidoth*, the wife of *Lapidoth*, which also translates as: "woman of the torch" (Judges 4).[4] Lazarus, who had started learning Hebrew in the 1880s, draws on it here along with another powerful and pivotal Jewish symbol. The poem's concluding image of the "lamp" is repeatedly associated in her work with the Chanukah lamp, the sign of freedom from Hellenist oppression.

The poem's opening image of the brazen giant takes on further meanings in this context. Lazarus poses her "New Colossus" against the ancient Colossus of Rhodes, pagan statue of the sun god. This figure is not only masculine, conquering, and pompous as against the statue's giant modesty. It is also Greek. But for Lazarus, as for Heinrich Heine, the opposing counterpart of Greek Hellenism is Hebraism. That the Greek giant acts in the poem as a figure for Europe implicitly contrasts America against it as Hebraic. America as asylum welcomes the Jews (among others) that Europe, in a phrase that suggests their point of view and not Lazarus' own, rejects as "wretched refuse." In contrast to Greece/Europe, America itself emerges as Hebraic site, with its history a mode of Jewish history.

In this way Lazarus' American discourse is made continuous with her Judaic one. Yet this is hardly an alien imposition. The Puritans themselves had done no less. As Jew, Lazarus would in fact have felt particularly called by the Puritan reading of biblical typology identifying America as the New Israel and promised land, providentially revealed at the very moment of Protestant Reformation. Indeed, Lazarus has special recourse to several distinctive—and not entirely congruent—strands in this complex rhetorical tradition. The Puritan venture was figured in typology as a new exodus of chosen people crossing the sea to found the "Kingdom of God." But it was also undertaken in pursuit of religious freedom, consecrating the New World Canaan as haven for the afflicted ("a refuge," in the words of the Psalmist [9:9], "for the oppressed.") The rhetoric thus supports election and asylum, a particularist and universalist vision at once.[5] On the one hand, the Puritans regarded their mission as an exclusive one. Yet if they were uniquely chosen, so could others be. America could be the promised land for all who would see it as such.

To be American thus becomes for Lazarus continuous with her Jewish commitments. As for Horace Kallen, inventor of the phrase "cultural pluralism," for Lazarus these identities need not clash; in fact, they reaffirm each other. It would be all but irresistible to recognize herself and her people in the Puritan image of the Israelites in Exodus, even as she would embrace the promise of asylum. But if thus far Lazarus' strategies seem mutually confirming and conforming between the Jewish and American traditions, just how complicated and potentially destabilizing the relation between them remains can be seen in the figure of Christ, which indeed stands at the center of all typology and which the "New Colossus" also evokes in its cry to "give me your tired, your poor." This phrase echoes, as Israel Zangwill remarks in his 1908 play, "The Melting Pot," the language of the Gospels (Matthew 11:28): "When I look at the Statue of Liberty, I just seem to hear the voice of America crying: 'Come unto me all ye that labour and are heavy laden and I will give you rest'."

Lazarus develops and confirms this connection in another sonnet composed at around the same time as the "New Colossus," called "1492." 1492, which the poem addresses as a "two-faced Year," marks the dual events of discovering America, but also the expulsion of the Jews from Spain after its Christian *Reconquista* from the Moors:

> Thou two-faced year, Mother of Change and Fate,
> Didst weep when Spain cast forth with flaming sword,
> The children of the prophets of the Lord,
> Prince, priest, and people, spurned by zealot hate.
> Hounded from sea to sea, from state to state,
> The West refused them, and the East abhorred.
> No anchorage the known world could afford,
> Close-locked was every port, barred every gate.
> Then smiling, thou unveil'dst, O two-faced year,
> A virgin world where doors of sunset part,
> Saying, "Ho, all who weary, enter here!
> There falls each ancient barrier that the art
> Of race or creed or rank devised, to rear
> Grim bulwarked hatred between heart and heart!"

In the poem, discovery and expulsion are linked in much the same way as Protestant historiography linked the opening of America providentially with the Reformation. America, again feminized as "virgin world," is prepared as future refuge for the Jews. The connection between the two events effectively makes the discovery of America an event in Jewish history.[6] Here again the "doors of sunset," opening in asylum, say in Christic echo: "Ho, all who weary enter here." Such conflation of Jewish Exodus, America, and Christ occurs elsewhere as well, most explicitly in a prose poem Lazarus wrote shortly before her death at the age of thirty-eight, called "The Exodus (August 3, 1492)." The expulsion from Spain reduces the Jews to "dusty pilgrims" who are spurned by all the nations. But the poem also prophetically "whispers" that, at that very historical moment, "a world-unveiling Genoese" sails "to unlock the golden gates of sunset and bequeath a Continent to Freedom." Among these Jewish exiles, as the very image of their suffering, is a "youth with Christ-like countenance," who "speaks comfortably to father and brother, to maiden and wife," while in his breast "his own heart is broken."

In invoking this figure of Christ, Lazarus is joining with many others who, in becoming American, adopt the typologies in which the voice of America merges with the voice of Christ.[7] But this ritual has for Lazarus particular exigencies, requiring strenuous revision of both the Puritan model and her ethnic alignments. Lazarus could discover in typology her Jewish identity within and indeed as founding her American one. But while in Puritan typology the Hebrews may serve as antecedents and typological ground, they do so in support of a structure that ultimately subsumes them. Especially in the American Puritan context, typology affirms biblical history as founding pattern. But to valorize as pattern is to subordinate as history. History becomes figure, indeed pre-figuration, of the Christian transformation that is its fulfillment.

In this sense, however, to be fulfilled is to be abolished. No independent historical course outside the pattern of its own subsuming is admissible for the ancient Hebrews. Meaning must pass from the Old Testament to the New One, from Judaic letter to Christian spirit, a passage that itself serves as paradigm for redemptive process. Indeed, to allow Jewish history any meaning independent of this figural, typological transformation is, as Augustine makes clear in *On Christian Doctrine*, sin. As to the Jews, their validity as model is guaranteed only by their relegation to the remote past. Independent Jewish history ends at the year zero. After that, the Jewish role is only to be anti-witness to the true Revelation and, indeed, the original and subsequent image of its denial. This is also to refuse its own figuralization, its typological transformation from historical reality to Christian prediction, another mode of its failure to integrate into sacral redemptive revelation. Thus, as ground for Christianity, Judaism participates in its sacred history. But as refusing Christian transfiguration, it is renegade, and sinful.

Compared to earlier eras, the Puritans had reclaimed the Old Testament and identified with it in ways that redefined their relation to the Hebraic past, and indeed to Jews.[8] But what emerges in Lazarus is the internal contradictions between granting the Jews continuous, valid, and autonomous historical life as against their traditional place in Christian sacral history. These two positions clash in their historical claims, which in turn implicate spiritual meanings and indeed redemptive possibility. This is a clash that looms through Lazarus' writings. It raises questions generally about how and whether multiple identities, made possible within American pluralist social structures, may indeed reside together given conflicts that may arise between them.

The poem "1492" signals Lazarus' own discovery of Jewish history. The expulsion from Spain is post-biblical, part of the ongoing Jewish narrative, although also presented in the poem typologically through imagery of the expulsion from Eden—Spain drives forth "the children of the prophets" by "flaming sword." But to Lazarus, discovering history was equally a moment of self-discovery, transforming her from a writer of more or less labored and decorous genteel verse (a decorum that prevented her all her life from reading her own verse in public; others did this for her) into a powerful polemicist. Lazarus had been born to wealthy and assimilated Portuguese-German Jews, whose milieu gave her a superb private education and social introduction to such prominent people of letters as Edmund C. Stedman, anthologist and editor; Richard Gilder, editor of the *Century Magazine* in which much of her prose writings appeared; Rose Hawthorne, daughter of Nathaniel; Thomas Wentworth Higginson, proctor to Dickinson; and most centrally, Emerson, whom she had met at a party given by Julia Ward Howe's brother, Samuel, in 1866. Emerson, despite wounding her deeply by failing to include her work in his *Parnassus* anthology of American verse, remained for her a presiding and confirming connection (later in her life she visited with Emerson and his daughter, and was probably the first Jew either had ever met).[9]

Lazarus' subsequent change has all the mystery and prepared suddenness of a conversion experience, but what she converts to is a historical rather than religious vision. In the wake of the mass immigration of Russian Jews escaping from pogroms in 1882, the Rabbi of the Portuguese synagogue (who had earlier approached her to contribute some verses to a Reform prayer book: she agreed to contribute English translations of German versions of Medieval Hebrew hymns[10]) had her accompany him to Ward Island. The scene transfigured her from an elite, decorous young lady to a combatant in public campaign.

Even before this turn, Lazarus had shown some consciousness of her Jewish identity. Among her first poems is her reply to Longfellow's "Jewish Cemetery at Newport." In "In the Jewish Synagogue at Newport," Lazarus answers his "dead nations never rise again" with, if not full resurrection, then at least a continued sacral presence: "Still the sacred shrine is holy yet . . . Take off your shoes as by the burning bush." But the new sciences of history just then emerging as German-Jewish *Wissenschaft des Judentums*, to which her Rabbi had also introduced her, provided Lazarus with direct weapons to confront the devastation of the "murder, rape, arson, [and] one hundred thousand families reduced to homeless beggary" that she describes in one of her first polemical pieces. Lazarus there is replying to one Mme. Ragozin—collaborator in Putnam's multi-volume *The Story of the Nations*, member of the Oriental Society, of the Societé Ethnologique de Paris, and of the Victorian Institute of London[11]—who, in an essay called "Russian Jews and Gentiles," had defended the pogroms as the appropriate response to an alien, subversive, heretical Jewish presence in Russian society. Lazarus's own essay, "Russian Christianity vs. Modern Judaism," already in its title alters the historiographic map by which Ragozin had divided all Jewry into "those who followed Jesus, and those who crucified him."[12] Lazarus instead asserts that Jewish history is alive, indeed is "the oldest among civilized nations."[13] This historicist approach to Jewish life had itself been an innovation of the *Wissenschaft* movement, whose original group included the young Heine.[14] Lazarus makes it the center of such poems as "The World's Justice" and "Gifts," which contrast Israel against the long defunct kingdoms of Egypt, Assyria, Greece, and Rome. In prose essays she similarly sets out, as she writes in "The Jewish Problem," to "review" Jewish history "since the Scriptural age, where ordinary readers are content to close it." Lazarus, moreover, addresses her historicized vision to both Jews and Gentiles, "convinced," as she writes in her *Epistle to the Hebrews*, "that a study of Jewish history is all that is necessary to make a patriot of an intelligent Jew."[15]

The new historiography, both German and Jewish, also provides Lazarus with the basis for rewriting typology. Her task is to find a place for Jews not only in history but also in America. This alters their typological place only as prefiguration fulfilled and absorbed into Christianity, to extend into their contemporary presence within American pluralism. Her historiography thus both joins her to and distinguishes her within the American community, and she requires a rhetoric that will allow for both impulses. What Lazarus must do is marshal the power of typological rhetorical patterns while resisting their historical erasures; she must recast the Jew as both antecedent and present, figure and history, type and living citizen.

One strategy in this project is to invoke Hellenism as contrast to Hebraism, as she does with the "brazen giant of Greek fame" in "The New Colossus." In poem after poem, Lazarus adopts a Greek/Hebrew opposition that contrasts the ancient, dead culture against her living one, identifying Europe with the first and America with the second. She especially privileges the Maccabees, who led the second century B.C.E. Jewish revolt against Greek imperialism and Hellenist culture. Lazarus substitutes for the typological correlation and then supercession of Jew/Christian, in which America is identified as Christian, an ongoing opposition between Greek/Hebrew, in which America is identified as Hebrew. The status of both America and Hebraism is thereby transformed, not only combining them but also making Judaism not a dead letter but a living culture.

At the center of these transformations, however, there remains the figure of Christ. Throughout Lazarus' later poetry, Christ emerges very oddly as the central image of Jewish history itself. Lazarus here draws on the newly contemporary and still controversial studies of the historical Jesus in his Jewish context. This had become a topic for German and German-Jewish historians alike, beginning with Hermann Reimarus' *The Aims of Jesus and His Disciples*, an historical reconstruction of the life of Jesus published by Lessing in 1778; and then elaborated by Jewish figures such as Moses Mendelssohn, Heinrich Graetz, and Abraham Geiger, as well as such Christian scholars as David Strauss and Ernest Renan in his *Life of Jesus* (1863).[16] Lazarus wrote an essay for *The American Hebrew* on "M. Renan and the Jews," where she approves Renan's view of Judaism as a prophetic religion (although Renan himself is in fact quite ambivalent about Jewish nationhood) and his description of Christianity as "Judaism adapted to Indo-European taste" (163–164). She also cites Mark Antokolsky in her *Epistle to the Hebrews* (35), a contemporary artist whose *Ecce Homo* innovatively portrays Jesus in ancient Jewish costume, with Semitic features, side curls, and a skullcap.

Lazarus is, if not the first, then certainly among the first to represent the historical and Semitic Jesus in literature.[17] She does more, however, than reclaim Jesus as an historical Jew. She makes Christ a defining figure of Jewish identity. He embodies Jewish history, and the Jews themselves, in their suffering, persecution, and martyrdom. Thus, "The Crowing of the Red Cock" represents the suffering of Christ as persecution of the Jews:

> Where is the Hebrew's fatherland?
> The folk of Christ is sore bestead;
> The Son of Man is bruised and banned,
> Nor finds whereon to lay his head.
> His cup is gall, his meat is tears,
> His passion lasts a thousand years.

The Jews as "the folk of Christ" are "sore bestead." They are personified as "the Son of Man," and their history as a prolonged "passion." The poem "The Valley of Baca" similarly presents Jewish historical suffering in the image of a "youth" whose head is "circled with a crown of thorn." In "The Supreme Sacrifice," Israel, enduring "the scorn of man" for two thousand years, "bows his meek head" and confesses "thy will be done." "Raschi in Prague" is "featured like the Christ," and in "The Death of Raschi," the great Rabbi, having been martyred by Christians, on the "third day" is said to have risen from the dead, "the life returned." This miracle of resurrection characterizes the whole of Jewish history, which shows "the miracles the Lord hath wrought / In every age for Jacob's seed."

Lazarus here enters typology at a different point from normative Christian patterns and redistributes the elements of its construction. In this, however, she also reverses its fundamental direction and values, and indeed changes the shape of its whole redemptive process and pattern. To identify the Jews with Christ is to lift them out of their anticipatory, pre-figural role and place them instead at the very center of history, the place of revelation, whose truths are not transferred from but instead realized through them. The sacred and indeed divine moment is retained in their continuing nationhood rather than eclipsing it. Christ becomes the prophetic figure of the Jews themselves as suffering remnant, the "remnant lost," as Lazarus names them in "The World's Justice," confirming rather than displacing Jewish prophecy and providential history.

Christian history is at the same time severely criticized. Instead of emerging as the people of Christ, the Christian becomes their persecutor through history. The crucified becomes the crucifiers, and those long accused as crucifiers become the crucified. Not Jews, but Christians, betray Christ. Thus Lazarus concludes her translation of "The Dance to Death," a play depicting the destruction of a German-Jewish community by its Christian citizens during the Black Plague, with a cry of Jewish martyrs to the "cruel Christ" against the Christian "child murderer." As she sums up in "The Crowing of the Red Cock": "When the long roll of Christian guilt / Against his sires and kin is known...What oceans can the stain remove / From Christian law and Christian love?"

Lazarus' treatment recasts typology as a mode of polemic, the central impulse of all her later writings. Yet Lazarus is aware that her revised version directly contests and is incompatible with the main tradition she nevertheless attempts to invoke and enlist. A crucial point of contention is anti-Semitism. Several poems directly confront Christian anti-Semitic history. In "The Guardian of the Red Disk," Lazarus brings to completion a narrative poem in balladic form begun by Heine. In the poem "Epistle," Lazarus, as she explains in a note, rewrites a letter to Paulus, a Jewish convert to Catholicism who had achieved high Church office and become active in its persecutions of the Jews of Seville. Based in a story she had read in Graetz's multi-volume *History of the Jews*, the poem systematically considers Christian beliefs, contrasting it against a Jewish understanding in light of their own history. As she quotes from Graetz: "Christianity gives itself out as a new revelation in a certain sense completing and improving Judaism...where [in Christian history] is the truth and certainty of revelation?" What makes the Christian claim to truth stronger than the Jewish one?

Lazarus thus enlists her polemic in defense of Jewish identity in history. Yet her position remains a complicated one. Her very model of history emerges as the clash of stances and conflicting claims—a clash that her writing in many ways reproduces rather than resolves. The Christic imagery she adopts allows her to negotiate a Jewish identity within American culture. But if she thus rewrites typology, she is also rewritten by it. Christ as encompassing center of history and culminating image is, after all, an odd figure for Jewish identity, not unlike the Christian one. Lazarus' reversals are in this sense unstable. Her work in other ways enacts, without resolving, conflicts within her multiple identity. She in fact institutes not one pattern, but two. Alongside the figure of suffering sacrifice, Lazarus introduces a contrary one of Jewish assertion, awakening, and heroism. This finds its ultimate expression in her vision, adopted from George Eliot, of a

Jewish restoration in the national homeland of Palestine. Incipient Zionism becomes a central feature of Lazarus's prose, from "The Jewish Problem," where she declares "all suggested solutions other than this of the Jewish problem [are] but temporary palliatives" (611), through her *Epistle to the Hebrews*, where she repeatedly urges "the signs of a momentous fermentation" (32), and the "prophetic intuition" of the "revival of the idea of a Restoration" (46).

Lazarus' Zionist commitment draws her particularly to images of the Maccabean revolt, recalled not only in the "New Colossus," but also in "The Banner of the Jew" and "The Feast of Lights." She wishes to "recall to-day / the glorious Maccabean rage" and to "chant psalms of victory till the heart takes fire, / The Maccabean spirit leap new-born." Most powerfully, "The New Ezekiel" transmutes the graveyard of two millennia of history into a prophetic scene of national rebirth:

> What, can these dead bones live, whose sap is dried
>   By twenty scorching centuries of wrong?
> Is this the House of Israel, whose pride
>   Is as a tale that's told, an ancient song?
> Are these ignoble relics all that live
>   Of psalmist, priest, and prophet? Can the breath
> Of very heaven bid these bones revive,
>   Open the graves and clothe the ribs of death?
>
> Yea, Prophesy, the Lord hath said. Again
>   Say to the wind, Come forth and breathe afresh,
> Even that they may live upon these slain,
>   And bone to bone shall leap, and flesh to flesh.
> The Spirit is not dead, proclaim the word,
>   Where lay dead bones, a host of armed men stand!
> I ope your graves, my people, saith the Lord,
>   And I shall place you living in your land.

Two millennia of history are made into a prophetic scene of national resurrection. History itself is cast as dead bones, here called to life against every reasonable expectation. Here Lazarus joins with, illuminates, and strengthens the public nature of nineteenth-century women's poetic roles. Hers is a prophetic voice addressed to her two people, Americans and Jews, trying to unfold before them a vision of renewed history. As prophet she specifically claims for herself a public, communal, and potent voice. She herself in a way is the "New Ezekial," called to "prophesy." It is through her that the Lord will "proclaim the Word." For who here is "psalmist, priest, and prophet," if not she? The image opens history to women and inscribes them within historical process.

The Bible figures large in this literary and political undertaking. Lazarus' verse becomes cadenced with biblical phrasings, references, images, and perhaps above all, authority. The result is a biblical poetics, shaping voice, image, language, and also poetic role and motive. As with other women poets, Lazarus comes to forge a public—indeed a prophetic—voice, calling Jews and Americans to political commitments and stances. Lazarus here comes closest to realizing a Hebrew poetics in which history and biblical text act as ethnic voice, spoken as a prophetic "word" that unites, rather than opposes, "flesh" and "spirit," history and pattern.

Yet a question remains even here: which land does she have in mind, America or Palestine? Lazarus does not relinquish her claim on America as the Promised Land. Indeed, she is careful to make clear in her *Epistle* that her Zionist program is not intended for American Jews ("There is not," she assures her readers, "the slightest necessity for an American Jew, the free citizen of a republic, to rest his hopes upon the foundation of any other nationality soever" [41]). It is only the problem of the Eastern European Jews that Zionism solves, since "their colonization en masse in the United States is impracticable" (44). Her plea for "the establishment of a free Jewish State has not the remotest bearing upon the position of American Jews," for "wherever we are free, we are at home" (72).

To Lazarus, these two promised lands are complementary, not competing. Nevertheless, their several claims lead to rhetorical ambivalence, if not confusion, in her verse. The poem "In Exile" celebrates the journey of refugees from the Egypt of Russia not to Palestine, but to Texas, there to enjoy the "freedom to love the law that Moses brought" and "drink the universal air" of American civil religion. But in having the refugees "link Egypt with Texas in their mystic chain," Lazarus is unclear in whether she intends their journey as one of exile or of exodus. "The New Year" tells how,

> In two divided streams the exiles part,
>   One rolling homeward to its ancient source,
>   One rushing sunward with fresh will, new heart.
>   By each the truth is spread, the law unfurled.

Two streams, two homecomings. Nonetheless, the journey the poem depicts as the fulfillment of "the prophet's promise," is the one from

the Russian "steppes" to the American "Sierras" (a somewhat confused geography), in a rhetoric that realizes Moses' plea to Pharaoh
through a "New Colossus" image of American asylum:

> To snow-capped Sierras from vast steppes ye went,
>   Through fire and blood and tempest-tossing wave
> For freedom to proclaim and worship Him,
>   Mighty to slay and save.

Lazarus' ambivalence finally derives both in herself and from her
America. She firmly articulates an ideal that allows participation in
American life while retaining distinctive ethnic identity. As she wrote
in her *Epistle*: "To combine the conservation of one's own individuality with a due respect for the rights of every other individuality is the
ideal condition of society, but it is a foolish perversion of this truth to
deduce therefrom the obligation to renounce all individuality." Yet,
her work poses questions regarding the extent to which ethnic identity
is absorbed, tolerated, or encouraged by American cultural forces in a
society where, as one writer puts it, ethnicity remains a "secret" that
somehow has "to exist and yet not to exist, to be needed and yet to be
unimportant, to be different and yet to be the same, to be integrated
and yet to be separate."[18] Even "The New Colossus" has a polemical
context, to assert as much as to confirm the American welcome to
the huddled masses. It was written at a time when the mass immigration from Eastern Europe intensified nativist agitation—a problem Lazarus acknowledges in her *Epistle*. The poem, moreover, was
enshrined at the Statue of Liberty's entrance only after the restrictive
Immigration Act of 1924 had put an end to mass immigration, and
after the destruction of Jewry and other peoples in Hitler's Europe
in 1945.[19] The two traditions so carefully intertwined in the poem of
asylum and election, universalism and nationalism, remained conflictual in the political history of immigration.

Lazarus herself was no immigrant, but an American expressing her
ethnic vision through the rhetoric of her native country. She throughout her career wrote for both Jewish and American audiences and resolutely dismissed what she calls, in her essay on Renan, "the whole
rotten machinery of ritualism, feasts and fasts, sacrifices, oblations
and empty prayers" for a rational, historicized national identity and
a prophetic tradition consistent with, and founding, "universal religion." The result is a discourse in which the American and the Judaic
remain conjunctive and disjunctive at once. The contrastive pressures
of the rhetorics she adopts can be seen when she lauds America as "a

society where all differences of race and faith were fused in a refined cosmopolitanism" (*Epistle*, 73), or when, at the very moment she calls for national restoration in "The Jewish Problem," she hastens to add: "From this statement I exclude American Jews, who have lost color and individuality, and are neither Jew nor Gentile." Here Lazarus reverts to a Pauline language that, while apparently universalist, is highly typological and acts to subsume every identity into the unity of Christ, as it is written: "But now also put off all these...And have put on the new man...where there is neither Greek nor Jew, circumcision nor uncircumcision...but Christ is all, and in all" (Colossians 3:8–11). The logic of typological rhetoric carries Lazarus at such moments to an erasure of Jew and Greek within a unified identity that remains, however, essentially Christian, rather than allowing her to assert her different, although related, Hebrew and American identities.

It seems relevant here to point out that there is as yet no collected works of Emma Lazarus. Emma Lazarus died in 1887 of cancer. The Lazarus sister, Annie, who controlled the copyright of her writings, declined permission when Bernard Richards in 1926 asked to edit a complete works. Herself having converted to Catholicism, she felt, as she wrote to Richards, that while Emma's

> politico-religious poems are technically as fine as anything she ever wrote, they were nevertheless composed in a moment of emotional excitement, which would seem to make their theme of questionable appropriateness today...There has been, moreover, a tendency, I think, on the part of some of her public, to overemphasize the Hebraic strain of her work, giving it thus a quality of sectarian propaganda, which I greatly deplore, for I understood this to have been merely a phase in my sister's development...Then, unfortunately, owing to her untimely death, this was destined to be her final word.[20]

Lazarus tries to sustain in her typology Jewish and Christian readings of biblical history that share common ground but are also incompatible. The result is a poetic that seems half confused, half prophetic; one which yearns, as Lazarus writes in a poem dedicating herself to the spirit of prophecy ("To Carmen Sylva"), to speak both "for poet David's sake" and also "for his sake who was sacrificed—his brother Christ."

CHAPTER 11

PAUL LAURENCE DUNBAR'S CROSSING LANGUAGES

Since their publication in the 1890s, Paul Laurence Dunbar's poems have been divided into two separate kinds: the poems in dialect as against those in Standard English. His first volumes, *Oak and Ivy* (1893), *Majors and Minors* (1895), and *Lyrics of Lowly Life* (1896) present each linguistic register in separate sections. This division has continued to compromise Dunbar's place among American poets, with each language raising questions about the authenticity of his poetic voice. When Dunbar writes in Standard English, he is suspected of betraying his African-American identity. Rather formal in their lyricism, his poems, moreover, seem to remain conventional ("genteel, slightly labored...set pieces and imitations") when compared with the modernist innovations that soon followed.[1] But when Dunbar writes in dialect, he is suspected of being complicitous with white stereotypes of black language, conforming to racist representations such as Joel Chandler Harris' plantation literature or minstrel shows.[2]

This split has haunted Dunbar's poetry since its very emergence, when a review by William Dean Howells at once announced and obscured it from view. Howells launched Dunbar into literary visibility, something against all odds for a young black writer. But Howells emphasized the division between Dunbar's Standard English, in which he saw nothing "especially notable except for the Negro face of the author," and the dialect poems, which he saw as accomplished, but only as displaying the "difference of temperament between the races." This difference he goes on to define as "appetite and emotion, with certain lifts far beyond and above it, which is the range of the race."

It was ultimately in his "humorous quality" that Howells saw Dunbar as "add[ing] to our literature." Thus, what Dunbar's dialect, while authentic, finally represents is a "finely ironical perception of the Negro's limitations."[3]

Dunbar felt the consequences of Howells' review for the rest of his short life. Ever after he considered himself typed as a dialect poet. As he told James Weldon Johnson, "I didn't start as a dialect poet. I simply came to the conclusion that I could write it as well, if not better, than anyone else I knew of, and that by doing so I should gain a hearing. I gained the hearing, and now they don't want me to write anything but dialect."[4] Gaining a hearing in dialect meant his eclipse in Standard English. In the end, either language Dunbar could choose became suspect. What Howells indirectly points to is the difficulty of Dunbar's having a language at all, akin to the invisibility that Ralph Ellison was later to expose. James Russell Lowell could use dialect in the *Biglow Papers* as another poetic language available beside, rather than in competition with, his Harvard English. Dialect and Standard English each expressed a continuous Yankee identity rooted in the New England village of Cambridge and ultimately claiming to be generally and authentically American. In Dunbar's case, in contrast, dialect is seen to express a racial identity in tension with established literary language remote from it. His dialect never ceases to be marginal, indeed subordinate, within American cultural life, and unrepresentative of American identity as a whole.

Dunbar's dilemma as caught and confined within this division between Standard English and black dialect restages fundamental issues of African-American identity. It embodies and enacts the complex of dual identities that W. E. B. Du Bois called ""double consciousness," containing "two souls, two thoughts, two unreconciled strivings, two warring ideals."[5] In Dunbar, this double consciousness takes on a specifically linguistic configuration. But rather than working at cross purposes in ways that deny him his voice, Dunbar's poetry explores the mutual relation between his languages in a complex form of poetic expression. While Dunbar's languages remain distinct, they are not simply opposed. Instead, they register the cross-cultural context in which both are finally situated. Moreover, Dunbar's poetic is bivocal not only between, but also within both Standard English and dialect pieces, bringing each to bear on the other in a richly hybrid and inter-cultural discourse. Each language is thus an expression of Dunbar's complex African-American identity. Each addresses and incorporates elements from the other. And each acts as a reflection of the other, exactly across their differences. Seeing the two in stark contrast is finally damaging to interpreting each group of poems, and to seeing Dunbar's work as a whole.[6]

Paul Laurence Dunbar was born in Dayton, Ohio, to parents who had been slaves. His father had escaped to Canada through the Underground Railroad and later fought in the Civil War in the 55th Massachusetts Regiment. His mother taught him to read and traditions of dialect. It is important to note that as Dunbar himself never lived in the South, dialect was something he learned and set out consciously to master as a literary technique. He approached black dialect as a craftsman, polishing his skill through writing exercises in German, Irish, as well as the Hoosier dialect of James Whitcombe Riley.[7] Dunbar was acutely aware that dialect had been appropriated to reinforce stereotypes in nostalgic visions of the lost plantation, glorifying white Southern culture and alienated from black perspectives. Indeed, dialect itself arose out of the suppression and loss of the African tribal languages in the passage to America and enslavement. Once in America, the black peoples had available only a dominant English language to which they had limited access. The anti-literacy laws and the conditions of slavery itself made attaining formal English very difficult.[8] Dialect, from this point of view, signaled cultural deprivation. This compromised history made subsequent black writers such as James Weldon Johnson and Sterling Brown critical of Dunbar's dialect verse. Johnson comes to describe Dunbar as "writing in the conventionalized dialect," and therefore as "dominated by his [white] audience . . . expressing only certain conceptions about Negro life that his audience was willing to accept."[9]

But Dunbar set out to contend against this linguistic appropriation, to recover an African-American history that was precious as well as problematic and painful. Like W.E.B. Du Bois, Dunbar recognizes dialect as an essential element in African-American historical consciousness, a rich and necessary medium for cultural expression and redemption.[10] The challenge was to destabilize stereotypic forms and reclaim his heritage for his own positive creation and identity. As he wrote to the poet Alice Moore during their courtship, theirs was a choice of "preserving by Afro-American writers these quaint old tales and songs of our fathers," or, "like so many others," to "ignore the past and all its capital literary materials."[11]

Dunbar's best work does not so much transcend this predicament of language as make it his subject. This is accomplished in a number of ways. Dunbar reclaims stereotypes by dramatizing viewpoints and transforming utterance into self-conscious acts of representation. He adopts and transforms genre forms in dual directions—that is,

from black to white and from white to black. And he uses richly reso-
nant figures tied to African and African-American culture, including
the mask, black religious modes, spirituals, and song. These cross-
cultural exchanges take place, moreover, in both his Standard and dialect poems, whose division itself moves from opposition and contrast
to mutual address and transformation.

"We Wear the Mask," one of Dunbar's most powerful poems in
Standard English, both addresses and represents the complex dilemmas facing him, not least in its implications for his poetic language.
"We Wear the Mask" repeats as a refrain through the poem. Cast in a
plural first person, the poem speaks for a whole people for whom the
mask "hides [their] cheeks and shades [their] eyes," and which they
"mouth with myriad subtleties." As with Du Bois' veil, the mask here
not only hides the speakers from those who see them, but also shades
and shadows how they themselves see. The obfuscation reaches from
vision to voice, to the "mouth" as also to "tears and sighs" in the next
stanza. The final stanza moves fully towards voice imagery:

> We smile, but, O great Christ, our cries
> To thee from tortured souls arise.
> We sing, but oh the clay is vile
> Beneath our feet, and long the mile;
> But let the world dream otherwise,
> We wear the mask.

The cries to Christ and singing recall the slave spirituals. But
here both African-American selfhood and language are masked
in Standard English. English itself is a mask. And yet the mask is
not only a figure of concealment. For the mask itself is also deeply
African, as both aesthetic and religious object. It therefore stands
here not only for self-concealment in conformity with white social
stereotypes, but also the assertion of unique African-American cultural modes of representation.[12] The mask hides and conforms, but
also prevents outsiders from seeing into a secret cultural world whose
mystery it at once affirms and protects. The poem's language, too,
adopts the mask of very high Standard English ("myriad subtleties"),
but through this English utters a cry from the inner "tortured souls"
of black folks.

Standard English here does not simply sacrifice African-American
identity to white linguistic and social norms. Rather, it claims English
as its own legitimate American identity, joining it to African cultural
forms to forge a specific and unique hybrid mode. The figure of the

mask, also as a figure for language, attests the continuing survival of African cultural forms within the surrounding society that would suppress them, and the claim to American forms for its own unique cultural expression.

But this is also the case for poems in dialect. Dunbar's plantation poems in particular have disturbed readers, who fear they betray black self-representation in complicity with white versions of it.[13] But Dunbar seeks in these poems to recover African-American history in accordance with his own poetic and cultural intentions. The outstanding feature of these poems is their formal constitution: they are almost entirely cast as dramatic monologues. Dunbar handles this form with a sophistication and mastery that antedates its development by modernists such as Pound and Eliot. By using the represented speech of dramatic monologue form, spoken by characters who are precisely situated in historical time and place, Dunbar is able to control, and reframe, what had become black stereotypes. This can be a tricky undertaking. Sometimes Dunbar mimes plantation stereotypes so well that they can be mistaken for his own. "The Deserted Plantation" and "Chrismus on the Plantation" feature images of the devoted slave familiar from white plantation literature. Even in these cases, however, Dunbar is not presenting, but stylizing one kind of black personae: masks that the slaves displayed to their masters as a certain type within African-American history and lore. Dunbar here has his black speakers act the way whites think they do, an imitation of an image, his enactment of an act to which blacks themselves might resort. Moreover, it is greatly significant that Dunbar, against the norms of plantation literature, situates the poems in terms of black and not white experience, thus challenging the hegemony of white culture, if not of white power, in the ante-bellum South. Dunbar, however, does not evade the fact of slavery. His plantation representations must be placed in a complex socio-history: coming to terms with slave history was a pressing problem at the turn of the century in the context of the failure of Reconstruction. Intensifying racism, political exclusion, and economic neo-enslavement disappointed the hopes and promises of emancipation. A desire to put slave history behind combined with the need to face and understand its effects on African-American communal life. Dunbar, again like Du Bois, does not flinch from facing the destructive force of slavery. At the same time, he emphasizes African-American humanity, endurance, and spiritual gifts even under slavery's dehumanizing anomie.[14] A poem such as "Little Brown Baby with Sparklin' Eyes," for example, is exquisitely balanced between painful recognition of powerlessness and the strength of human devotion. Thus the slave father addresses his baby:

> Come to yo' pallet now—go to yo' res';
> Wisht you could allus know ease an' cleah skies;
> Wisht you could stay jes' a chile on my breas'--
> Little brown baby wif spa'klin eyes.

This poem is powerful and tense in its tragic contradiction between personal dignity and social powerlessness, as a slave father can never guarantee to his slave baby "ease and cleah skies," however longingly he desires to do so.

The formal constitution of the dialect poems, as dramatic monologues situating speech acts of specified individuals, allows Dunbar to investigate nostalgia rather than asserting it. His dialect poems reconsider negative or servile images in order to employ them polemically, subversively, or contentiously, to the disadvantage of the (white) outsider to the discourse. "Signs of the Times" asks of Thanksgiving what Frederick Douglass asked about the Fourth of July: what do these American holidays mean to the slave?[15] In the poem, moreover, the turkey, unaware of its coming fate as Thanksgiving dinner, stands as figure not for the South in its ownership, but in its own coming doom.

The dialect poems conduct an investigation into African-American identity. But so do the Standard English poems. What is striking through Dunbar's work is the continuity of intention between the two poetic groups. The black identity that dominates the dialect poems also provides a base matrix in Standard English poems. If the African-American identity is dual, then Standard English is Dunbar's heritage as much as dialect. Dunbar sets out to re-claim the Anglo-American tradition in creative relation to his African-American one. In this he does not present a synthesis, but controversial and contrapuntal strands interwoven through his texts.

Some dialect poems are complicated as polemical answers to white racist assumptions. Others draw on European modes. This is especially the case in Dunbar's use of Renaissance models. Among his earliest verse experiments are such elaborate troubadour forms as the madrigal and roundeau.[16] These are more important to Dunbar than is the Romantic tradition more usually cited. Especially interesting is Dunbar's recasting of Renaissance lyric in dialect poems. "Parted," for example, offers a dialect lament at being sold "down de stream" as a formal address to "my lady": "De ship hit teks me far away / My lady, my lady." Conversely, many Standard English poems feature powerful emblems of African- American experience, such as the mask or, in another moving poem, the cage:

> I know why the caged bird beats his wing...
> I know why the caged bird sings, ah me...
> It is not a carol of joy or glee...
> But a plea, that upward to Heaven he flings.

The cage evokes America itself in all its preventions and restrictions of its black citizens; and also evokes Standard English itself, which in one sense constrains the poet's song, but which he here also makes a vehicle of his own expression, overcoming those who would deny him his voice, both as black and as American.

Bivocalism emerges as a central concern in Dunbar's self-reflexive poems on writing poetry. These are constructed in both dialect and Standard English and are also about the relationship between the two languages. These poems have been interpreted as voicing Dunbar's ambivalence in being restricted to and by dialect. His "The Poet" is most often cited, with its lament against a world deaf to him when he "sang of life, serenely sweet" to praise only "a jingle in a broken tongue." But the failure here is in the audience who sees dialect as broken jingle, not Dunbar's own attitude towards it. Against them he insists that he has "voiced the world's absorbing beat," an embrace of African-American musical culture. Dunbar's senses of betrayal, difficulty, and mission come together in the poem "Compensation," written as he faced death from tuberculosis at the age of thirty-three. "Because I had loved so deeply," he writes, God gave him "the gift of song." But

> Because I have loved so vainly,
> And sung with such faltering breath,
> The Master in infinite mercy
> Offers the boon of Death.

The figure of song, in religious invocation, implicitly places this poem in a tradition of African-American experience. Its Standard English, however, agonizingly registers Dunbar's senses of his cultural identity as constricted and defeated, and yet, almost against itself, also transmits and movingly expresses that life. Song remains Dunbar's core trope for poetry, connecting him to the African-American culture in which music and song plays so central a role and which he recreates in his own melodic structures.[17] Dunbar's lyrics take shape in relation to ballad, serenade, lullaby, children's song, dirge, hymn, or love song, with Dunbar's special Renaissance quality, and in special relation to the spirituals tradition. Dunbar, unusually in African-American writing of his time, is both skeptical of and strongly invested in religion.[18] His poems "A Plantation Melody" and "A Spiritual" come close to a re-creation in dialect of spiritual faith, as do various hymns in Standard English. Other dialect poems suggest the otherworldly dimension of the spiritual tradition, in a "longing to go home" that indicts this world of enslavement. But in "Mare Rubrum," the spirituals' topic of Moses at the Red Sea is rendered in an elaborate Petrarchan sonnet, and opens into a rupture that contests faith even as it evokes the saving and providential "Word" through history. The poet awaits the "sound of that sustaining word / Which long ago the men of Israel heard;" but for him the "barrier waters" do not open. He is left asking whether "struggling faith may die of hope deferred?" Redemptive hope structures the poem, but also remains a hiatus within it.

Dunbar's treatments of the spirituals conjoin Standard English with African-American culture. These poems register the biracial, syncretist nature of the spirituals themselves, in which African-American religious forms developed both from and against white norms.[19] He repeatedly plays on distinctions between slave religion and white interpretations of it, showing black religious life as it responds to and also resists white religious values. Some poems, such as "Deacon Jones' Grievance," address the controversy over dance and music, in which African-based rhythmic worship was seen as contrary to church decorum.[20] In another poem, "Angelina" is warned off of fiddling. Such tensions eventually were resolved into rhythmic worship as adopted by both black and white religious groups, with strong mutual influences penetrating in both directions.[21]

"An Ante-Bellum Sermon" serves as an outstanding example of Dunbar's acute historical sense, rendered through a stunningly complex linguistic act. This poem recalls and reworks both the slave spiritual and the black sermon traditions. Written in dialect, it conducts an elaborate biblical exegesis that in one performance actually splits in its address: on the one hand to slave worshipers, for whom it brings a biblical message of hope and freedom; on the other and at the same time to white masters overseeing them, including and indeed especially in church, to make sure no such message takes place. The result is a multiple discourse around the Bible, in both its political and spiritual significances, as these divide between distinct audiences.

The figure of the preacher, so central to African-American religious history, is dramatized, while poetic form reaffirms important ties to spiritual song.[22]

Like so many spirituals, the "Sermon," "chooses fu' ouah subjic' "—that is, takes as its text, Moses and the Exodus.

> Dis—we'll 'splain it by an' by;
> "An de Lawd said, 'Moses, Moses,"
> And de man said, "hyeah am I." (13)

The preacher will " 'splain" his subject (i.e. conduct an exegesis). The readings he goes on to offer range through biblical history from Exodus to Gabriel's Last Trumpet, typologically linking events together—as in the spirituals—through a message of deliverance. God's infinite redemptive power is attested throughout a providential history, with promise and hope for release from slavery. But the preacher, even while he delivers this message to his slave audience, must disguise it so as to keep it from the white overseers whose job it is to prevent exactly such subversive messages.

The result is a virtuoso multiplication of meanings, each directed toward the sermon's different audiences. Towards the slave audience, there is a call to freedom and to faith, shown through comparisons and continuities between past deliverance and present hope: "Fu' de Lawd will he'p his chillun / You kin trust him evah time." Toward the white audience, the preacher hastens to deny what he has just asserted:

> So you see de Lawd's intention,
>   Evah sence de worl' began,
> Was dat His almighty freedom
>   Should belong to evah man,
> But I think it would be bettah,
>   Ef I'd pause agin to say,
> Dat I'm talkin' 'bout ouah freedom
>   In a Bibleistic way.

The figure of the preacher finally evokes some of the ambivalence towards Dunbar's own position that made him say near the end of his life, "I am a black white man." Dunbar's life was deeply strained by financial need, a struggle with tuberculosis that killed him at the age of thirty-three, marital breakdown, and his often-frustrated search for modes of expression that led him to write novels, librettos, songs, and essays in addition to poetry for a range of audiences, none of whom completely accepted him. His historical position at the time of Jim Crow faced him with acute disappointment against the vision of equality and integration that emancipation had seemed to offer.[23] Like the preacher in "Sermon," Dunbar in one sense, accommodates his means of expression to an inimical and hostile social order. Yet in another sense, he exposes and challenges the structures that demand such accommodation, and controls his meanings within and despite their hierarchies of power.

Dunbar's poetry resides within this complex orchestration of audiences and linguistic meanings. He negotiates contrary forces of assertion and accommodation. Complicity and creative command of language engage each other, often painfully. Yet he boldly claims as his own an American language that others would deny him. His languages act as an arena for exposing and indicting, resisting and also negotiating Dunbar's double American experience. His most accomplished poems finally attain a delicate and indeed excruciating balance between promise and betrayal, exclusion and transformation, in which his two languages engage each other: antagonistic and reflexive; mutually confronting, mutually constituting.

CHAPTER 12

HARVARD FORMALISM

There is a good deal of Harvard throughout nineteenth-century poetry. Longfellow, Lowell, and Holmes all spent most of their lives there; first as students and then later as professors. But in the 1890s, Harvard became the seat of a peculiar concentration of poetic activity, which on one side signaled a particular contraction, but on the other inaugurated strong future trends. Genuine poetic departures within the nineteenth century took place on the whole outside Cambridge: Whitman's, Dickinson's, Dunbar's, Crane's. 1890s Harvard was, nevertheless, a matrix out of which emerged a range of the next century's diverse, and in many ways conflicting, modernisms (oddly, but not exclusively, from among students who passed through but did not complete degrees: E.A. Robinson [1891–1893], Wallace Stevens [1897–1900], Robert Frost [1897–1899)], and T.S. Eliot, who completed his B.A. and M.A. from 1906–1914, also teaching philosophy courses, but did not return from London to defend his completed doctoral dissertation, thus ceding his PhD). All these poets can be said to reflect and revise the aesthetics of Harvard at the century's end.

What connects Harvard's nineteenth-century poets is their commitment to a formal poetics, which became by the end of the century rigid in practice but also ideologically innovative, not to say aggressive. The central ideologue was George Santayana, a poet, a philosopher, but above all a custodian of ideas. These different roles worked rather at cross purposes. Santayana's commitment to what he saw as the main traditions of Western civilization ultimately sealed his poetry to the point of suffocation. His poetic faults include stilted diction, predictable rhyme, strained syntax, garbled sequences, unnatural and unmusical phrasing, and derivative imagery and sentiment. Indeed, Santayana, so disdainful of the genteel tradition he himself named, also very much embodies it. In many ways, his most astute critical remarks apply first to himself. And yet, his poetic interests project the aesthetic concerns that become fundamental and energetic in poetry after him.

Santayana in general may be said to have disliked. He disliked natives and immigrants, the masses and the elite, Jews, women, the devout and the secular. As Van Wycks Brooks sums up, Santayana disliked America. "He was repelled by everything that characterized American life...his smiling contempt for the efforts of men to better the world and humanity was reflected in a host of Harvard minds that were reversing the whole tendency of the great New England epoch."[1] This disdain no doubt originated in Santayana's horrible childhood of abandonment and displacement, which was deepened through an adult life of homelessness and suppressed homosexuality.[2] He was left by his American mother in Spain with his father at the age of five so that she could return to Boston to raise the children from her first, elite New England marriage. At age eight he was taken to Boston to live with his wealthier half-brother and sisters. Catholic in a Protestant environment, Santayana grew up on the borders of wealth, social position, and religious affiliation.[3] Remaining at Harvard as a professor after completing his studies there, his mother's death in 1912 at last freed him to return to Europe. He died in a convent in Rome in 1952.

Santayana introduced the notion of the genteel tradition in a lecture delivered at Berkeley in 1911, as he was departing America. The term is not closely or rigorously defined. But it focuses a core problem for American poets and indeed for America at large: the split in the "American Mind" such that, as he describes it in "The Genteel Tradition in American Poetry," one half—the main one—is occupied "intensely in practical affairs," while the other half remains "slightly becalmed...floating gently in the backwater."

> The American Will inhabits the sky-scraper; the American intellect inhabits the colonial mansion. The one is the sphere of the American man; the other, at least predominantly, of the American woman. The one is all aggressive enterprise; the other is all genteel tradition.

Santayana's gendered language here is neither accidental nor inconsequential. It recurs when, in a later essay on "Genteel American Poetry," Santayana describes the genteel as a

> frank and gentle Romanticism which attached it to Evangelines and Maud Mullers...a simple, sweet, humane, Protestant literature,

grandmotherly in that sedate spectacled wonder with which it gazed at
this terrible world and said how beautiful and how interesting it was.[4]

Santayana points here to Longfellow as the exemplar of the genteel.
Yet Santayana is himself caught in Longfellow's anxiety that poetry in
America has no place, that it does not count. American sensibility not
only splits into practical life as opposed to a high culture, but regards
the latter as essentially irrelevant, or, as he says, feminine. Genteel
poetry is "grandmotherly"—which is to say, for Santayana, American
poetry is a separate sphere.

But Santayana is less disturbed by the separation than by its hierarchies. Santayana does not really desire an integration of American
business and American art, as Whitman does (in ways Santayana
steadfastly disdains). What annoys Santayana is not the division of
American life into a commercial mass culture as against an elite literary one, but the fact that the first dominates rather than the second.[5]
Not the separation of its sphere, but its powerlessness, feminizes literature for Santayana. He would not mind its being separate and male,
like the exclusive Laodicean Club he founded at Harvard that mirrored and rivaled other exclusive men's clubs (and whose journal, the
Harvard Monthly, refused to publish special-student E.A. Robinson).
But he would substitute poetry for money as the counter of prestige.
Santayana endorses elite culture. However, he wishes it to be effective
in ways that he feels in America it is not. His solution, or advocacy,
will be to intensify poetry as an elite, separate realm for which he will
make greater and greater claims.

Santayana brought out a collection of poems and sonnets in
1894. A second sonnet cycle began in 1896 with the publishing of
his aesthetic treatise, *The Sense of Beauty*. Then, in 1900, came his
Interpretations of Poetry and Religion, which was followed by many
other prose works, but no poetry, in the new century. The 1890s
works are of a piece. In both the poetry and the aesthetics, formalization emerges as the dominant commitment. In Sonnet I, "I sought
on earth a garden of delight / Or island altar to the Sea and Air,"
the earthly garden and isolated "island altar" is the sonnet itself. But
what its "prayer" and "rite" mark is a metaphysical space that has been
emptied of its force. A Christic figure is invoked, but

> though his arms, outstretched upon the tree,
> Were beautiful, and pleaded my embrace,
> My sins were loth to look upon his face.
> So came I down from Golgotha to thee,

> Eternal Mother; let the sun and sea
> Heal me, and keep me in thy dwelling-place.

Christianity is shown to have waned as an effective myth, but the turn to the earth as "Eternal Mother" can only be nostalgic. "I would I had been born in nature's day," he complains in Sonnet IV. But he was not. Olympian heaven remains unreal, "a thousand beauties that have never been," even as they "haunt me with hope and tempt me to pursue" (Sonnet XVI).

What recurs in Santayana is the coming apart of Christian suffering and Christian redemption, while retaining a sense of Christian sin. Divine love fails to rise above the flawed world, but sin prevents him from accepting or embracing the earth, either. The two elements of sin and redemption that govern traditional Christian structure in Santayana cancel each other out. His mythologizing never really sanctions nature. "Birth," as he writes in Sonnet XXV, is to him a "great disaster." "Do you suppose the slow, painful, nasty, bloody process by which things in this world grow, is worth having for the sake of the perfection of a moment?" he wrote a friend in 1887.[6] The mythological world he invokes remains very much literary allusion. Similarly, the Neo-Platonist-troubadour-Renaissance Italian tradition that he endorses in his chapter on "Platonic Love in Some Italian Poets" in *Interpretations of Poetry and Religion*, remains ghostly in Santayana's lack of an impelling Neo-Platonic or troubadour "beloved," and also of a genuine Platonist metaphysical ladder of ascent. These linger on in the poems only as a kind of décor, a "battlements of heaven" in Sonnet IX that ultimately is "passion-quelling," or a "ghostly mistress" (Sonnet XXXIX). As Santayana himself puts it, he is

> Unmindful of the changing outer skies,
> Where now, perchance some new-born Eros flies
> Or some old Cronos from his throne is hurled
> I heed them not. (Sonnet XIV)

Santayana's ultimately seems a poetry of Eros without the Eros ("I heed them not."). Several sonnets suggest that his closeted homosexuality may be one source for this stillborn eroticism (e.g., XXXVI and XXXVII). Instead, he presents an aestheticized love such as appears in "Chorus," one of the "Various Poems" that are not sonnets and show rather more linguistic flexibility. There he devotes to "immortal love" a series of items of which he has little experience: an "antelope," a "horne'd bull…bellowing to his herd," concluding with an aesthetic image:

> The painted bird
> For thee hath music and to thee addressed,
> And the brief sadness of his dying note
> Is for thy bitter absence and thy pain.

The "painted bird" as aesthetic object is image and product of the death and painful absence of Eros. Santayana speaks of a conversion or "metanoia" in his life that "rendered external things indifferent," a mode of renunciation where "the whole world belongs to me implicitly when I have given it all up, and am wedded to nothing particular in it."[7] In many ways, his is an ascetic dualism. However, it lacks metaphysical frameworks, preserving renunciative sacrifices while granting few of the rewards of genuine ascent (see Sonnet VI—"Love not as do the flesh-imprisoned men"; or VII—"I would I might forget that I am I, / And break the heavy chain [of] the body's tomb"). This suggests less renunciation than repression; with form its ultimate image and self-referring goal. Art is

> A wall, a wall to hem the azure sphere
> And hedge me in from the disconsolate hills!…
> Come no profane insatiate mortal near
> With the contagion of his passionate ills.   (XV)

Formalism, erected like a wall against passion, nature, and world in a kind of facsimile of monastic retreat from profane mortality, becomes in Santayana an intentional aesthetic.

Even before Santayana, Harvard had other poets of formal commitment if not aesthetic theory. First, the genteel Fireside poets, but also Frederick Goddard Tuckerman (1821–1873), who enrolled at Harvard in 1839, where Jones Very was briefly his tutor. In 1842 Tuckerman graduated as a lawyer, but a rich inheritance saved him from having to choose between the different halves of Santayana's American mind. He was thus freed for culture as an amateur botanist, astronomer, and poet, living increasingly the life of a recluse after the early death of his wife.

Tuckerman's greatest distinction is to have his ode on "the Cricket" named by Ivor Winters as "the greatest poem in English of the century."[8] But Tuckerman's poetic focused on sonnets. These are intricate linguistic structures, densely interwoven with details from a naturalist's notebook. Particularly successful is his double-sonnet, "The starry flower, the flowerlike stars that fade," in which minute floral patterns find their counterpart in the cosmological heavens. But Tuckerman's world, like Santayana's, is one of collapsed metaphysical space.[9] While he often offers a Hopkinsesque naming of parts of the world, there is little sense of transcendent logos holding them together. Only the sonnet form itself can attempt to do so, figured as an enclosed garden with "dark fens of cedar, hemlock branches gray" that form a dense "darkness, shut from strife" (Part I, VII).

Other of Harvard's formalist poets include Trumbull Stickney, whose 1890s Harvard association with Santayana's Laodicean Club covers the greater part of a career cut off by sudden death in 1904. Stickney's work is poised between the nineteenth and twentieth centuries. Both European and American like Santayana, Stickney was privately tutored by his professor father as the family moved restlessly between various European cities. Entering Harvard in 1891, he joined an intellectual circle that included Santayana, Henry Cabot Lodge, and Henry Adams as further associates. After Harvard he became the first American to earn a *Doctorat des Lettres* at the Sorbonne, editing fifteenth century letters in Latin from a Venetian ambassador to Rome and writing a thesis on gnomic, aphoristic elements in Greek verse.[10] He lived one year at Harvard as an instructor in Greek before dying of a brain tumor at the age of thirty in 1904.

Strickney's Harvard formalism emerges most clearly in his sonnets, such as the *Sonnets from Greece*, but classicism deeply penetrates all his work. "Lucretius" and "Kalypso" feature dramatic speakers. "Oneiropolos" offers a kind of dialogue between Indian and Greek cultures, both of which Stickney studied. "In the Past" seems to re-stage without naming the river Styx, evoked as an interior stagnation:

> There lies a somnolent lake
> Under a noiseless sky,
> Where never the mornings break
> Nor the evenings die . . .
>
> And the hours lag dead in the air
> With a sense of coming eternity
> To the heart of the lonely boatman there:
> That boatman am I.[11]

To Stickney, the present characteristically emerges as such a solitary and abandoned dead scene, a "cold," "empty," "lonely," "dark" present "country" in autumn contrasted against, as in the poem "Mnemosyne," the "long sun-sweetened summer days" of memory. But this is less personal nostalgia than historiography. The ancient world is for Stickney a cultural point of view, and it is this he feels his own world to have lost. A poem such as "Song," with its refrain: "A cuckoo said in my brain: 'Not Yet,'" (repeated as "so soon," and then "too late;") shows Stickney's promise in lyric music and structure, but also his sense of temporal displacement and nostalgia. His "An Athenian Garden," in which "leaves are echoes" and the "earth / Is packed with footsteps of the dead," can almost stand for his own work. On the other hand, in his poems on Greece and specific sites there, nostalgia merges into the concrete present, giving his Greek sonnets a clearer, scenic focus than is otherwise the case. His sonnet on "Eleusis," revisiting the place of "a thousand years processional / Winding around the Eleusinian bay," provides a glimpse of how the natural world was alive and sacral within Greek experience:

> As then the litanies antiphonal
> Obscurely through the pillars sang away,
> It dawned, and in the shaft of sudden day
> Demeter smiling gave her bread to all.
> They drew as waves out of a twilight main,
> Long genuflecting multitudes, to feed
> With God upon the sacramental grain.

Natural pillars open intrinsically into antiphonal celebration. Past ceremony enriches the present. Mystery penetrates the mundane as "sacramental grain." This immediate classical experience of the imminent world Stickney opposes against what he condemns, in an essay on "Herakleitos" for the *Harvard Monthly* (February 1895), as the Romantic "provincialism" of "metaphysical abstractions, investing the world with strange values, elaborating explanations for insane hypotheses."

Reading backwards, it is possible to discern in Stickney, as in Santayana, the beginnings of what later became a sharp drawing of battlelines between Romanticism and Classicism for Eliot, Pound, and T. E. Hulme. Stickney describes his poems as a "revival of self-restraint," a poetry of concrete containment he contrasts against Wordsworth, whose world Stickney describes as a repository of vague powers.[12] This containment is finally realized as aesthetic formalization itself. Stickney's sonnet on "Eleusis," in its imagery of "litanies antiphonal," is self-referring. The sonnet "Sunium" converts the whole scene of mountain and cloud into art object, as "Aegean lyre" whose "strings" stretch "across the sky and sea." The Greek world is presented here as its own becoming into art. This transmutation, however, remains an after-image of a lost past. The "flutings" of this world-lyre can be felt "now" only as "strained and dubious." Its magnificence is consumed within its own declared moment.

Formalization begins in Stickney to take shape as an enclosed world, containing its own elements in a classical restraint. In Santayana, these impulses become an express aesthetic program. Santayana's treatise, *The Sense of Beauty*, devotes a long section to "form," defined as symmetry and unity, in an art "object" increasingly geometric, spatialized, totalized, and static.[13] "Beauty" is "value positive, intrinsic, and objectified" (51), in which "form" is "the unity of a manifold" (98). Through symmetry, "the parts, coalescing, form a single object [of] unity and simplicity" (95). As he reiterates in his theoretical discussions in *Interpretations of Poetry and Religion*, "human reason and human imagination require a certain totality" (163).[14] Poetry is measure, where

> measure is a condition of perfection, for perfection requires that order should be pervasive, that not only the whole before us should have a form, but that every part in turn should have a form of its own, and that those parts should be coordinated among themselves as the whole is coordinated with the other parts of some greater cosmos.   (252)

As in the High Modernism of the new century, Santayana's emphasis on unity and totality emerges as a polemical attack against Romanticism, which he sees as "vague" and "incoherent," displaying "less mastery" in the artist (*Sense*, 131). Beauty is essentially formal for Santayana: "We can only see beauty in so far as we introduce form" (145). Only an "illusion, proper to the Romantic temperament, lends a mysterious charm to things which are indefinite and indefinable" (145). Any work of art that "remains indeterminate is a failure...The emotion, not being embodied, fails to constitute the beauty of anything" (148). This is what makes Romanticism little more than a "loose and somewhat helpless state of mind" (146), an "example of aesthetic incapacity" (148).

That Santayana's ideal of perfected formal unity is essentially ahistorical and atemporal emerges as another foreshadowing of High Modernism. Symmetry, he writes in *The Sense of Beauty*, must contribute to "the unity of our perception," in a manner that is "instantaneous" (97). History itself is nothing but a collection of "indeterminate material" and only attains value when, "like poetry," it asserts "beauty, power, and adequacy of form in which the indeterminate material of human life is presented (140–141). As against the Romantics, he is pleased to "prefer the unchangeable to the irrecoverable" (145). This formalist ahistoricism underlies Santayana's attacks on Walt Whitman. Santayana, it is true, cites Whitman as the one American poet who escapes the genteel tradition. But this escape is for Santayana an aesthetic failure. To Santayana, Whitman represents an "attitude utterly disintegrating," his imagination nothing more than a "passive sensorium for the registering of impressions" in which "no element of construction remained," leaving only a "lazy, desultory apprehension" (*Genteel*, 53). "Everything" in Whitman "is a momentary pulsation of a liquid and structureless whole" (*Sense*, 113). Santayana thus rejects Whitman's art as formless, as nothing but "sensation...without underlying structure" (179), where form is defined as subsuming time and sequence into unitary wholeness. Whitman, as Santayana complains, offers "no total vision, no grasp of the whole reality" (*Interpretations*, 168). Santayana prefers a mind that "does not easily discriminate the successive phases of an action in which it is still engaged; it does not arrange in a temporal series the elements of a single perception, but posits them all together as constituting a permanent and real object." (170)[15]

The configuration that emerges in Santayana's essays, as in his poetic writing, is one that opposes form against history, against time, detached from nature in a distinct, alternative world. In a sonnet called "The Power of Art," Santayana contrasts the beauties of nature "that by changing live" against what art produces. Natural beauties "in their begetting are o'erthrown, / Nor may the sentenced minutes find reprieve." But in art "our hands immortalize the day" and "save from utter death / The sacred past that should not pass away." The sonnet form itself is the best, although still inferior, modern equivalent to classical unity through its interlinking of rhyme and parts (*Sense of Beauty*, 170). Despite this, even Shakespeare is criticized for failing to present "fragments of experience [as though] fallen together into a perfect picture [in which] the universe is total" (*Sense of Beauty*, 154). Nature instead should be eclipsed in an art that offers an "eternal whole" (VI, cf. VIII, XIX). Art should be nature's antagonist, an immortal "day" that removes the "shifting light of life" into a totality of the lost, "sacred past" as in a kind of formaldehyde.

On one level, Santayana's aesthetic makes increasingly ambitious claims for art. As a unification of its materials, art stands outside of time, representing a totalized culture that he, like Eliot after him, names tradition. This tradition forms an ahistorical context to which the individual artist must "discipline" himself, something Whitman wrongly refuses to do (*Interpretations*, 176). But Santayana's claims for art as an independent realm, self-controlled and absolute, is in the end constructed as an obverse image for the world Santayana felt to be commercial, crass, and victorious—a world that left little room for art, or for him. And yet in this it derives from and mirrors that world. In its detachment, its enclosure, its self-sufficiency, Santayana's high culture in effect reproduces the genteel irrelevance it is meant to protest. Santayana denounces poetry's cultural place as little more than a holiday "relaxation," with artists performing feast day functions on the order of "cooks, hairdressers, and florists" (*Interpretations* 267).[16] But his aesthetic is itself a product and mirror of that split in the American mind against which he protests. Masquerading as aesthetic autonomy, his conception of art is socially determined. Longing for the "perfect human discipline…of a Greek city or of the British upper classes" (*Genteel*, 140), Santayana is faced instead with the "material restlessness" of "a new type of American…the untrained, pushing, cosmopolitan orphan" (86), "Jewish, Irish, German, Italian, or whatever they may be…[arriving] not in the hope of founding a godly commonwealth, but only of prospering in an untrammeled one" (101). Not only Whitman's writing, but Whitman's democracy, is "a mass of images without structure," collapsing "all extraordinary gifts of genius or virtue" into "material improvement" and, horrors, "an actual equality among all men" (*Interpretations*, 181–2). Tradition is thereby demoted to a genteel, which is to say in Santayana's gendered language, a feminized margin, mere "academic luxuries, fit to amuse the ladies" (123) lacking both authority and power.

What Santayana's work suggests is that the other side of the coin of formalism is money. The more rigidly self-constituted, autonomous, and absolute the claims for poetic form, the more it mirrors, inversely, a commercial culture that denies it cultural priority. Some of Santayana's best writing occurs when this cultural confrontation comes to the surface. Of his poems, the most readable are the looser "Odes," less straight-jacketed than his sonnet writing and openly opposing "this labouring nation" against an "inward gladness…in some Persian / Garden of roses" (Ode I). Ode II denounces "my generation / that talks of freedom and is slave to riches," who "wretched

themselves, they heap, to make them happy, / Many possessions."
Ode III frankly names Columbus as villain:

> He gave the world another world, and ruin
> Brought upon blameless, river-loving nations,
> Cursed Spain with barren gold, and made the Andes
> Fiefs of Saint Peter;

Trumbull Stickney similarly writes a sonnet against Columbus, as one who "rash and greedy took the screaming main / And vanished out before the hurricane / Into the sunset after merchandise." Stickney's preferred outcome to this betrayal of culture to money is apocalyptic destruction, in which its world would "pass before us like a cloud of dust." Just so, Santayana concludes his "Ode to the New World" in apocalyptic dust and almost Gnostic denial of the natural world for some remote, inhuman, and absolutely composed realm:

> Until the patient earth, made dry and barren,
> Sheds all her herbage in a final winter,
> And the gods turn their eyes to some far distant
> Bright constellation.

In the wake of Santayana, a group of modern writers emerged out of Harvard, each facing the formal and cultural problems Santayana in many ways foretold. Edward Arlington Robinson's first volume of poems, published without much notice during the 1890s, is able to restore to formalism some natural language and a dramatic (which is to say more temporalized and historicized) focus. Robert Frost most fully achieves a language at once formal and natural; while Wallace Stevens and T.S. Eliot each rejects Santayana's conflation of religion with art: Stevens finally to abandon metaphysical space, Eliot finally to reclaim it. Eliot in particular then developed an aesthetic whose notions of autonomous self-enclosure, discipline, and unity in many ways echo Santayana's, even as he was able to find a new accommodation between formalized and natural poetic language. But the yawning gaps Santayana witnessed as opening between modernity and tradition remained for the modernists an aesthetic and cultural crisis.

CHAPTER 13

WALT WHITMAN'S REPUBLIC OF
LETTERS

Walt Whitman cuts so large a figure that readings of his work seem doomed to be fragmentary. What often emerges is a splitting apart of Whitman into contradictory and opposing poses. There is Whitman the solitary singer as against Whitman the political journalist; Whitman the imperial self as against Whitman the poet of democracy; Whitman the Romantic and/or antinomian ego as against Whitman the wound dresser; Whitman the homoerotic radical as against Whitman the defender of the "American Way."

What these opposing categories largely dissociate is Whitman's work as autonomous from his social involvements. But it is his particular commitment to bring these two, as well as the myriad other experiences that make up American experience, into mutual configuration. Whitman's work can appear a "scrapbasket," as one early reviewer described it, as if he merely wrote down whatever came into his head or caught his eye.[1] But Whitman's is a highly orchestrated poetics, constructed to bring into alignment the vast range of materials he introduces into his texts. He does this by proposing each level of engagement—public and private, political and poetic, religious and sensual and material—as a figural reflection of each other. In his art, different levels of experience are meant to mutually evoke, image, and transform each other. This figural reflection is registered in *Leaves of Grass* through core words ("tally," "echo," "hint," "transparent") that suggest links and extensions between terms. Through them and their figural energy, Whitman imagines America as just this possibility for different dimensions of experience to enforce and enlarge each other. The private and the public, the material and the creative, the physical and the emotional, the prosaic and the poetic all can emerge as modes, developments, and elaborations of each other. Whitman's figural poetics sets out to draw together exactly the oppositions seen to divide him. His project is precisely to redefine and overcome these divisions, in the face of tensions and conflicts gaping wide across the country he inhabited.

In this project, political terms are foundational, although not exhaustive. Whitman's imaginative vision is directed towards an America in which individual integrity founds rather than splinters community. His poetic is central to this venture: creating a language in which self and community mutually constitute and transfigure each other. His poetry offers both model and conduct toward this mutual construction, in an America whose diverse commitments and impulses are reciprocally confirming rather than conflicting. This political-poetic project is closely allied with a republican tradition in which liberty means not personal "property" in the Lockean sense, but participating in self-government through a civic virtue that realizes the self through the common good. It is on this political model that Whitman constructs his poetic voice. Through that voice he addresses every reader, in the effort and hope to awaken each to his/her individual place and responsibility within the American polity and possibility. It has long been remarked, and the text itself proposes, that *Leaves of Grass* pursues a journey and process of self-construction that it conducts but never concludes, a journey it invites and incites each reader to undergo in his/her own right.[2] The poem in fact is constructing not only selves, but polities as well. The structures and images of the poems are directed towards balancing and harmonizing pluralities of selves and meanings within communal allegiances and mutual commitments. Whitman's goal is to have diversities mutually correspond and affirm each other. This is one of the senses in which Whitman claims America itself to be a poem. Like a poem, and through his poetry, he envisions America as bringing its many different components and ventures into complex but affirmative relationship, casting each as figures for the other in mutual transformation and confirmation.

Whitman's poetic subject is, then, the diversity of America; plural cultures as the foundation of a common society that each individual would be committed to building. But Whitman by no means claims this task to have been already accomplished. The self and society as it currently exists are not what he is celebrating. Whitman's heroic and exuberant verse is always conducted through a no less profound critique and skepticism regarding the America that confronts him. This skepticism, far from surfacing sporadically as an anomaly or a kind of bad mood, exerts a continuous pressure throughout Whitman's work. It penetrates the mutual relationship between his figure of the self and the figure of America. Whitman's self is not euphoric and smug, and neither is his America. At most, he offers a promise of each as still to be attempted and accomplished through the very processes the poem inaugurates. Neither the America nor the self of Whitman's poem has been already achieved. Each is no more (but also no less) than the promise that the poem, in the face of severe threats, sets out both to attest and to guard from despair.[3] What the poetry celebrates is a self and nation as yet to be created, not least through Whitman's own writing.

A key figure in this undertaking to constitute an 'America of Promise' is Whitman's "Myself." But Whitman's Myself is multiple and complex.[4] Far from merely being an image of Whitman himself (and it is striking that we learn almost nothing in the poem about Whitman in any personal sense. Even his name only appears in the 498th line, and the original edition carried his picture, not his name), Myself stands forth as a figure for America and for Americans. It is in this sense that Myself repeatedly speaks as America. Whitman's is a rhetoric of gargantuan personification, not as engulfing, imperial ego or as propagandist voice for an imperial America, but as the multiple and hence exemplary representative of American diversity and energy.[5] The role of Myself is to be delegate, exemplar, type, representative—roles that open out from their poetic center to extend deeply into American history, political philosophy, and culture. It reaches toward every reader as potential poet, delegating him/herself in paths the poem will open and ways that it will show, not to completion, but to generation. "The greatest poet," Whitman writes,

> is he who in his works most stimulates the reader's imagination and reflection, who incites him the most to poetize. The greatest poet is…he who suggests the most; he, not all of whose meaning is at first obvious, and who leaves you much to desire, to explain, to study, much to complete in your turn. (*CPP* 1022)[6]

In this and many other passages, Myself figures America, and America Myself. The rhetorical strategy of personification structures the mutual embodiment announced in such *Leaves of Grass* titles as "I hear America Singing." In the poem's journeys through America, in its catalogue formations, its vistas, landscapes, and record of character types, Whitman's "I" stands not only for Whitman as an individual or even as a poet, but for the country as a personified figure. "I" can reach to include all varieties of American experience because, on at least one figural level, "I" is America speaking. This is not to incorporate and engulf or even encompass, but rather to recognize and summon. The 1855 preface specifies these courses, introducing both personification and catalogue as techniques for spanning American geographical, social, historical, and political configurations:

> A bard is to be commensurate with a people...He spans between them also from east to west and reflects what is between them...To him enter...past and present events...the first settlements north or south...the haughty defiance of '76, and the war and peace and formation of the constitution...the endless gestation of new states—the convening of Congress every December, the members duly coming up from all climates and the uttermost parts.

The political evocations here are not merely illustrations, but foundations of Whitman's venture. He speaks specifically for and to America's settlement, its revolutionary and current history, invoking specific cultural and political models. "The poet is representative," Emerson writes in "The Poet," "He stands among partial men for the complete man, and apprises us not of his wealth, but of the common-wealth." Whitman realizes both poetic and political directions of this analogy. Whitman's "bard" is "commensurate with a people," as a Congressional representative is to his constituents.[7] He stands not for his own interests, but for the "common-wealth" he and each American help to define, and whom he emblemizes and leads towards their own republican self-realization.

Whitman's poetic project draws upon, furthers, and in many ways derives in his political commitments.[8] He came to poetry after a career as political journalist and activist (though he also worked as a carpenter, a schoolteacher, a small businessman, and other sundry jobs).[9] His affiliations were with the Democratic Party and its newspapers as editor, reporter, and reviewer. His newspaper writings through the 1840s and 1850s trace his political course from a centrist position increasingly to the margin of anti-extension, anti-slavery politics, and finally breaking away from the Democratic Party to join the Free-Soil Party. He actively campaigned for Martin Van Buren's presidential run, and for Silas Wright, a New York Barnburner gubernatorial candidate, in 1846, and participated as a delegate to the first Free-Soil Convention in 1848.[10] Whitman had been writing fiction through the 1840s: short stories and the wildly successful temperance novel

Franklin Evans, or the Inebriate, which sold 20,000 copies (more than all the editions of *Leaves of Grass* in Whitman's lifetime).[11] His plunge into poetry was from this political activism and its frustration, as a mode of appeal, intervention, and participation carrying forward his political vision and commitments. His work reflects and re-works not only current topics but also very much the roles of political involvement, including the democratizing transformations taking place through the Jacksonian period and the contradictions and exclusions this no less marked.

It is slavery, of course, that ruptures the claims of American republicanism, defeating the vision of equal individuals joining together in self-governing community. Whitman has been criticized for weakness in his anti-slavery position. He resisted radical abolitionism: a *Brooklyn Eagle* editorial denounces the "wicked wrong of abolitionist interference with slavery in Southern states" (*UPP*, 160). But this was, like Lincoln, due to what he understood as constitutional restraints on direct interference in states where slavery was already established. And, like Lincoln, he was adamant against the extension of slavery into new territories—although he certainly supported expansion itself. Both North and South believed that without extension slavery would die out; and it is certain that the South would have ceded political power as new territories came to be admitted as free states.[12] Legislative history tracks efforts at restriction and compromise on slavery through the Northwest Ordinance, the Missouri Compromise, the Wilmot Proviso, the Compromise of 1850, and the Kansas-Nebraska Bill, as each section faced increasing pressure from the country's expansion to define and control the national character in political, economic, and cultural terms.

But whatever his other political considerations, such as constitutional issues and his concern for Free (white) Labor, Whitman opposed slavery, and did so on republican grounds. Slavery betrayed the fundamental vision of both self and self-government on which he felt America to be founded. Southern society itself constituted an unrepublican aristocracy, the "interests of the few thousand rich 'polished,' and aristocratic owners of the slaves at the south," as he wrote in one editorial, against "the grand body of white workingmen." (*BE*, Sept 1, 1847; UPP, I 208). "What is this American Republic for?" writes Whitman in an early manuscript, using the language of social contract that his notes show he had studied in Rousseau. The Confederacy stands against "the meaning and direct purpose of our supreme compact, [in which] when not impeded by special State sovereignty (and then always in contempt of their letter and spirit) that the hopple shall fall away from the legs of the slave."[13] Though unfortunately protected by constitutional state sovereignty, Whitman considers slavery "in contempt of [the] letter and spirit" of American law. Slavery, he goes on to say, is "the greatest undemocratic un-Americanism of all," establishing "the odious distinction of an inferior class, composed of all who are not owners of slaves." In notes on "the true American character" dating from 1856, Whitman contrasts those who are "easy and friendly with his workmen" against "the stern master of slaves" and all who make "ignominious distinctions." Slavery, to Whitman, stands as the last, hideous vestige in the New World of a feudal, old European order, the

> relics of imported feudal manners, the taking off of hats in any presence, and all sirring and Mr.-ing with all their vast entourage that are foreign to These States [and] are to go the same road hence as the idea and practice of royalty have gone. (*NM*, VI 2147)

Whitman's poetry, written at a different time and in a different medium than was his newspaper prose, is continuous with his journalism. The haunting figures of slavery in 1855's *Leaves of Grass* emphasize the essential humane equality of person to person: in the runaway slave of *Song of Myself*, housed in "a room that enter'd from my own," and fed "next me at table" (Song 10); or, in the image of the poet himself as "the hounded slave" ("I wince at the bite of the dogs...hell and despair are upon me" [Song 33]). Whitman is most subversive and transformative in "I Sing the Body Electric" (VII), where he turns the very language of the auction against itself. "I help the auctioneer—the sloven does not half know his business." What the auctioneer degrades as property Whitman reveals as personhood, unveiling the sanctity of selfhood, that epitome of volition, body, sense, and possibility that stands at the center of every human person:

> A man's body at auction,
> (For before the war I often go to the slave-mart and watch the sale,)
>
> I help the auctioneer, the sloven does not half know his business.
>
> Gentlemen look on this wonder.
> Whatever the bids of the bidders they cannot be high enough for it...
>
> In this head the all-baffling brain,
> In it and below it the makings of heroes...
>
> This is not only one man, this the father of those who shall be fathers
>   in their turns,

In him the start of populous states and rich republics,
Of him countless immortal lives with countless embodiments and
enjoyments. (VII)

In 1848, Whitman had spent three months in New Orleans (his only
visit to the deep South) working for the newspaper the *Crescent*. The
poem's "body," of course, intends the body politic as well, which the
poet sets out to "discorrupt." "Electric" is one of Whitman's poetic images of dense interrelation. It evokes at once sexual attraction,
spiritual extension, figural connection, and scientific energy. But
these are confuted and interrupted by the auctioneer's reduction of
the human being to a material, economic commodity. Yet Whitman
commandeers this very language and transforms it into a declaration
of illimitable and infinite value. He builds his appeal out of traditions
of religious moral sanctity of the individual as created "wonder," then
realized in traditions of a political citizenry each of whom contributes
to "populous states and rich republics." But "rich" here is a subtle
term. What Whitman does not mean, what he is polemically countering, is economic measure as asserting itself to be the determining
value in America, and not only in terms of slavery. "Countless"
rebukes economic gain and the reductive flattening of the person to
calculated value, to say nothing of the denial of personhood for the
slave. Earlier in the poem he insists: "The love of the body of man
or woman balks account, the body itself balks account." Whitman's
poem poses monetary against poetic accounting. Section 7, in a stun-
ning rhetorical inversion, converts the auction scene of utmost degra-
dation and reduction to the revelation of the incalculable value of the
individual, each one "the makings of heroes."

Slavery imports a feudal order that ruptures and negates the moral,
religious, and political heritage and commitments Whitman sees as
defining America. Whitman, adopting a term with specific political
resonance gathered to it throughout the post-revolutionary period,
and specifically echoing Lincoln, calls America an "experiment" in
government by, for, and of the people (e.g., *DV*, 407). Whitman registers the incredible excitement of the invention of popular sovereignty,
of government in which power is delegated up from below rather than
allocated down from an authoritarian power above.[14] Strengthening
and extending the political structures of popular sovereignty had been
the core trend of the Jacksonian democracy that formed Whitman's
political background—including, for example, term limits and rota-
tion of office to curtail the entrenchment of power and to open it
to a greater number of people. Jackson's own First Annual Message

(Dec. 8, 1829) calls for the direct, popular election of both President and Vice-President in the name of the "experiment" of the American system of government, defining the President as "the direct representative of the American people."[15] He similarly called for direct election of the Senate, election of judgeships, the revocation of property requirements both for holding public office and for voting in a 'universal' (white male) suffrage, and supported instructions from constituents to direct the votes of their representatives.[16] So Whitman describes in the 1855 Preface to Leaves of Grass, "the President's taking off his hat to [the people] not they to him." "We elect Presidents, Congressmen, &c.," he writes in "Notes Left Over," "not so much to have them consider and decide for us, but as surest practical means of expressing the will of majorities on mooted questions, measures, &c" (*CPP* 1067).

T. S. Eliot remarked, "Just as Tennyson liked monarchs, Whitman liked presidents." But Whitman's president is more like a republican delegate than a British monarch. Or rather, a republican president is like Whitman himself: he casts the presidency in the image of the poet. It was the failed presidencies of Fillmore, Pierce, and Buchanan that drove Whitman from politics to poetry. He rails in "The 18th Presidency" against a "deferential" public which allows itself to "be managed in many respects as is only proper under the personnel of a king and hereditary lords" (1308). The presidency itself is corrupt, imposing itself upon the people in the name of ruling interests ("Every trustee of the people is a traitor" [1309].). Against the current and actual case, he goes on to conjure a "redeemer president," who "fullest [sic] realizes the rights of individuals," and who "is not to be exclusive, but inclusive" (*CPP* 1321). This is uncannily proleptic of Lincoln, the president with whom Whitman is most closely associated.[17] These two great writers (Whitman praised Lincoln's literary skill at "indirections," his own fundamental poetic technique, CPP 1072) both opposed abolition but also slavery, both supported the constitution and Union, and both grounded their vision in a republican sense of equal right to individual initiative and participation in government. As Lincoln stated in his final debate with Douglas at Alton:

> No matter in what shape it comes, whether from a king who seeks to bestride the people of his own nation and live by the fruit of their labor, or from one race of men as an apology for enslaving another race, it is the same tyrannical principle.

And yet, in "The 18th Presidency," the president Whitman ultimately nominates is himself. If America is the greatest poem, then the poet is its president. There is a characteristically Whitmanian self-description in his call for

> some heroic, shrewd, fully-informed, healthy-bodied, middle-aged, beard faced American blacksmith or boatman [to] walk into the Presidency, dressed in a clean suit of working attire, and with the tan all over his face, breast, and arms. (1308)[18]

Earlier in his career, Whitman had in fact written editorials such as one where he pictures "a nation of loafers," with himself "getting up a regular ticket for President and Congress and Governor and so on for the loafer community in general" (*UPP* 45). Another article entitled "Hero Presidents" reminds that in times past "the poet, the priest and the warrior exercise[d] more influence over men's minds than the statesman and legislator" (*UPP*, 196–197). These images of poetic office finally burst forth in the Preface to the first edition of *Leaves of Grass*: "Of all nations the United States with veins full of poetical stuff most need poets...their Presidents shall not be their common referee so much as their poets shall" (33).

The liberal-republican structure of political representation penetrates both Whitman's politics and his poetics. These make up two of the multiple dimensions that are the substance and structure of Whitman's figural poetics: the political and poetic are figures for each other. This figural mirroring constitutes "Myself" as the presiding structure of "Song of Myself," as announced in its opening lines:

> I celebrate myself, and sing myself,
> And what I assume you shall assume,
> For every atom belonging to me as good belongs to you.

To "celebrate" suggests a holiday, especially a public one, and, if personal, shares a private occasion with others in a common life.[19] Similarly, when Whitman writes, "What I assume you shall assume," he does not intend "assume" to mean "impose," but rather in a sense of taking on, as in assuming office. The "I" here invites each "you" to celebrate each self and each other. This becomes a radically egalitarian declaration. Every "atom" is recognized, where "belonging" does not mean ownership but taking part with "me" and "you" as equally "good."

As with "celebrate" and "assume," Whitman's poetic vocabulary often takes up and reworks terms drawn from political usages. The most obvious example of this is liberty, central first to the discourse of republican ideology and then of sectional conflict. Whitman's

American Primer calls on American writers to "show far more freedom in the use of words" (35). The 1855 Preface names the poet "the voice and exposition of liberty. They out of ages are worthy the grand idea...the attitude of great poets is to cheer up slaves and horrify despots" (44). Whitman in "Song of Myself" calls himself "turbulent, fleshy, sensual...whoever degrades another degrades me" (Song 24), where turbulence was a catchword for revolutionary and republican agitation.[20] In the "18th Presidency," Whitman opposes the "owners of slaves" against the "fierce and turbulent races" of America's working people, whom "Liberty has nursed in these States," and who slavery betrays (*CPP* 1322). As to poets, in his "Letter to Emerson" (1856), Whitman calls on them to walk "freely out from the old traditions, as our poetics has walked out" into an America "agitated and turbulent" (*CPP* 1335–1336).[21]

Poet and people together enact liberty. Yet the first has a special role of leadership, not as imposition on liberty, but as opening paths towards it. Leadership means to Whitman acting among the common people, not apart from them—or rather, of acting both among and apart. He represents people as their deputy, one of them in ways that clarify and pursue their common lives. This is the strong image that concludes the "Song of Myself" in its final, 52nd (like the weeks of the year) section: leadership at once before and among the people he addresses:

> I bequeath myself to the dirt to grow from the grass I love,
> If you want me again look for me under your boot-soles.
>
> You will hardly know who I am or what I mean,
> But I shall be good health to you nevertheless,
> And filter and fibre your blood.
> Failing to fetch me at first keep encouraged,
>
> Missing me in one place search another,
> I stop somewhere waiting for you.

"Song of Myself" opens with any and every "I." It closes with each and every "you." The poem itself traces a trajectory from the one to the other. "You" is addressed by a poet as common as dirt and grass. Yet he is also before and ahead, "somewhere waiting for you."

This leadership is conducted through hints: "You will hardly know who I am or what I mean." Both identity and meaning are events, never final, toward which the poet summons us. In "Slang in America," Whitman had denounced "bald literalism." Against such literalism, Whitman opposes "indirection" as the power to "express itself illimitably, which in highest walks produces poets and poems." No single level or final meaning will suffice. "Song of Myself" is itself a kind of primer in educating readers to such creative imagination. It involves both multiple dimensions and ongoing extension of meanings. "What is the Grass" in Section 6 offers a demonstration and induction. It is a series of displacing images of the grass: as flag of disposition, as romance handkerchief in divine sign, as hieroglyph of democratic equality. No one of these is final or definitive. Each points to each, invoking and aligning different levels of experience. Not least is the grass as sign of death, of physical bodies in graves. But death here is not end erasure. Whitman offers it rather as ultimate and radical transformation.

Section 6 enacts sequences of displacing, generating figures. Section 5 offers figures not in processional transformations but rather as dream vision, in which different images overlay each other in a dense interweaving. Invoking long traditions of mystical visionary experience, Whitman invokes spiritual and physical love, but exactly against dualisms that would pose them against each other, where one dimension excludes and denies the other:

> I believe in you my soul, the other I am must not abase itself
> to you,
> And you must not be abased to the other

Self and other are themselves open figures: body and soul, person and person, self, neighbor, stranger. "A kelson of creation is love" is this section's declaration of interdependence.

"Crossing Brooklyn Ferry," written in 1856, is perhaps boldest and most energetic in its visionary binding together of diverse elements while yet respecting the integrity of each. The poem opens with a dazzling multidimensional figure at once religious, commercial, poetic, and natural. The ferry links Brooklyn to Manhattan as a place of work, surrounded by the industry and commerce of the East River. "On the river the shadowy group, the big steam-tug closely flank'd on each side by the barges...On the neighboring shore the fires from the foundry chimneys burning high and glaringly into the night" (Section 3). But this is a scene of visionary transformations, refracted through the opening Self seeing its own reflection in the water, which is to say, seeing itself and its own seeing:

> Flood-tide below me! I see you face to face!
> Clouds of the west—sun there half an hour high—
> I see you also face to face.   (section 1)

> The impalpable sustenance of me from all things at all
>   hours of the day,
> The simple, compact, well-join'd scheme, myself
>   disintegrated, every one disintegrated yet part of the
>   scheme,
> The similitudes of the past and those of the future,
> The glories strung like beads on my smallest sights and
>   hearings, on the walk in the street and the passage over
>   the river,..
> The others that are to follow me, the ties between me and
>   them,
> The certainty of others, the life, love, sight, hearing of others.   (section 2)

The image in the water is of radiant individual selfhood. In one dimension, it focuses the poetic act, as the surrounding sea and city
comes into configuration through his vision ("The glories strung like
beads on my smallest sights and hearings."). But there is also a religious figure here, implicit in the "face to face," and further clarified
in the next section when the reflection takes form as "fine centrifugal
spokes of light round the shape of my head in the sunlit water" like
a halo. Whitman in fact had, in a June 1857 notebook entry, named
his project in *Leaves* as "The construction of a New Bible" "Song
of Myself" Section 3 seems a specific rewriting of passages from
Romans. But the halo-like "spokes of light" in "Crossing Brooklyn
Ferry" do not signal a religion divorced from the senses and the body,
which Whitman always insists on as yet another dimension his poetry
addresses and another level of its meanings: "The life, love, sight,
hearing of others." Yet all these levels are never simply integrated. If
there is "a simple, compact, well-join'd scheme," then there is also
"myself disintegrated." There is the paradox yet promise—social, political, religious, poetic, of "every one disintegrated yet part of the
scheme."

This vision of the commercial ("Thrive, cities...Expand") with
the spiritual ("Being than which none else is perhaps more spiritual")
of the sensual and the poetic, the self and the "others" is not a present one, but rather projects into a future that the ferry crossing, as a
figure for Whitman's own poetic voice, itself enacts: "The others that
are to follow me, the ties between me and / them." Just how fragile
this vision remains emerges in Section 6:

> The dark threw its patches down upon me also,
> The best I had done seem'd to me blank and suspicious,
> My great thoughts as I supposed them, were they not in
>   reality meagre?

> Nor is it you alone who know what it is to be evil,
> I am he who knew what it was to be evil,
> I too knitted the old knot of contrariety,
> Blabb'd, blush'd, resented, lied, stole, grudg'd,
> Had guile, anger, lust, hot wishes I dared not speak.

In this confession, personal and sexual sins threaten social-poetic integration. The "knot of contrariety" blocks the figural "ties" of the earlier section. Transformative vision is reduced to a "blank" that ruptures, interrupts, reduces, and negates.

But despite this interruption, what emerges with overriding force in "Crossing Brooklyn Ferry" is Whitman's double commitment both to divinized individual selfhood and to a community of love. Making good the poem's earlier promise of "similitudes of the past and those of the future" (2), Whitman enfolds time into the structure of simile, crossing in the ferry "just as" others will cross, endlessly, into an open-ended future. He carefully constructs a figure of "you" to match that of self, in a rhetoric of address that enacts the crossing from self to other, from present to future.[22] Is Whitman's a rhetoric of imposition, forcing his selfhood upon the other, with simile and analogy acting here as coercive uniformity? In "Crossing Brooklyn Ferry," his fantasy is for the democratic crowd to come into free and personal relationship with each other, each on every level and dimension, each an image and extension of each:

> Consider, you who peruse me, whether I may not in unknown
>   ways be looking upon you,...
> Fly on, sea-birds! fly sideways or wheel in large circles
>   high in the air;...
> Diverge, fine spokes of light, from the shape of my head, or
>   any one's head, in the sunlit water!...
> Flaunt away, flags of all nations! be duly lower'd at sunset
> Burn high your fires, foundry chimneys! cast black shadows
>   at nightfall!...
> You necessary film, continue to envelop the soul,
> About my body for me, and your body for you, be hung out
>   divinest aromas,

Political flags and foundry chimneys conjoin with the transfigured individual whose "fine spokes of light" form a halo around "any one's head." Emersonian "circles" of the seabird trace energies that expand in body and soul, in sexuality and materialism. "Black shadows" and "film" take part in rather than erase this scene, which is also a scene of poetry as "you peruse me" in some future time linked to this moment by this very text.

"Crossing Brooklyn Ferry," as its very title doubly announces, marks a moment of intense intersection and intercrossing. Yet Whitman's integrative vision—between self and community, leader and people, different American sections and identities, commerce and creativity—is daring, radical, and also deeply fragile. There is a darker side. Whitman's poetic does not attempt to deny rupture and dislocation. Nor does he attempt to resume diversity into unitary totality. As with poet and president, he attempts to match figures from different spheres of experience. Yet he also senses their mismatch, which threatens to explode his entire poetic vision. There is a haunting sense that the different levels of experience, instead of echoing, may subvert each other; that individuals may remain in their separate spheres, failing to join together in a multiple venture:

> The past and present wilt—I have fill'd them, emptied them.
> And proceed to fill my next fold of the future...
>
> Do I contradict myself?
> Very well then, I contradict myself,
> (I am large, I contain multitudes.) (Song 51)

Whitman's figural poetics fill and are filled with past and present, but also empty them. This may be necessary to make place for the next "fold"—in paper as well as in time, each an image of the other. But Whitman is also worried as to whether the "contradictions" he so ecstatically yawps can indeed reside together in productive and creative energy; whether the poem of America can "contain" its contradictions, its plural interests and individuals, or will be rent apart by them.

This in fact is what Whitman's 1850s poems were facing, and what indeed occurred. The celebration of the ferry neither finally nor fully reconciles the divisions so masterfully negotiated through its rhetoric. 1856 is not a happy American year. Whitman writes in the face of ruptured Union, which he, far from ignoring, is attempting to offer a way of negotiating. Slavery explodes claims to republican selfhood and community. Whitman further casts their contradiction as emblematic of a general counter-pull between private interest and public, materialism and creative selfhood. Such tensions are clearly present in Whitman's early poem "Pictures." A catalogue of his mind, it ranges from personal family history to what Whitman announces as "a historic piece," in which "Thomas Jefferson of Virginia sits reading Rousseau, the Swiss, and compiling the Declaration of Independence, the American compact," then moving to "Emerson," and to the "Congress in session in the Capitol" (lines 104–106). The poem composes this history as a continuous and evolving American political tradition of social contract among equals. But the lines before and after this passage are disruptive:

> And there, in the midst of a group, a quell'd revolted
>   slave, cowering,
> See you, the hand-cuffs, the hopple, and the blood-stain'd
>   hopple… (lines 99–100)

Just how a Rousseaun-Jeffersonian tradition of social compact, equality, and self-government is to be squared with "the hopple and blood-stain'd cow-hide" of the captured slave, or with the following picture of "mansions of the planters" behind an old black man who "sits low at the corner of a street, begging, / humming hymn-tunes" (lines 107–109) is, to say the least, unclear. For all its rhythmic chant, the verse rhythms cannot hold these pieces together.

"Pictures" also proleptically includes a self-portrait that is strongly homoerotic:

> And again the young man of Mannahatta, the celebrated rough,
> (The one I love well—let others sing whom they may—him
> I sing for a thousand years!). (lines 102–103)

The "celebrated rough" of "Mannahatta" inevitably evokes Whitman himself, even as the lines also suggest a homoerotic confession. "Love" here, as generally in Whitman, asserts a social-eroticism no less than any individual one. And yet, can love be "adhesive" in the way Whitman envisions?[23] Can it indeed bind wounds and divisions? The question comes back disturbingly at the conclusion of "Pictures:"

> But here, (look you well,) see here the phallic choice of
>   America, a full-sized man or woman—a natural, well-
>   trained man or woman
> (The phallic choice of America leaves the finesse of cities,
>   and all the returns of commerce or agriculture, and the
>   magnitude of geography, and achievements of literature and art)

Do these figures, strung together, correlate? Does the "magnitude of geography" (and Whitman supported Manifest Destiny) confirm the "finesse of cities"? Does Whitman's homoerotic confession have place in a society that rejects it? Does the erotic vision, for which he bids to leave all else, truly encompass these variances? Can the figure of the man stand for, represent, and convert into the figure of the woman, especially when the "choice" and song of America are seen to be so emphatically "phallic?"[24] Not least, do the "returns of commerce" indeed accord with the "achievements of literature and art"? And does the status of Whitman's vision as "pictures" in the house of his mind compose them in any way beyond his own subjectivity?

These tensions erupt. Whitman's 1860 "Sea Drift" poems stare into historical chasm. "Out of the Cradle" stunningly opens with a single long sentence in which sea, bird, child, and then poet each figure the other as together "fitful risings and fallings," weaving a "musical shuttle" of past memories and present song. But the music has arisen out of rupture: the death of a bird, significantly set in winds that blow "South and North, white and black," is what gives birth to the poet. The poem was originally named "the Word out of the Sea," and that word is revealed at the end to be death.

"As I Ebb'd with the Ocean of Life" returns to the seashore, not as in "Crossing Brooklyn Ferry," as a place of revelation, but rather as the scene of its eclipse:

> I musing late in the autumn day, gazing off southward,
> Held by this electric self out of the pride of which I utter poems,
> Was seiz'd by the spirit that trails in the lines
>   underfoot,...
>
> Fascinated, my eyes reverting from the south, dropt, to follow those
>   slender windrows
> Chaff, straw, splinters of wood, weeds, and the sea-gluten,
> ...there and then as I thought the old thought of likenesses
> These you presented to me you fish-shaped island,
> As I walk'd with that electric self, seeking types.

The poem reworks many key Whitman terms for visionary transformation, exposing their fragile foundation. Is his vision all subjective projection? As he walks poetically "musing," the "old thought of likenesses" loses its hold, the "electric self seeking types" finds not intelligible "types" of the world—with resonance in terms of both religious meanings and poetry itself. The intense intersections of the "electric self" at once physical, poetic, and spiritual, may be only a delusory desire for them. The seashore is strewn with debris. All these become "trails in the lines underfoot," undoing his poetic journey, dissolving into the sea's "hoarse" and "sibilant" cries.

The poem openly acknowledges itself as a reflection not of correspondence, but negativity. These are shores "I know not," haunted by "wreck'd" voices of men and women. Neither self nor world stands coherent, or even accessible. The "echoes" that elsewhere signify figural relationships (the "loud echoes" and "hints" of "my songs" [Song 18]) here are no more than the tautological "recoil" of a voice that expresses no world, only itself. Yet without the world, even that self dissolves, "untouch'd," in a defeat of Whitmanian sexuality elsewhere evoked by the sea. Here it can only "sting" rather "dash with amorous wet" (Song 22) or, in the erotic vision of the "Song's" twenty-eight bathers, "souse with spray" (Song 11). The "real Me . . . untouch'd, untold" is less a metaphysical figure of final Being than the lost possibility of personal and poetic coherence (with "untold" an undoing of tally, in the sense of to tell, to take or give account). The self as a figure for poetic, or any other coherence, is now "withdrawn far, mocking me with mock-congratulatory signs and bows."

The skepticism of "As I Ebb'd" is aesthetic and epistemological, but also immediately historical, as the poem's 1860 composition and reference to "gazing off southward" reminds. The skeptical gap between self and world, self and self, self and others; the tensions between self-referring subjectivities; the problem of building a community out of diversity and the forces of disintegration opposed to it, found their most specific political corollary in Civil War. The secession crisis obviously took America's centrifugal forces to the furthest extent of nightmare. Whitman's own Unionism has been seen as mirrored in his poem's absorbing powers.[25] But when, in "As I Ebb'd," Whitman writes, "I too but signify at the utmost a little wash'd up drift/a few sands and dead leaves to gather/gather, and merge myself as part of the sands and drift,"the "merge," far from denoting the ingesting of the world into the imperial poet, here dissolves the self into the "sands and drift"

The Civil War's schisms marked a failure of America's liberal vision, reaffirmed however by Lincoln's reconciliatory vision. But post-war, Whitman increasingly sees schismatic forces within that very liberalism. The economic individualism present in America from the Puritan beginnings gained increasing ascendancy through the nineteenth century. The Jeffersonian tradition of limited government (what Isaiah Berlin has called "negative liberty") meant to ensure space for individual freedom. This Whitman strongly upholds. The "sum and substance of the prerogatives of government" are, in Whitman's newspaper formulation of negative liberty, that

no one's rights [be] infringed upon. . . .All that is necessary in government; [is] to make no more laws than those useful for preventing

a man or body of men from infringing on the rights of other men.
(July 26, 1847)

Whitman's *Brooklyn Eagle* editorials sum up this vision of individual
rights as freedom from others in the popular Jeffersonian formula
that "the best government indeed is 'that which governs least.'"
    It is telling that Whitman opens the *Democratic Vistas* (1871)
with reference to John Stuart Mill's Essay, "On Liberty." Mill's
notion of a "truly grand nationality" requires, Whitman writes,
"1st, a large variety of character—and 2nd, full play for human
nature to expand itself in numberless and even conflicting directions" (*DV*, 389). But Whitman also worried as to just how these
principles of "variety and freedom," as expressed in discreet individuals protected from each other, are to build a common good.
Democratic Vistas, written after the Civil War, turns its attention
towards the increasing power of economic materialism in American
society as a disruptive force. On the one hand, Whitman is committed to American prosperity as an emblem of creativity and individual realization. "Not the least doubtful am I on any prospects
of [American] material success," he insists, which will "outstrip all
examples hitherto afforded, and dominate the world" (*DV*, 391).
Yet the promise of America must be realized beyond material development and acquisition, and even liberal rights, as these frame
and support economic possession and initiative. *Democratic Vistas*
is essentially launched from this motive:

> to alarm and caution even the political and business reader...against
> the prevailing delusion that the establishment of free political institu-
> tions...do, of themselves, determine and yield to our experiment of
> democracy the fruitage of success. (*DV*, 398–399)

Whitman embraces the heady liberal promise of personal independence and endless opportunity, of government's role as "not merely
to rule, to repress disorder, etc., but to develop, to open up to cultivation, to encourage the...aspiration for independence, and the pride
and self-respect latent in all characters" (*DV*, 411). But he sees this
expression of independence not in narrow self-interest but in "really
grand religious, moral, literary and aesthetic results" (400). All the
"objective grandeurs of the world" must be transfigured through
"the mind, which alone builds the permanent edifice." Only then
"are conveyed to mortal sense the culminations of the materialistic,
the known, and prophecy of the unknown" (440).

But distressingly, the vista opening before Whitman from the 1870s onward is the "hollowness" (*DV*, 399) of American life, overwhelmed by the "depravity" of business, which in its "hectic glow" is "all-devouring" (399–400). The "unprecedented materialistic advancement, society, in these States, is cankered, crude, superstitious, and rotten," (399) endowing America with a "vast and more and more thoroughly appointed body" that has left it "with little or no soul" (400). Instead of redemptive conversion, America is threatened with demonic inversion: "Our modern civilization, with all its improvements, is in vain, and we are on the road to a destiny, a status, equivalent, in its real world, to that of the fabled damned" (467). Division, isolation, and even mutual destruction are potential forces within liberalism itself. Within the "independence" Whitman defines as "freedom from all laws or bonds except those of one's own being" (*DV* 450), there is a latent "pride, competition, segregation, willfulness, and license beyond example" (*DV* 464). The enterprise, not least of all Whitman's poetic one, in which material and individually creative engagements would extend each other in a society of mutually confirming selves—a nation of poets—also contains the danger of solipsistic self-enclosure and competitive disintegration. If each individual pursues his and her own interpretation in a negative liberty of imagination, as individual business entrepreneurs do theirs, what guarantees mutual participation and community? But Whitman violently rejects the alternative of hierarchical, imposed order, "authority and . . . . cohesion at all cost," as these have through "political history" been based on "order, safety, [and] caste" (*DV* 404). They would defeat the very goals of community they are supposed to be upholding.

Whitman's dissent and critique of America very much remains within the compass of its own ideological commitments. As is common to American dissent, Whitman's is a call to America to return to and realize its best energies, not a rejection of American ideals.[26] For Whitman, the individual neither simply opposes social institutions, nor is he/she engulfed by them.[27] Enterprise, even as business, is not something Whitman wishes to repudiate, but rather to ensure as the effort of unique individuals, with the polity precisely being their joint diverse efforts. The effort to project relationships that both respect and join together diverse constituents remains the central hope, and also the central anxiety, for Whitman's poetic creation and for the world of America it variously represents.

Whitman repeatedly claims America to be a poem: "These States are the amplest poem,"("By Blue Ontario's Shore"). The "United States today," he writes, have become a "poetry with cosmic and dynamic features of magnitude and limitlessness suitable to the human soul...never possible before" (*BG* 371). But in the course of his exuberant "tallying"—one of Whitman's core words for figural creativity—Whitman is aware that even while "politics.... religious forms, sociology, literature, teachers, schools, costumes, etc., are of course to make a compact whole, uniform, on tallying principles," he must still ask: "For how can we remain, divided, contradicting ourselves, this way?" (*DVC*, 448).

At issue in some sense is the status of poetic vision altogether. As with other nineteenth-century American poets, Whitman's task included not only finding a poetic language and mode to match the emerging national identity, but also finding a place for poetry in America's developing culture. This had made Longfellow anxious, and also timorous compared to Whitman, who dares more. He responds to poetry's threatened displacement by claiming for it an integral part in the American venture—indeed, claiming it to be that venture's ultimate expression and result. Whitman offers a poetic interpretation of America and also a poetic preeminence within it. For him, poetry and poetic language has a civic role to play. In unpublished notes called *Rambles with Words*, through his *American Primer* and the essay "Slang in America," Whitman endorses "popular speeches and writings, [as] for unhemmed latitude, coarseness, directness, live epithets, expletives." His own poetry contains an unusual range of dictions, etymologies, regional words, and slang. Whitman as poet launches such living, expanding, democratic language, engages to construct it, and addresses the people through it. But this also means negotiating the division and even violence potential in a liberty that may free individuals from each other to release a competitive battle against one another.

The community of poetic language Whitman hopes to construct must acknowledge the conflict and division within the liberal-individualism of America to which he, however, remains committed. Perhaps the most poignant and difficult of these efforts is his elegy to Lincoln. "My Captain, My Captain" is an anomaly in its conventional construction. "When Lilacs Last in the Dooryard Bloom'd" offers an elegy more intrinsic to Whitman's poetic methods and purposes. Lincoln stands as emblem, and not only for Whitman, of how America's pluralistic strands may be woven together in political union: individual rights, opportunity, and self-advancement with commitment to a joint civic life. Lincoln's death conversely registered the forces opposing a community of differences. But it also became a scene for gathering together and overcoming division in mutual loss.

It is in a way absence, not fullness, that emerges as a common ground; retraction of self making space for others rather than self-assertion. Seen as fully Christic by many (he was shot on Good Friday), Lincoln's death is treated by Whitman not as suffering that is justified or redemptive, but as a confrontation with rupture and loss that creates a common mourning.

"Lilacs" conducts one of Whitman's most intense interplays among mutually invoking multiple figures: Lincoln as "O powerful western fallen star," the bird as poet-figure, the sprig of lilac as the poem itself, the poem as the public sphere in which many different voices are woven. Whitman had written throughout the Civil War poems both militant in the Union cause and also bereaved at the incredible losses, which Whitman (of all the Northern writers) had personally witnessed and tried to ameliorate in his role as wound dresser. In "Lilacs," he emerges as the solitary singer who is often seen in opposition against his public self, yet here it is exactly as a solitary mourner that Whitman is driven to public song. As in the "Sea Drift" poems, it is death, negation, and rupture that impel bonds to others:

> Song of the bleeding throat,
> Death's outlet song of life, (for well dear brother I know
> If thou wast not granted to sing thou would'st surely
> die).   (Section 4)

In "Out of the Cradle," the death of the bird, the rending of the nest, is what marks the birth of the poet. So here, out of the hole torn in the fabric of the republic, the poet is driven to sing. But the song is not a private one. As the poem proceeds, the poet passes before and among surrounding mourners, representing them, transforming their voices through his "tallying." The thrush may sing solitary, but elegy is a public ritual—here quite factually in the cortege whose course the poem follows, which carried Lincoln's coffin across the states to its burial place in Springfield.[28] As the poet moves, "passing" among scenes of battle and mourning, the song becomes the community's while the community itself comes into being through the song:

> Passing the visions, passing the night,
> Passing, unloosing the hold of my comrades' hands,
> Passing the song of the hermit bird and the tallying song of
>   my soul,
> Victorious song, death's outlet song, yet varying ever-
>   altering song, . .

"Lilacs" is almost a poetic version or response to Lincoln at Gettysburg. Loss creates a bond of dedication, a community of commitment: "It is rather for us to be here dedicated to the great task remaining before us—that from these honored dead we take increased devotion to that cause for which they gave the last full measure of devotion." The poet's "tallying song of my soul" tallies his soul with those of other citizens. The procession itself becomes a figure for the song and vice versa, as the poet's voice, like and with the coffin "passes through lanes and streets" of America, interweaving as it gives form "with dirges through the night, with the thousand voices / rising strong and solemn." The core figures exfoliate into and through each other: president and poet, hermit bird and people, sprig and song. Yet its song remains a song of "night." "Lilacs" does not deny rupture. Indeed, the poem's strange appeal to "sane and sacred death" gives place to what can never be integrated, what therefore safeguards difference and the disjunctions that inevitably remain within a community of discourse. Nor does it deny wounds. Rather it sets out, as Lincoln said in his Second Inaugural, to bind them up. No full conversion of loss into gain is declared, nor isolation into comradeship, or difference into unity. Whitman is committed to time's motion, the "varying ever-altering song" that necessarily entails change, and hence loss, negation, and death. Whitman's response, but not solution, to this is love. The last section of "Lilacs" calls to "comrades mine, and I in the midst, and their memory ever I keep—for the dead I loved so well; / for the sweetest, wisest soul of all my days and lands ... and this for his dear sake" (20). The death of the loved figure becomes a shared experience across, although not erasing differences.

"Lilacs" figurations and their relationships is strangely mirrored and yet reversed in Whitman's *Calamus* poems of 1860. These poems are intensely private. Taking up his position in the solitude into which the thrush of "When Lilacs" withdraws itself, in *Calamus* Whitman is "away from the clank of the world," off at a margin ("In the growth by margins of pond-waters") socially and, as he implies ("Resolv'd to sing no songs to-day but those of manly attachment"), sexually. Sexuality had been throughout *Leaves of Grass* a multi-dimensional figure: autobiographic, poetic, social, and if a central drive to love, also registering divisions that both threaten and constitute it. In the *Calamus* poems,

> the soul of the man I speak for rejoices in comrades,
> Here by myself away from the clank of the world,

> Tallying and talk'd to here by tongues aromatic.
> ("In Paths Untrodden")

The "tallying" and talking is vividly sensual, the "tongues" bodily as well as poetic.

This homoerotic rejoicing "in comrades" may stand in tension not only against conformity (as if to "tell the secret of my nights and days" is to tell something guilty), but also as dividing male from female. Whitman's sexual figures, and also his poetic ones, are highly phallic. In the 1855 Preface, Whitman urges "the perfect equality of the female with the male." But his poetry tends to envision women as mothers, or, in the somewhat astonishing poem "A Woman Waits for Me," as the site where he may "pour the stuff to start sons and daughters fit for these states ... I dare not withdraw till I deposit what has so long accumulated within me."[29] This male sexual paradigm serves as figure for Whitmanian creativity: as explosive outburst of "pent-up rivers of myself." At issue is not so much Whitman's personal homoeroticism as his use of it to represent experiences beyond his own, to represent others even while respecting the negative space of difference from them.

The *Calamus* poems in this and other ways appear almost to retreat from, or fracture, Whitman's larger figural project. They often seem situated in a psychical interiority, a personal space remote from Whitman's public concerns and especially vulnerable to solipsistic threat and subjective self-enclosure. "Of the Terrible Doubt of Appearances" makes such solipsism and skeptical challenge its explicit topic. In it, "reliance and hope," as well as "identity beyond the grave" and even "the things I perceive," emerge as uncertain. They may be "only apparitions." They may be merely subjective, one's own limited and distorted viewpoint:

> May-be seeming to me what they are (as doubtless they indeed but seem) as from my present point of view, and might prove (as of course they would) nought of what they appear, or nought anyhow, from entirely changed points of view....

This poem is almost technical in its presentation of epistemological doubt. All that we see dissolves into "colors, densities, forms," mere "appearances" and "apparitions." The very world seems to fall apart, "the sense that words and reason hold not, surround us and pervade us," while what is truly "real" and beyond mere "appearances" remains unknown. All reduces to a Romantic subjectivity. "My present point of view" need not correlate with "changed points of view."

The "identity beyond the grave" is just as uncertain as everyday perception, as though both were equally a matter of faith.

Yet the poem does not attempt to settle or dispel its terrible doubt of appearances in philosophical terms—terms that, once set up a certain way, almost exclude settling the doubts raised by them. Whitman concedes: "I cannot answer the question of appearances or that of identity beyond the grave." What he does instead is to turn to "lovers" and "dear friends." In them his skeptical doubts are "curiously answer'd":

> To me these and the like of these are curiously answer'd by
>   my lovers, my dear friends,
> When he whom I love travels with me or sits a long while
>   holding me by the hand,
> When the subtle air, the impalpable, the sense that words
>   and reason hold not, surround us and pervade us,
> Then I am charged with untold and untellable wisdom, I am
>   silent, I require nothing further,
> I cannot answer the question of appearances or that of
>   identity beyond the grave,
> But I walk or sit indifferent, I am satisfied,
> He ahold of my hand has completely satisfied me.

Whitman, in his skepticism, finally appeals not to abstract epistemology, but social community. At the end of "Lilacs," the poet turns. "with the holders holding my hand," to "comrades mine and I in the midst." So here the poet turns to "he whom I love . . . while holding me by the hand." Hand, often a trope for the poet writing, is offered here as social, sexual, and also political. Homoeroticism itself enacts issues of conformity and its resistance, through which Whitman addresses the social world and presses it towards transfiguration. "Not that half only, individualism, which isolates," Whitman writes in *Democratic Vistas*, but "another half, which is adhesiveness of love, that fuses, ties, and aggregates" (*DV*, 414). Ties open among individuals, who press, each in his and her own manner, to define and redefine the aggregate.

Whitmanian poetics brings into relation many different dimensions: sexuality, politics, and poetics itself as the enactment in language of these and yet further dimensions. For language has been, since ancient Greek democracy, itself the agora, the public sphere, in which participation takes place.[30] Poetry emerges as both image and enactment of participation in the space of language. The poet stands as representative self, before and ahead of others, but he does so in order to invite them into the discourse that founds and provides the arena for a community of unique individuals. This project points not beyond the world or time toward eternity or unity, but within the generations and displacements of time and of language. Whitman thus confirms the common and historical world "under your boot-soles," and in discourse, where the representative "I" of "Song of Myself" stops always "waiting for you."

POSTSCRIPT

CHARTING AMERICAN TRENDS: STEPHEN CRANE

In nineteenth-century America, poetry both takes part in and charts unfolding cultural developments. The nineteenth century is a time of radical transformation. Industrialization, urbanization, and immigration; revolutions in communication, transportation, and distribution make the America of the century's beginning almost unrecognizable by its end. The effects of the Revolution penetrated and reshaped American religion, politics, and social, territorial, and cultural definitions. These changes mark the poetry that variously reflects and directly participates in urgent questions regarding the directions and significance of an extremely volatile nineteenth-century America.

American culture can be seen as a particular configuration and contention between core religious, civic, and economic trends. All share historical and ideological backgrounds but pursue distinct courses of development—and often compete and conflict. In the nineteenth century, economic interests begin increasingly to press to the side earlier forms of religious and civic society. Economic interests had, of course, been present in America from the outset. The first settlements were launched as joint stock companies representing investors' hopes for profitable returns. But in the course of the nineteenth century, economic interests begin to dominate, overwhelming religious and civic trends that had been equally foundational to American society and which the American Revolution had brought to new political formation. Self-government was an Enlightenment project and republican experiment. But its sources went back to Puritan theology, especially Puritan church polity, in which members "covenanted"

202 Poetry and Public Discourse in America

with each other in a church at once voluntary and called, with a leadership of ministers elected by the members and ultimately accountable not only to God but to them. These intercrossing traditions of civic and religious participation strongly defined American community. The nineteenth century witnesses an increasing hegemony of economic culture as against both civic and religious traditions. Senses of the self steadily break away from earlier constraints. Purpose and achievement come to be defined more and more in terms of economy and self-interest.

This ascent of economy is acutely felt in American poetry through its voices of protest against the encroachment and displacement of other values by economic ones. Such protest is especially prominent in the writing of women. To the extent that women's verses focus on domesticity, they often do so in opposition against the increasing definition of American life as acquisition and material possession. Domesticity has long been treated as a mode of female confinement, with its central topics seen to be frustration and conflict over its own limitations. While recent discussion has broadened to consider "sentimental" literature as political appeal, this continues to frame female writing within the private sphere. But a considerable range of verse by women directly addresses public issues, and is particularly concerned with defending resources for community beyond individual self-interest. This poetry—including Emily Dickinson's reclusive and cryptic work—holds up a counter-mirror against the elimination of values other than material ones from American public life. Women's verse in this way consistently opposes the restriction of American promise to economic pursuits in the name of broader commitments promised by earlier visions of America, both civic and religious, and particularly within the possibilities opened by the American Revolution.

Resistance to the reduction of what Jefferson had imagined as a "pursuit of happiness" to economic interests is also a strong force in much writing by men. Even Longfellow's polished verses are shot through with anxiety about the displacement of art and culture by economic drives. Where in American life would there be space for poetry and culture? Longfellow thus did not simply incarnate the split in the American mind, as Santayana claimed, but was engaged by it—that is, by the reduction of poetry to a leisured hiatus, estranged from the world of venture and economic desire.

Santayana's reaction to this shrinking cultural space was to launch in the 1890s a new aesthetic that harbingered twentieth-century formalism: the cult of the art object as turned in on itself, an art about art's own structures in endless self-reflection. Poe, early in the nineteenth century, had already outlined such an enclosed, self-reflecting aesthetic. Both his and the later formalism was, despite a resistance to history, very much engaged in a critique of social culture increasingly shadowed by the glare of money. In Poe's case, this was situated through his own severe displacement within both Southern and Northern societies. By the century's end, poetry found itself in a profoundly defensive posture, taking shape in an aesthetic self-consciousness where cultural engagement, although by no means eliminated, became subsumed into formal experiment and rigor.

As against such formalist investment, nineteenth-century poets were generally direct in their address to the counter-posing and competing claims of their society. Revolutionary visions of a new political order challenged poets to create both a language and an art in which it could be realized. But this proved a fraught enterprise. The post-revolutionary generation found themselves facing civil and cultural division. The revolutionary heritage, splintered between North and South, was deflected through different usages and meanings granted to the central words of America's foundations—a divergence of language expressed in poetry in the different regions, among different groups, and along different cultural trajectories. In these usages, the various American trends coincide and collide in words such as "liberty," which conjures civic self-determination, but also the right to "property," which was interpreted in the South as slaveholding but everywhere else as economic pursuits against constraints, and finally religious traditions of conscience but also of authority.

Indeed, religious discourses loom as large in American poetry as in the American public life of the nineteenth century, and are integrally involved in attempts to define American directions. By the nineteenth century, religious energies defied central authority as well as state interference, with denominations and sects wildly multiplying through every region—a situation that both intensified regional/cultural differences and yet pointed toward peculiarly American modes for ultimately negotiating them. The Second Great Awakening confirmed earlier forms of American religion as intensely activist. Highly provisional and decentralized religious movements weakened and challenged hierarchies, with preachers moved by personal call addressing large informal groups, and an emphasis on religious experience and conversion that granted authority even to women and African-Americans. Such religious call often formed the basis of poetic vocation as well, perhaps especially, but not only among, women. This is the case strikingly for Frances Harper. An African-American woman abolitionist, Harper pioneered dialect and ethnic voice in

African-American poetry. In her work, the civic and religious together direct poetic vision in protest against the gravest economic reduction of all: humankind to slavery.

Religion, especially the Bible, while a shared cultural inheritance, contributed to America's severe divisions as well. Cited by abolitionists and women, but also by Southern slaveholders, the Bible was an authority that all were eager to claim. Liberal egalitarian readings of equality before God and individual conscience contrasted with subordinationist ones teaching obedience and submission to an institutional hierarchy structured with superiorities at once racial, gendered, and economic. Yet within Protestant commitments to personal call and individual access to the Bible, interpretive discipline proved impossible to enforce. Even conservative interpretations enacted liberal interpretive rights to the text, which came to include women, African-Americans, and varieties of immigrants from whatever backgrounds.

Thus the Bible and religious discourses joined civic traditions of rights and participation in an increasingly differentiated American communal and political life. After the Civil War, poetry particularly resonates with such intensified pluralist American identity. Sectional division gave way to regional setting in a newly centralized federalism. Influxes from abroad and into cities, steady if grudging movement toward women's rights, and of course emancipation and the freeman's contested entry into private rights and public roles shifted earlier balances in the polity and the poetry. Minority voices, such as Emma Lazarus and Paul Laurence Dunbar, begin to claim and also reshape American idioms. But this is not just to bring diverse identities to expression. American pluralism pledges to negotiate new conceptions of identity itself, involving freedom of movement between groups and multiple senses of the self within individuals.

The three trends of economic, religious, and civic society and the selfhood they construct come into stark relief—and contradiction—in the work of Stephen Crane. Far better known as a writer of prose than of poetry, Crane's verses are radically experimental in ways that seem expressly formalist, but which remain deeply and intimately tied to immediate cultural context and cultural critique. The poems are usually interpreted, following modes of understanding Crane's fiction, as existential and heroic cameos of stoic man, alone and isolated, confronting an indifferent and alien universe.[1] In practice, they offer a radical representation of American trends of individualism in their increasing conflict. This is accomplished through a number of foci. Individualist claims are exposed as self-constricting, religious contexts as drained of meaning. Perhaps above all, Crane represents an economy that is consuming the very individuals who pursue it, in notable imagery of money and prostitution.

Crane's poems are often situated as if in emptied landscapes–wilderness, high place, highway, sea. In this apparently stripped scene, the texts are structured as confrontations between self-enclosed subjectivities, each with its own faulty viewpoint:

> I saw a man pursuing the horizon.
> Round and round they sped.
> I was disturbed at this;
> I accosted the man.
> "It is futile," I said,
> "You can never—"
> "You lie," he cried,
> And ran on.   (CP 24)

In this poem, each speaker remains caught in his own irreconcilable point of view, with irreconcilable claims: one, that the man pursuing the horizon is deluded, the other, that his accuser is blind to idealism.[2] Crane has described one of his intentions as refusing to resolve such dilemmas, leaving them to the reader. "If there is any moral or lesson," he wrote in a letter, "I let the reader find it for himself."[3] One result is to insist on the limits of any single viewpoint, exposing self-reliance as a kind of solipsism. The Emersonian circle proves self-enclosing, not expanding. But this abstract critique is situated in a concrete, historical one. The man pursuing the horizon also suggests any American pursuing the American Dream. Crane's desert places here evoke the biblical, national mission of American Errand.[4] The biblical resonance seems to promise revelation; the American one, calling. But here it emerges as an obsessive drive of the self to achievement, revealed in another poem to have peculiar affinity to monetary measure. When

> A man saw a ball of gold in the sky;
> He climbed for it,
> And eventually achieved it—
> It was clay.

The ball of gold may be the sun, but it is cast in the image of precious metal. And, even as the poem exposes this to be "clay" the man, when he returns to earth and looks again,

> Lo, there was the ball of gold.
> Now this is the strange part:

> It was a ball of gold.
> Aye, by the heavens, it was a ball of gold.   (CP 35)

Is this delusion or devotion? The gold may be an emblem of imagination. And yet the pursuit here seems to lead to a dead end. Nothing has been transformed. The round is endless and self-enclosed. And its object, suspiciously, is named as that most seductive item of the Gilded Age, gold, which, instead of standing for imaginative possibility, may displace and betray it.

Crane's skepticism of the American self is equaled by his skepticism of religion. Crane's angry attacks on God as the source of punishment rather than mercy caused scandal when the poems were first published. Crane denounces the God who visits "the sins of the fathers...upon the heads of the children": "Well, then, I hate Thee, unrighteous picture" (CP, 12). But Crane's interests are less theological, less weighing the Old Testament against the New or his father's God against his mother's as cruel or saving, than they are social.[5] There is in Crane no sustained metaphysical analysis, such as Emily Dickinson undertakes in her work. Crane's concern instead is with the way these images of God direct human actions or, even more, are exploited by them. Rather than elevating people or founding communities, religious claims are exposed as instituted through or used in support of structures of power. What interests Crane is what the word "god" is taken to mean from instance to instance; what vision of the world seems implicit in those who claim to know God, especially in the vindictive ways of the "stern spirit" condemning the human devotion of a weeping maid (CP, 25). The divine can act as an inner voice "that whispers in the heart," (CP, 39), a "god of his inner thoughts" (CP, 51). But religion largely emerges in Crane as a debased social discourse, a sale by "strange peddlers," each

> Holding forth little images, saying:
> "This is my pattern of God.
> Now this is the God I prefer."   (CP, 34).

Crane rejects sin and any metaphysical space representing moral degrees:

> I stood upon a high place,
> And saw, below, many devils
> Running, leaping,
> And carousing in sin.
> One looked up, grinning,
> And said: "Comrade! Brother!"   (CP, 9)

When Crane's first publishers insisted he edit out the "blasphemy," he protested that this would "cut all the ethical sense out of the book. All the anarchy, perhaps. It is the anarchy which I particularly insist upon."[6] Anarchy stands against hierarchy, and for Crane, anti-hierarchy is a social and ethical position, not a metaphysical one. What he upholds instead is responsibility and responsiveness. These, however, he finds almost everywhere betrayed:

> With eye and with gesture
> You say you are holy.
> I say you lie;
> For I did see you
> Draw away your coats
> From the sin upon the hands
> Of a little child.
> Liar.   (*CP*, 57)

Crane takes sides, against those with holy pretensions and fine coats, and for those most sinned against. Here, they are represented by the "little child," a figure at once Christic and realistic. It finds its association in Crane's novel *Maggie* (1893), when Maggie, already ruined and walking the street, appeals to "a stout gentleman in a silk hat and chaste black coat," having "heard of the Grace of God." But the gentleman gives "a convulsive movement and save[s] his respectability with a vigorous side step" (pp. 141–142).

What do men pursue besides gold? Women. Now this is the strange part. For all his macho image, Crane, perhaps more than any other nineteenth-century male poet, writes a poetry that is deeply gendered—that is, poetry that recognizes the social experiences of women (and men) as structured through gender divisions. Crane's love poetry is usually and apologetically bracketed way from the rest of his work. But it is in many ways a true poetry of Eros. The imagery of wandering, of seeking, of pursuit is also Eros-longing for the remote beloved. In his own life, Crane's loves tended to fall into categories of the unattainable. His first, youthful, unrequited loves were for women belonging to social classes above him. Later he extended gallant protection to fallen women, whose prior sexual experiences made sole possession impossible—a love, as he wrote of his eventual companion Cora, a former Madam of a brothel: "always [in] the shadow of another lover" (*CP*, 107). This is love seen through "the ashes of other men's love," hence a "temple" on whose "altar" his self and heart can be sacrificed (*CP*, 103 "Intrigue").

Crane's gendered imagery is mainly of poor and abused women, exploited through sexuality and poverty, especially harlots. Indeed, Crane, like many women writers, is a poet of the double standard:

> I. There was a man and a woman
> Who sinned.
> Then did the man heap the punishment
> All upon the head of her,
> And went away gayly.

Only the woman is punished. Yet, as the poem pursues, if the man were to share the woman's excoriation, he would be denounced as "fool" or abandoned to death. As to the comfortable, reader, the poem concludes:

> Let it be your grief
> That he is dead
> And your opportunity gone;
> For, in that, you were a coward.   (CP 61)

Here the term "opportunity," like pursuit before, evokes an American code of values, but forces its meaning from economic ambition to ethical obligation, here betrayed. What slavery is to Whitman, prostitution is to Crane: the most extreme case of reduction of one person by another; of aggressive self-assertion at another's expense; of self-interest as particularly expressed through money. But prostitution is only one point on a continuum. A cluster of late texts propose questions of material interests as images of social abuse. "The outcry of old beauty / whored by pimping merchants" is, after all, only one instance of "the impact of a dollar upon the heart" (*CP*, 96). "Flesh painted with marrow" is only one "trivial bow" bought by "the successful man....slimed with victories over the lesser / a figure thankful on the shore of money" (*CP*, 92). In this world, the "real cross" is "made of pounds, dollars or francs" (*CP*, 135). Friendship, heaven, welfare, and curse all become modes of "crying their wares" (*CP*, 122). Poverty opposes wealth across a "chasm of commerce" (*CP*, 130). "Carts laden with food" mock those reduced to alms (*CP*, 128).

Crane continues to praise the courage of the self and the American promise of individual freedom and self-discovery. It is better to "be a toad" rather than to "think as I think" (*CP*, 47); to choose a "new road" apart from those who go in "huddled procession," even if the result is to die in "dire thickets" (*CP*, 17). But Crane also sees that this individualist value, without restraint or responsibility, becomes destructive with nothing to contain aggression and appetite.

The result is war, which haunts Crane's work. War is continuous with Crane's other concerns of money, religion, and the abuse of women. The title poem of Crane's second volume of poetry, "War is Kind" (does he also mean of human kind?) addresses the maiden, the orphaned child, the mother, each enjoined not to weep even as the poem makes their doing so inevitable:

> Do not weep, maiden, for war is kind...
> Little souls who thirst for fight,
> These men were born to drill and die.
> The unexplained glory flies above them,
> Great is the Battle-God, great, and his Kingdom—
> A field where a thousand corpses lie.   (*CP*, 76).

War here and elsewhere in Crane is the destitution of women, family, and community, sanctioned, as more explicitly in Crane's own version of a "Battle-Hymn of the Republic," by a "Battle-God" whose power is measured by the dead (*CP*, 129). This is a betrayal of those very ends for which war was presumably acting as a means. It is registered not in heroic self-assertion, but in the lives that are devastated, in the "tears of her who loved her son / even when the black battle rages" (*CP*, 124), in "crimson clash" where "women wept" and "babes ran, wondering" (*CP*, 14). As he writes in his "Battle-Hymn," "The chanting disintegrate and the two-faced eagle" (*CP*, 129). There is a coming apart of values, such that the heroic destroys the very world it claims to rescue.

Against these forces: what Crane can offer is what might be called a kind of modesty.

> In the desert
> I saw a creature, naked, bestial,
> Who, squatting upon the ground
> Held his heart in his hands,
> And ate of it.
> I said: Is it good, friend?
> "It is bitter—bitter," he answered;
> "But I like it
> Because it is bitter,
> And because it is my heart."   (*CP*, 3)

This text presents a complicated and polemical texture in which the Christian image of fallen man is at once invoked and questioned while the "heart" of inner conversion (Jeremiah; Paul) is equally revoked and recast. Crane in one sense recalls the older Christian suspicion of self-love in favor of humility.[7] But Crane's humility is not a Christian one, as he rejects both its institutional definition and its metaphysical hierarchy, and above all its required submission to higher authority. Yet there is a profound commitment to self-limitation: a bitterness to be embraced.

Crane sees art itself as written in the "red muck" of his heart (46), the "bastard mushroom / sprung from a pollution of blood" (79) into which he dips as ink. It is an art of immense responsibility and self-chastening in the face of the atomistic trends that had, by the 1890s, seem to overcome and consume the common commitments of America's energies. In this he, along with Poe, Dickinson, and Melville, provides a dark shadow to the American vision as pledged, even if against odds and alarm, by Whitman. As against Crane's min-imalism, in Whitman, all the century's trends intersect gigantically. They are collected in his hope that they will ultimately not only con-tend against but also complete each other in a grand enterprise of American diversity and possibility. His is the self that most strives to reflect and negotiate (rather than incorporate and absorb, as is often claimed) the range of Americans and America, with the nation itself declared to be the greatest poem. By this Whitman intends its ability to allow the greatest differences to reside together not only non-violently but creatively. Yet his poems, which call for the awakening of each self in ways that draw on both civic and religious traditions of participation, teeter on the edge of the conflicts and ruptures he, writing before and in the aftermath of the Civil War, knows to be in-herent in the very diversity he hopes to celebrate. Different identities threaten not to complement or enrich but to exclude and destroy each other. And, increasingly after the war's conclusion, both individual and community seem to Whitman in danger of being consumed in a reductive materialism corrosive of both public and private life. But it is Whitman's courage to pledge himself to the continued possibility of an American life in which all forms of possibility, in every sphere, remain open and mutually enhancing. Whitman's thus remains the grandest and most daring attempt to at once negotiate and encom-pass, yet respect and retain the possibilities of diverse commitments and identities within a liberal and pluralist America.

NOTES

PREFACE: POETICS, CULTURE, RHETORIC

1. Theodore Adorno, "Lyric Poetry and Society," *Telos* 20 (1974), 56–71, pp. 56–57.

1 MODEST CLAIMS

1. See chapter 3 for fuller discussion.
2. Modesty is a central term in most discussions of women and women poets, usually in a repressive sense. Thus Cheryl Walker sees modesty as a "denigration of ambition," *The Nightingale's Burden* (Bloomington: Indiana University Press, 1986) by which women were "deeply debilitated by their own internalized sense of guilt over their desire for power," p. 34. Alicia Ostriker sees a retreat into "Female powerlessness" after the Revolution had succeeded to "override the claims of modesty." *Stealing the Language* (Boston: Beacon, 1986), pp. 21, 23, although she also sees a dialectic between "assertion and self-effacement," p. 3. Suzanne Juhasz, *Naked and Fiery Forms* (New York: Harper and Row, 1976) laments that "women lack that sense of self," the "Ego" which men writers claim p. 2. Mary Kelley identifies literary domesticity with a deep seated modesty that led women to "demean their literary efforts and themselves by limning them as the humble efforts of humble creatures" p. 295. *Private Woman, Public Stage* (New York: Oxford University Press, 1984), p. 335. Sandra Gilbert and Susan Gubar consistently use "modesty" to describe female self-effacement, blocking the self-assertion necessary to poetic production. *The Madwoman in the Attic* (New Haven: Yale University Press, 1979), pp. 23, 61–63.
3. Cotton Mather, *Ornaments for the Daughter's of Zion* (Boston: S. Green and B. Green, 1692); John Bennett, *Letter to a Young Lady on Useful and Interesting Subjects* (Warrington: 1803), p. 44. Advice books are quoted in Angeline Goreau, *The Whole Duty of a Woman* (New York: Dial, 1985), pp. 36, 10, 44, 52.
4. Barbara Welter lists piety, purity, submissiveness, and domesticity as comprising "The Cult of True Womanhood," all modest virtues, *American Quarterly* 18:2 (Summer 1966), 151–174, p. 152. Mary Beth Norton, *Liberty's Daughters: The Revolutionary Experience*

of American Women (Boston: Little, Brown and Company, 1980) equates "femininity" with women as "modest, chaste, cheerful, sympathetic, affable, and emotional," p. 112

5. Jean Bethke Elshtain provides a history of gendered division between public and private realms in *Public Man, Private Woman* (Princeton: Princeton University Press, 1981).

6. On legal and political rights of women, see, for example, Norma Basch, *In the Eyes of the Law: Women, Marriage and Property in the Nineteenth Century* (Ithaca: Cornell University Press, 1982). Peggy A. Rabkin, *Fathers to Daughters: The Legal Foundations of Female Emancipation* (Westport, CT: Greenwood, 1980). Also Linda Kerber, "A Constitutional Right to be Treated like Ladies," in *U.S. History as Women's History*, ed. Linda Kerber (Chapel Hill: University of North Carolina Press, 1995), pp. 17–35. The laws for women were based in couverture: "The very being or legal existence of the woman is suspended during the marriage, or at least is incorporated and consolidated into that of the husband: under his wing, protection and cover, she performs everything." *Blackstone's Commentaries of the Laws of England*, Book the First, Oxford 1765, p. 442.

7. Ruth Bernard Yeazell *Fictions of Modesty* (Chicago: University of Chicago Press, 1984) sees modesty mainly as a "sexual virtue" for women (p. 8). Nancy Cott however distinguishes "Passionlessness" from modesty as a sexually active mode, *A Heritage of Her Own.* ed. Nancy Cott and Elizabeth Pleck (New York: Simon and Schuster, 1970), pp. 162–181.

8. On the evolution of manners in the changing society of nineteenth-century America, see especially John F. Kasson, *Rudeness and Civility* (New York: Hill and Wang, 1990); also Karen Halttunen, *Confidence Men and Painted Women* (New Haven: Yale University Press, 1982).

9. George Savile, Lord Marquess of Halifax, *The Lady's New Year's Gift* (first printed London 1688; reprint Stamford, CT: Overbrook, 1934), p. 61.

10. Mary Ryan, *Women in Public* (Baltimore: Johns Hopkins University Press, 1990), pp. 63–64.

11. Sarah Josepha Hale, *Manners, or Happy Homes and Good Society*; (Boston: Tilton and Company, 1868; reprinted New York: Arno Press, 1972, pp. 241–2); Eliza Ware Farrar, *The Young Lady's Friend* (Boston: American Stationer's Company, 1836; reprinted New York: Arno Press, 1974), p. 343; John R. Kasson on women's dress, pp. 121, 128–129. *The Ideology of Conduct*, ed. Nancy Armstrong, Leonard Tennenhouse (New York: Methuen, 1987). Cf. Roger Thompson *Women in Stuart England and America* (London: Routledge, 1974). See Christine Stansell, *City of Women* (Urbana: University of Illinois Press, 1987), for a discussion of laboring as against middle-class women.

12. Carroll Smith-Rosenberg, "The Female World of Love and Ritual," *Disorderly Conduct: Visions of Gender in Victorial America* (New

York: Alfred A. Knopf, 1985), 11–52; Nancy Cott, *The Bonds of Womanhood: "Women's Sphere" in New England 1780–1835* (New Haven, Yale University Press, 1977), pp. 84, 98, 200–201.

13. Daniel Scott Smith, "Family Limitation, Sexual Control, and Domestic Feminism in Victorian America," in *A Heritage of Her Own*, ed. Nancy Cott and Elizabeth Pleck (New York: Simon and Schuster, 1979), 222–245; pp. 231, 236–239.

14. Lori Ginzberg, in *Women and the Work of Benevolence* (New Haven: Yale University Press, 1990) charts women's many political and public activities outside of electoral politics.

15. Carl Degler, *At Odds: Women and the Family in America from the Revolution to the Present* (New York: Oxford University Press, 1980) as well as many other writers on nineteenth-century women's history, emphasize this continuity between public activities and domestic roles.

16. Mary Beth Norton, *Liberty's Daughters* and Linda Kerber, *Women of the Republic* (Chapel Hill: University of North Carolina Press, 1980) discuss the new roles as educators available to women out of the Revolutionary experience.

17. On the failure of women's suffrage see Carl Degler, *At Odds: Women and the Family in America from the Revolution to the Present* (New York: Oxford University Press, 1980); also Estelle Freedman, "Separatism as Strategy: Female Institution Building and American Feminism 1870–1930," *Feminist Studies* 5:3 (Fall 1979), 512–529; Aileen Kraditor, *The Ideas of the Woman's Suffrage Movement* (New York: Columbia University Press, 1965).

18. For discussion of Beecher, see Jeanne Boydston, Mary Kelley, and Anne Margolis, eds., *The Limits of Sisterhood: The Beecher Sisters on Women's Rights and Woman's Sphere* (Chapel Hill: University of North Carolina Press, 1988), p. 20. Kathryn Kish Sklar, *Catherine Beecher: A Study in American Domesticity* (New Haven: Yale University Press, 1973). Gillian Brown, *Domestic Individualism* (Berkeley: University of California Press, 1990), pp. 3–5, sees Beecher's as an emphasis on personal, private autonomy as contributing to an emerging ideology of individualism.

19. On Sarah J. Hale, see Ruth E. Finley, *The Lady of Godey's: Sarah Josepha Hale* (Philadelphia: Lippincott, 1932); Isabelle Webb Entrikin, *Sarah Josepha Hale and Godey's Lady's Book* (Philadelphia: Lancaster, 1946); Nicole Tonkovich Hoffman, "Sarah Josepha Hale" *Legacy* 7 (1990). See also Frank Luther Mott, *History of American Magazines* (Cambridge, MA: Harvard University Press, 1938); Nina Baym, "Sarah Hale, Political Writer" *Feminism and American Literary History* (New Brunswick: Rutgers University Press, 1992), 167–183; who argues that "Hale was very much an active political writer," who we now see from the "wrong side," p. 168.

20. *Godey's Lady's Book*, ed. Sarah J. Hale and Lydia Sigourney, Godey and Co., Publishers, XII, p. 7 (XIV, p. 212). Sarah J. Hale, *Manners, or Happy Homes and Good Society* (Boston: Tilton, 1868; reprint New York: Arno, 1972), pp. 176, 357.

21. Hale, *Manners*, p. 359.

22. See Mary Beth Norton, "The Paradox of "Woman's Sphere," in *Women of America: A History*, eds. Carol Ruth Berkin and Mary Beth Norton (Boston: Houghton, Mifflin, 1974), pp. 139–146. pp. 145–146.

23. Quoted in Wendy Martin, "Anne Bradstreet's Poetry: A Astucy in Subversive Piety," in *Shakespeare's Sisters*, eds. Sandra Gilbert and Susan Gubar (Bloomington: Indiana University Press, 1979), p. 26.

24. Mary Kelley, *Private Woman, Public Stage* (New York: Oxford University Press, 1984), pp. 126–7.

25. Quoted Goreau, *The Whole Duty of a Woman*, pp. 17, 43, 39.

26. The emphasis on hypocrisy structures Karen Halttunin, *Confidence Men and Painted Women* and Yeazell.

27. See Joanne Dobson, *Dickinson and the Strategies of Reticence* (Bloomington: Indiana University Press, 1989).

28. Cott, "Passionlessness," p. 166. See also Kasson, pp. 121, 129.

29. For this double argument, see Linda Kerber, "Separate Spheres, Female Worlds, Woman's Place: The Rhetoric of Women's History," *Journal of American History* 75:1 (June 1988), 9–39. pp. 16–18.

30. Gordon S. Haight, *Mrs. Sigourney, the Sweet Singer of Hartford* (New Haven: Yale University Press, 1930), p. 34. For biography see also Mary De Jong, "Legacy Profile" *Legacy* 5:1 (Spring 1988), 35–43.

31. Aaron Kramer dismisses Sigourney's success as a "spectacularly lucrative trade" in sentiment," *The Prophetic Tradition in American Poetry* (Rutherford, NJ: Fairleigh Dickinson University Press, 1968) p. 346. Ann Douglas Wood generally excoriates Sigourney but sees her "endless series of tributes to feminine modesty" as "the most approved way for a woman to succeed." "Mrs. Sigourney and the Sensibility of the Inner Space," *New England Quarterly* June 1972, 163–181.

32. Ann Douglas Wood, "Mrs. Sigourney," p. 163, who sees the death imagery as "the final form of anesthetized sublimation," p. 177. Barton Levi St. Armand, *Emily Dickinson and Her Culture* (New York; Cambridge University Press, 1984) sees Sigourney as a writer of the "popular gospel of consolation" p. 47. Cheryl Walker, *The Nightingale's Burden* (Bloomington: Indiana University Press, 1982) similarly describes Sigourney as a sentimental writer with "an overfondness for idealizing children and the dead, a tendency to take comfort in simplistic conceptions of life and pious platitudes," p. 57. Susan Phinney Conrad, *Perish the Thought: Intellectual Women in Romantic America 1830–1860* (New York: Oxford University Press, 1976) sums up Sigourney as a writer using "the same cloying themes and the floral aspects of nature as analogues to the exquisite female sensibility," p. 26.

33. Quoted in Haight, pp. 99, 90.

34. Nina Baym redefines Sigourney as a "historian," emphasizing how she is an "activist and interventionist" writer." "Re-inventing Lydia Sigourney" in *The (Other) American Traditions*, ed. Joyce W. Warren (New Brunswick: Rutgers University Press, 1993), 53–72. See also Sandra A. Zagarell, "Expanding America: Lydia Sigourney's *Sketch of Connecticut* and Catherine Sedgewick's *Hope Leslie*," *Tulsa Studies in Women's Literature* 6: 2 (Fall 1987), 225–245.

35. Carol Smith Rosenberg "Female World"; Mary Ryan, *Cradle of the Middle Class* (New York: Cambridge University Press, 1981).

36. Mary Beth Norton, "The Paradox of the Woman's Sphere," in *Women of America: A History*, eds. Carol Ruth Berkin and Mary Beth Norton (Boston: Houghton, Mifflin, 1974), describes the shift from fathers to mothers as the primary power in child-rearing as one of the paradoxical extensions of power within the limits of domestic ideology, p. 145.

37. Baym claims that for Sigourney, "elegy forms part of a public occasion," "Re-inventing Lydia Sigourney," p. 57.

38. Mary Ryan, *Womanhood in America* (New York: New Viewpoints, 1975), p. 84.

39. Haight, p. 51.

40. Haight, p. 46.

41. Carol Gilligan's *In a Different Voice* (Cambridge, MA: Harvard University Press, 1982) importantly proposes care as a feminist moral model.

42. Quoted in Yeazell, *Fictions of Modesty*, p. 9.

43. See Gilbert and Gubar's chapter on "The Aesthetics of Renunciation" in *The Madwoman* for such a polarization, for example, p. 575.

2   EMILY DICKINSON AND AMERICAN IDENTITY

1. Mary Ryan, *Women in America* (New York: Viewpoints, 1975), p. 94.

2. Wendy Martin counters the image of Dickinson as victim by emphasizing her resistance to gendered conformity, thus creating "conditions for her own art, *An American Triptych: Ann Bradstreet, Emily Dickinson, Adrienne Rich* (Chapel Hill: University of North Carolina Press, 1984), p. 80. Cf. Suzanne Juhasz, *The Undiscovered Continent* (Bloomington: Indiana University Press, 1983) who describes Dickinson as withdrawing "to achieve certain goals and overcome certain forces in her environment" and to gain a "perfect control over her life," pp. 4–5. Cf. Juhasz, "Introduction" to *Feminist Critics Read Emily Dickinson* (Bloomington: Indiana University Press, 1983), p. 10. Cf. Barbara Mossberg, *When a Writer is a Daughter* (Bloomington: Indiana University Press, 1982), who sees Dickinson's as a "facade of filial obedience" enacting a "mode of rebellion."

3. Dickinson's reclusion has been read as madness and breakdown by John Cody, *After Great Pain* (Cambridge, MA: Harvard University Press, 1971) and George Whicher, *This Was a Poet* (New York: Charles Scribner's, 1938). Sandra Gilbert and Susan Gubar also present Dickinson as an agoraphobic madwoman, although they see Dickinson as converting her madness into triumph, *Madwoman in the Attic* (New Haven: Yale University Press, 1979).

4. Clark Griffith, *The Long Shadow* (Princeton: Princeton University Press 1964).

5. Joanne Dobson, *Dickinson and the Strategies of Reticence* (Bloomington: Indiana University Press, 1989) compares Dickinson with other women writers.

6. Robert Weisbuch describes Dickinson's analogical poetics as finally resolving into unity, "self-conflict in the service of a final wholeness," *Emily Dickinson's Poetry* (Chicago: University of Chicago Press, 1972), p. 10.

7. Suzanne Juhasz's article on "Reading Dickinson Doubly" clearly presents some of the methodological issues of such doubling in Dickinson texts, in *Emily Dickinson: A Celebration for Readers*, ed. Suzanne Juhasz and Christina Miller (New York: Gordan and Brack, 1989), 217–221.

8. David Porter *The Modern Idiom* (Cambridge, MA: Harvard University Press 1981) describes Dickinson's as "the significance of incoherence" in "retreat from reality into words," p. 8. Cf. Margaret Dickie, *Lyric Contingencies* (Philadelphia: University of Pennsylvania Press, 1991), Sharon Cameron, *Choosing Not Choosing* (Chicago: University of Chicago Press, 1992) and others.

9. Limitation becomes redeeming expansion in Jane Donahue Eberwein *Dickinson and the Strategies of Limitation* (Amherst: University of Massachusetts Press, 1985).

10. David Porter describes Dickinson's as a "lack of an advancing, coherent, and complicated intention," p. 83; and a "taste for individual excitements as against overall design," p. 106.

11. The question of Dickinson's lesbianism was early broached and has been widely discussed. See especially the work of Martha Nell Smith.

12. St. Armand, *Emily Dickinson and Her Culture* (New York: Cambridge University Press, 1984) particularly absorbs Dickinson into a sentimental love religion. He describes Dickinson's as "a romantic submission to the divine will of Phoebus" and as "a slave to her religion of romance" from which "only death could emancipate her," p. 101. Vivian Pollak, *The Anxiety of Gender* (Ithaca: Cornell University Press 1984) also speaks of Dickinson's as a "religion of love," pp. 166, 169. Sandra Gilbert, "The Wayward Nun beneath the Hill," in *Feminist Critics Read Emily Dickinson* likewise speaks of a "complex theology of secular love," p. 27. Of course, Dickinson does elide the

figures of God, Father, and Lover, but not in a sentimental love religion. As Clark Griffith remarked, what they all have in common is that they all betrayed her, p. 281.

13. See especially Joanne Feit Diehl, *Dickinson and the Romantic Imagination* (Princeton: Princeton University Press 1981).

14. Feminist moral psychology, as launched by Carole Gilligan's *In a Different Voice* (Cambridge, MA: Harvard University Press, 1993) has made this critique of self-sufficiency a central topic.

15. See Karl Keller, *The Only Kangaroo among the Beauty* (Baltimore: Johns Hopkins University Press, 1979) for general discussion of Dickinson's reading of Emerson. On Dickinson's departures from Emerson, see Glauco Cambon, "Emily Dickinson and the Crisis of Self-Reliance" in *Transcendentalism and its Legacy*, ed. Myron Simon and T.H. Parsons (Ann Arbor: University of Michigan Press, 1967), 123–131.

16. Joyce Appleby, *Liberalsim and Republicanism in the Historical Imagination* (Cambridge, MA: Harvard University Press, 1992) p. 29.

17. Cf. J 617 / Fr 681. For an overview of imagery of sewing, see Elaine Hedges, "The Needle or the Pen," 338–364. She quotes Eliza Farrar's advice book, *The Young Lady's Friend*: "A woman who does not know how to sew is as deficient in her education as a man who cannot write," p. 122.

18. See Shira Wolosky, *Emily Dickinson: A Voice of War* (New Haven: Yale University Press, 1984). Also Sharon Leder and Andrea Abbott, *The Language of Exclusion* (New York: Greenwood Press, 1987). There is a great deal of new writing on Dickinson and her contemporary politics. For a recent overview see Faith Barrett, "Public Selves and Private Spheres: 1884–2007" *Emily Dickinson Journal* 16:1, 207, 92–104.

19. For Edward Dickinson's career, see Sewall, *Life*, pp. 52, 55, 67, 1222, 336, 444–445, 469 n 644. Dr. Josiah Holland, an intimate correspondent of Dickinson's for many years, wrote one of the first biographies of Lincoln. Higginson, known to Dickinson scholars as the man who refused to publish her work, was a leading activist in both the antislavery and the women's rights movements, and was the officer of the North's first black regiment when Dickinson began writing to him.

20. For general discussion of literary interpretations of the Civil War, see Daniel Aaron, *The Unwritten War* (New York: Alfred A. Knopf, 1973) and George M. Fredrickson, *The Inner Civil War* (New York: Harper and Row, 1965).

21. Sewall, *Life*, p. 536.

22. *The Rebellion Record*, ed. Frank Moore (New York: Arno Press, 1977).

23. Thomas Ford's early, and for long unique, article on "Emily Dickinson and the Civil War," *University Review of Kansas City*, 31,

Spring, 1965, estimates four poems as directly deriving from the war, p. 199. But recent work increasingly uncovers more and more political references.

3 Public and Private: Double Standards

1. Linda Kerber, *Women of the Republic* (New York: Norton, 1986) on Republican Motherhood.
2. Anne Douglas Wood in "Fanny Fern: Why Women Wrote," *American Quarterly* 23 (1971), 3–24, explores this problem of conforming to publisher's expectations. Cf. Margaret Ezell, *Women Writing Literary History* (Baltimore: Johns Hopkins University Press, 1993).
3. Mary Kelley, *Private Woman, Public Stage* (New York: Oxford University Press 1984), p. ix.
4. Jane Tompkins, *Sensational Designs* (New York: Oxford University Press, 1985) launched the reading of sentimental literature as proposing a distinctive ideological vision, in opposition against Ann Douglas's presentation of sentimentalism as "the political sense obfuscated or gone rancid [which] never exists except in tandem with failed political consciousness," Ann Douglas, in *The Feminization of American Culture* (New York: Anchor, 1977), p. 254. Cf. Richard Brodhead, "Sparing the Rod: Discipline and Fiction in Antebellum America," *Representations* 21 (Winter 1988). Nina Baym, *Women's Fiction* (Ithaca: Cornell University Press, 1978); Philip Fisher, *Hard Facts* (New York: Oxford University Press, 1987). Laura Wexler reviews the Anne Douglas/Jane Tompkins debate in "Tender Violence: Literary Eavesdropping, Domestic Fiction, and Educational Reform," in *The Culture of Sentiment* ed. Shirley Samuels (New York: Oxford University Press, 1992), pp. 9–38.
5. Amy Kaplan, *The Anarchy of Empire in the Making of U.S. Culture* (Cambridge, MA: Harvard University Press 2002), 23–50. On complicity between domesticity and imperialism see Gayatri Chakravorty Spivak, "Three Women's Texts and a Critique of Imperialism," *Critical Inquiry* 12:1 (Autumn 1985), 243–261. On ideologies of domestic fiction see: Ann Romines, *The Home Plot* (Amherst: University of Massachusetts Press, 1992); Nancy Armstrong, *Desire and Domestic Fiction* (New York: Oxford University Press, 1987); Caren Kaplan, *Questions of Travel: Postmodern Discourses of Displacement* (Durham, NC: Duke University Press, 1998); Lora Romero, *Home Fronts: Domesticity and Its Critics in the Antebellum United States* (Durham, NC: Duke University Press, 1998); and Isabelle Lehuru "Sentimental Figures: Reading Godey's Lady's Book in antebellum America" *The Culture of Sentiment*, pp. 73–91, p. 75 explore the complex mix of the progressive and the restrictive. Most of these discussions focus on sentimental and domestic writing, not on women's public writings, and on fiction, not poetry.

6. Mary Ryan suggests complicity between women's literature as "gilded literary package[s] of domestic piety and pathos," and restrictive domesticity, *Womanhood in America* (New York: New Viewpoints, 1975), p. 76. Cf. Mary Ryan, *Empire of the Mother* (New York: Howarth, 1982).

7. Paula Benett, *Poets in the Public Sphere* (Princeton: Princeton University Press, 2003) offers a range of verse types, but most remains within the rubric of genteel and sentimental in various ways. Her interests are "complaint" literature that focuses on domesticity as constraining, through an equality-feminist political orientation.

8. Nina Baym underscores this historical dimension in women's writing in *Feminism and American Literary History* (New Brunswick, NJ: Rutgers University Press, 1992), p. 109. Cf. her *American Women Writers and the Work of History 1790–1860* (New Brunswick, NJ: Rutgers University Press, 1995. Emily Stipes Watts, *The Poetry of American Women 1632–1945* (Austin: University of Texas Press, 1977) describes some social involvements, but sees women to lack a "male" involvement with "broad philosophical and social concerns," p. 67.

9. See especially Jean Bethke Elshtain, *Public Man, Private Woman* (Princeton: Princeton University Press, 1981).

10. Ruth Bloch suggests this transference to women of public virtue, at least in the eighteenth-century aftermath of the Revolution. "Virtue in Revolutionary America," *Signs* 13:1 (1987), 37–57, pp. 56–57.

11. Joanne Dobson's "Reclaiming Sentimental Literature," *American Literature* 69:2 (June 1997), 263–288 importantly interprets sentimentality as celebrating "human connection" p. 266 and "social bonds" beyond (male) "individual existence" but in personal rather than civic contexts. See also Elizabeth Patrino, "Nineteenth-Century American Women's Poetry," in *Cambridge Companion to Nineteenth-Century American Women's Writing*, eds. Dale M. Buer and Philim Gould (New York: Cambridge University Press, 2001), 122–144.

12. Keith Thomas, "The Double Standard," *Journal of the History of Ideas* 20:2 (April 1959), 195–216.

13. Only two persons were arrested under the seduction law passed in New York in 1848. Mary Ryan, *Women in Public*, pp. 100–102. For discussion of the moral purity movements see Carroll Smith-Rosenberg, *Religion and the Rise of the American City* (Ithaca: Cornell University Press, 1971); Lori Ginzberg, *Women and the Work of Benevolence* (New Haven: Yale University Press, 1990); Barbara Meil Hobson, *Uneasy Virtue* (New York: Basic, 1987); David T. Pivar, *Purity Crusade* (Westport, CT: Greenwood, 1973).

14. Carol Smith-Rosenberg documents the history of the early New York Female Reform Society and its centrality, "Beauty, the Beast, and the Militant Woman: A Case Study in Sex Roles and Social Stress in Jacksonian America," *American Quarterly* 23 (October 1971), 562–84, p. 583.

15. Joan Sherman, *Invisible Poets* (Urbana: University of Illinois Press, 1974), pp. 62–72. Also Elizabeth Ammons, "Profile of Frances Harper," *Legacy* 2:2 (1985), 61–66; Hallie Brown, *Homespun Heroines and Other Women of Distinction* (1926—rpt. Arno, 1971).

16. This political dimension of sentiment is also discussed by Claudia Tate in *Domestic Allegories of Political Desire* (New York: Oxford University Press, 1992).

17. Bruce Dickson, Jr. *Black American Writing from the Nadir* (Baton Rouge: Louisiana State University Press, 1989), p. 19. Mary Dearborn, *Pocahontas's Daughters* (New York: Oxford University Press, 1986) discusses Harper's gentility, pp. 44–47; see also Susan K. Harris, "But Is It Any Good," in *The (Other) American Traditions*, ed. Joyce Warren (New Brunswick, NJ: Rutgers University Press, 1993), pp. 263–275.

18. Walker, *Nightingale's Burden*, p. 128.

19. Charlotte Perkins Gilman, *Women and Economics* (New York: Harper & Row, 1966), pp. 63, 171.

20. Adrienne Rich *Of Woman Born* (New York: W. W. Norton, 1976), p. 236.

21. Mary Wollstoncraft, *A Vindication of the Rights of Woman*, in *Works*, London; William Pickering, 1989, pp. 191–193.

22. J.G.A. Pocock's *The Machiavellian Moment* (Princeton: Princeton University Press, 1975); Donald Pease, in *Visionary Compacts* (Madison: The University of Wisconsin Press, 1987) notes "individuals who conceive of the life they can share together as a threat to their personal freedom cannot organize any vital community at all," p. 25.

4   Genteel Rhetoric, North and South

1. Noah Webster, *On Being American*, ed. Homer Babbidge, Jr. (New York: Ferderick A. Praeger, 1967), p. 101.

2. Noah Webster, *Dissertations on the English Language* (Boston: 1789). This national vision is reiterated in the prefaces to his Dictionaries.

3. Marc Shell, "The Politics of Language Diversity," *Critical Inquiry* (Autumn 1993), 103–127, p. 105.

4. Daniel Boorstin, *The Americans: The Colonial Experience* (New York: Random House, 1958), p. 273.

5. Michael Kramer discusses Webster's work in *Imagining Language in America* (Princeton: Princeton University Press, 1992).

6. See Edward C. Hirsh, *Henry Wadsworth Longfellow* (Minneapolis: University of Minnesota Press, 1964); Edward Wagenknecht, *Henry Wadsworth Longfellow: His Poetry and Prose* (New York: Ungar, 1986); and Newton Arvin, *Longfellow: His Life and Work* (Boston: Little, Brown and Co., 1963).

7. Newton Arvin, *Longfellow*, p. 28.

8. Henry James, *William Wetmore Story and His Friends* (1903; rpt. New York: Grove Press, n.d.), pp. 312–313.

9. Angus Fletcher makes this point on the most thoughtful essay available on Longfellow's poetry in "Whitman and Longfellow: Two Types of the American Poet," *Raritan* 10:4 (Spring 1991), 131–145.

10. Philip Fisher describes this as "a thickly sedimented historical product" "Democratic Social Space: Whitman, Melville and the Promise of American Transparency," *Representations* 24 (Fall 1988), 60–101, p. 61.

11. George Santayana, *The Genteel Tradition*, ed. Douglas L. Wilson (Cambridge, MA: Harvard University Press, 1967), pp. 73, 40.

12. William Charvat, *The Profession of Authorship in America*, ed. Matthew Bruccoli (Columbus: Ohio State University Press, 1968), p. 118.

13. Quoted Carl Degler, *Out of Our Past* (New York: Harper, 1984), p. 40.

14. See Charvat on Longfellow's commercial acumen.

15. Lawrence Buell discusses this tension between being "both marginalized and pedestalized," *New England Literary Culture* (New York: Cambridge University Press, 1986), pp. 115.

16. Ed. Winfield Parks, *Henry Timrod* (New York: Twayne, 1969), p. 79; *The Last Years of Henry Timrod*, ed. Jay B. Hubbell (Durham, NC: Duke University Press, 1941).

17. See Sacvan Bercovitch, *The Puritan Origins of the American Self* (New Haven: Yale University Press, 1975) for comparison and contrast between Southern and Northern visions of American destiny, pp. 137–139.

18. Quoted from: James McPherson *Battle Cry of Freedom* (New York: Ballantine, 1988).

19. See David Brion Davis, *The Problem of Slavery in the Age of Revolution*, 1770–1823 (Ithaca: Cornell University Press, 1975), p. 258.

20. Miriam Rossitersmall, *Oliver Wendell Holmes* (New York: Twayne, 1962).

21. On titles see Robert Middlekauff, "The Ritualization of the American Revolution," in *The Development of an American Culture*, ed. Stanley Coben,, Lorman Ratner (Englewood Cliffs, NJ: Prentice-Hall, 1970), 31–43, p. 31

22. *Atlantic Monthly* 65 (1890), 549–560.

23. Martin Duberman, *James Russell Lowell* (Boston: Houghton Mifflin., 1966); also Richmond Croom Beatty, *James Russell Lowell* (Nashville, TN: Vanderbilt University Press, 1942).

24. Jack de Bellis, *Sidney Lanier* (New York: Twayne, 1972); Jane S. Gabin, *A Living Minstrelsy: The Poetry and Music of Sidney Lanier.*

25. Lewis Leary, *John Greenleaf Whittier* (New York: Twayne, 1961).

26. Edmund Morgan, *American Slavery, America Freedom* (New York: W.W. Norton, 1975).

27. See Emily Budick, "The Immortalizing Power of Imagination: A Reading of Whitteir's "Snow-Bound," *ESQ* 31:2 (1985), 89–99.

28. "Introduction," *Victorian America*, ed. D. Walker Howe (Philadelphia: University of Pennsylvania Press, 1976), pp. 3–27, on genteel cultural anxiety.

29. F. O Matthiessen, *The American Renaissance* (New York: Oxford University Press, 1941), p. 23.

30. Mark Twain, "The Story of a Speech," *Mark Twain's Speeches, The Complete Works of Mark Twain* (New York: Harper and Brothers, 1923), 63–76. Van Wyck Brooks remarks that "between academic pedantry and pavement slang, there is no community, no genial middle ground," *Three Essays on America* (New York: E.P. Dutton, 1934), pp. 17–18. Cf. Malcolm Cowley, *After the Genteel Tradition* (New York: W.W. Norton, 1936).

5   EDGAR ALLAN POE: METAPHYSICAL RUPTURE AND THE SIGN OF WOMAN

1. Baudelaire's translations of Poe come to 5 volumes. Mallarmé translated 36 of 50 Poe poems; Valéry called Poe "perhaps the most subtle artist of this century." Lois Davis Vines, "Poe in France," and "Mallarmé and Valéry," in *Poe Abroad*, ed. Lois Davis Vines (Iowa City: University of Iowa Press, 1999), pp. 9–18, 171–176.

2. Cf. T.S. Eliot "From Poe to Valery," *To Criticize the Critic* (Lincoln: University of Nebraska Press, 1965), 27–43.

3. William Carlos Williams, *In the American Grain* (New York: New Directions, 1956), p. 216. cf. Harry Levin, *The Power of Blackness* (Faber and Faber, 1958), p. 87: "Poe was never more the child of his century than when he was denouncing it."

4. Rufus Wilmot Griswold, from "Memoir of the Author," in *Critical Essays on Edgar Allan Poe*, ed. Eric W. Carlson (Boston: G.K. Hall, 1987), pp. 52–57, p. 57.

5. Edward H. Davidson, *Poe: A Critical Study* (Cambridge, MA: Harvard University Press, 1957), p. 94.

6. On repetition and its aesthetic implications, see Barbara Johnson, "Strange Fits: Poe and Wordsworth on the Nature of Poetic Language," *The American Face of Edgar Allan Poe*, eds. Shawn Rosenheim and Stephen Rachman (Baltimore: Johns Hopkins University Press, 1995), pp. 37–48.

7. Cf. Perry Miller, *Nature's Nation* (Cambridge, MA: Harvard University Press, 1967): "Vraisemblance required the Romancer to portray actual scenes, not to make up fictitious ones as did that renegade from the Romance, Edgar Allan Poe," p. 260.

8. See Valéry's discussions on Poe's *Marginalia* and his "The Place of Baudelaire," *Leonardo, Poe, Mallarmé, Collected Works*, ed. Jackson

Mathews (Princeton: Princeton University Press, 1972), pp. 177–193. Cf. T.S. Eliot's discussion, "From Poe to Valéry," p. 40.

9. Allen Tate distinguishes Poe's obscurity from "the belief that language itself can be reality, or by incantation can create a reality: a superstition that comes down in French," p. 117. *The Man of Letters in the Modern World* (New York: Meridian, 1964).

10. Cf. J. Gerald Kennedy, "Phantasms of Death in Poe's Fiction," and *Poe, Death, and the Live of Writing* (New Haven: Yale University Press, 1987).

11. William Mentzel Forrest, *Biblical Allusions in Poe* (New York: Macmillan, 1928), p. 16. Cf. John Lynen, *The Design of the Present* (New Haven: Yale University Press, 1969) describes Poe's cultural milieu as one in which "the Puritan tradition was still dominant," p. 213.

12. Jeffrey Meyers, *Edgar Allan Poe: His Life and Legacy* (New York: Charles Scribners, 1992), pp. 9–10.

13. Tate, pp. 143, 114. Tate observes that "in the Virginia of Poe's time the subjects of conversation and reading were almost exclusively politics and theology," p. 349.

14. For discussion of Poe and apocalyptic, see Douglas Robinson, *American Apocalypses* (Baltimore: Johns Hopkins University Press, 1985), p. 111–122; and John Lynen, *The Design of the Present*, New Haven, Yale University Press, 1969).

15. Harold Bloom refers to Poe as a "Gnostic self before the fall into creation" in his "Introduction" to *The Tales of Poe*, ed. Harold Bloom (New York: Chelsea House, 1987), 1–15, p. 12. Cf. Barton Levi St. Armand's "Usher unveiled: Poe and the Metaphysics of Gnosticism," *Poe Studies* 5:1 (June 1972), 1–8 describes *Eureka* as a "gnostic escape," p. 1. Also Hyatt Waggoner, *American Poets* (Boston: Houghton Mufflin, 1968), p. 146, who sees Poe's as a "gnostic positive."

16. D.H. Lawrence, *Studies in Classic American Literature* (New York: Viking, 1961), p. 68. Tate, pp. 121, 349.

17. Lawrence, p. 67.

18. Tate, p. 135.

19. J. Gerald Kennedy speaks of "the poetic evocations of the beloved's blissful presence" in Poe's poetry as against his prose, "Poe, 'Ligea,' and the Problem of Dying Women" in *New Essays on Poe's Major Tales*, ed. Kenneth Silverman, pp. 113–129, p. 118. Cf. Kennedy's *Poe, Death and the Life of Writing* p. 88; J. Gerald Kennedy, "Phantasms of Death in Poe's Fiction," in Bloom, 111–133. 125. Daniel Hoffman's *Poe Poe Poe Poe Poe* (New York: Doubleday, 1972) discusses Poe's women as ideal ones, pp. 63–64. Leland Person *Aesthetic Headaches* (Athens: University of Georgia Press, 1988) seems to wish to argue that Poe's women resist objectification (p. 7), but then describes them as images of "perfection" that seek to transcend life as body, sexuality, and mutability (p. 19).

20. Cf. Glenn Omans, "Poe's Ulalume: Drama of the Solipsistic Self," in *Papers on Poe*, ed. Richard Veler (Springfield, OH: Chantry Music Press, 1972),62–73 sees "To Helen" as a "successful vision of the ideal," p. 64. Cf. Floyd Stovall, "The Conscious Art of Edgar Allan Poe," in *Poe: A Collection of Critical Essays* ed. Robert Regan (Englewood Cliffs, NJ: Prentice Hall, 1967), sees "To Helen" as "restoring Poe to his artistic home through the beauty of woman," p. 175.

21. Joan Dayan argues for Poe's irony as exposing rather than reproducing gender types, "Poe's Women: A Feminist Poe," *Poe Studies* 26:1–2 (June/December 1993), 1–12. Cf. G.R. Thompson's discussion of Poe's irony in *Papers on Poe* "Poe and Romantic Irony" 28–41; and *Poe's Fiction: Romantic Irony in the Gothic Tales* (Madison: University of Wisconsin Press, 1973). Evan Carton, *The Rhetoric of American Romance* (Baltimore: Johns Hopkins University Press, 1985) questions Poe's as pure irony: "Idealistic quest and parodic self-exposure are interwoven almost seamlessly in Poe's fiction." p. 132, Cf. p. 271.

22. *The Purloined Poe: Lacan, Derrida, and Psychoanalytic Reading*, ed. John P. Muller and William J. Richardson (Baltimore: Johns Hopkins University Press, 1988).

23. Charles Pierre Baudelaire, "New Notes on Edgar Poe," *Critical Essays on Edgar Allan Poe*, ed. Eric W. Carlson (Boston: G.K. Hall, 1987), pp. 63–77, pp. 65, 69.

24. On Poe in Southern contexts see David Leverenz, "Poe and Gentry Virginia," *The American Face of Edgar Allan Poe*, ed. Shawn Rosenheim and Stephen Rachman (Baltimore: Johns Hopkins University Press, 1995), pp. 210–236; Leland S. Person, "Poe and Nineteenth-Century Gender Constructions," in *A Historical Guide to Edgar Allan Poe*, ed. J. Gerald Kennedy (New York: Oxford University Press, 2001).

25. Joan Dayan, "Amorous Bondage," *The American Face of Edgar Allan Poe*, eds. Shawn Rosenheim and Stephen Rachman (Baltimore: Johns Hopkins University Press, 1995), pp. 179–209.

6   CLAIMING THE BIBLE: SLAVE SPIRITUALS AND AFRICAN-AMERICAN TYPOLOGY

1. D.K. Wilgus, "The Negro-White Spiritual," *Mother Wit from the Laughing Barrel*, ed. Alan Dundes (New York: Garland, 1981), p. 69.

2. On spiritual's music see Eileen Southern, *The Music of Black America* (New York: Norton, 1971), especially pp. 35–43; George Robinson Ricks, *Some Aspects of the Religious Music of the U.S. Negro* (New York: Arno, 1977); Jon Michael Spencer, *Sacred Symphony* (New York: Greenwood Press, 1988) and *Black Hymnody* (Knoxville: University of Tennessee Press, 1992); Thomas Earl Hawley, *Slave Tradition of Singing* (1993).

3. Lawrence Levine, *Black Culture and Black Consciousness* (New York: Oxford University Press, 1977), p. 6. George Robinson Ricks examines the balances between "African musical traits" and the "Euroamerican musical values" in *Some Aspects of The Religious Music of The United States Negro*, pp. 6–7, 27–29; Cf. Melville J. Herskovits, *The Myth of the Negro Past* (Boston: Beacon,1958), p. 268.

4. George Pullen Jackson made the claim that the spirituals are merely derivative from white hymns and gospel songs, *White and Negro Spirituals: Their Life Span and Kinship* (Locust Manor, NY: J.J. Augustin, 1943). Mechal Sobel, *The World They Made Together* (Princeton: Princeton University Press, 1987) clarifies the hybrid and syncretist contexts, p. 205. Eric Sundquist, *To Wake the Nations* (Cambridge, MA: Harvard University Press, 1993), pp. 5–6. Most historians of slavery accept the "hybrid" character of "Afro-Christianity," in which, as Raboteau puts it, at the end of a long "dual process"...the slaves did not simply become Christian; they creatively refashioned a Christian tradition to fit their own peculiar experience of enslavement in America." Albert J. Raboteau, *Slave Religion: The Invisible Institution in the Antebellum South* (New York: Oxford University Press, 1978), pp. 126–7. Cf. also Eugene D. Genovese, *Roll Jordan Roll* (New York: Pantheon, 1974), and John W. Blassingame, *The Slave Community* (New York: Oxford University Press, 1972)

5. W.E.B. Du Bois, *The Souls of Black Folk* (New York: Bantam, 1989), p. 182.

6. See Marcus Jernegan, "Slavery and Conversion in the Colonies," *American Historical Review* 21:3 (April 1916), 505–527 on the attempt by planters to regard their slaves as "incapable of instruction" and even as "without souls," p. 519. Cf. C.C. Jones *The Religious Instruction of the Negroes in the United States* (Savannah: Thomas Purse, 1942), p. 24; Eugene D. Genovese, p. 207. Raboteau offers a full review of white resistance to conversion of the slaves, pp. 100–129.

7. Eileen Southern (pp. 173, 216) and James Weldon Johnson, preface, discuss the difficulties transcription of music in its multiple variations. See Miles Mark Fisher on textual problems in the transition from oral to written forms, *Negro Slave Songs in the United States* (New York: Cornell University Press, 1953), pp. 13–15.

8. Le Roy Moore, "The Spiritual: Soul of Black Religion," *American Quarterly* 23 (1971), 658–676, p. 660.

9. Paul F. Laubenstein, "An Apocalyptic Reincarnation," *Journal of Biblical Literature* (December 1932), p. 245.

10. Thomas Wentworth Higginson, *Army Life in a Black Regiment* (Detroit: Michigan State University Press, 1960), pp. 27, 205.

11. Harold Courlander, *Negro Folk Music* (New York: Columbia University Press, 1963), p. 38. Johnson, p. 1

12. Sacvan Bercovitch, *Puritan Origins of the American Self* (New Haven: Yale University Press, 1975); *American Jeremaid* (Madison: University of Wisconsin Press, 1978).

13. Werner Sollors, *Beyond Ethnicity: Consent and Dissent* (New York: Oxford University Press, 1986), pp. 40–55, 59.

14. Raboteau, p. 26; Robert Liston, *Slavery in America* (New York: McGraw Hill, 1970), p. 45.

15. Jones, p. 14.

16. Frederick Douglass, *My Bondage and My Freedom* (New York: Dover, 1969), p. 266.

17. Frank J. Klingberg, *The Appraisal of the Negro in Colonial South Carolina* (Washington, DC: Associated Publishers, 1941), p. 69; Jones, p. 66; Raboteau, p. 147.

18. Cited by Janet Cornelius, *When I Can Read My Title Clear* (Columbia: University of South Carolina Press, 1991), p. 62.

19. Henry Louis Gates explores this issue in *Figures in Black* (New York: Oxford University Press, 1987), pp. 4, 11, 17.

20. W.E.B. DuBois, *Black Reconstruction* (New York: Harcourt, Brace, 1963, reprint 1935), p. 638. For differing assessments of slave literacy see George Robinson Ricks, pp. 17, 20; C. G. Woodson's *The Education of the Negro Prior to 1861* (New York: Arno, 1968, reprint from 1919), pp. 226–228.

21. Cornelius, pp. 9, 33–34.

22. Blassingame, p. 63.

23. Howard Thurman, *Deep River* (New York: Harper and Brothers, 1945), p. 16.

24. John B. Cade, "Out of the Mouths of Ex-Slaves," pp. 328–329.

25. Albert Raboteau underscores the "biblical orientation of slave religion" with the desire to read the Bible leading slaves to regard "education with a religious awe," p. 239. Cf. Janet Cornelius "We Slipped and Learned to Read:" Slave Accounts of the Literacy Process, 1830–1865," *Phylon* 44:3 (1983), 171–86, pp. 171–172.

26. Jon Michael Spencer, *Sacred Symphony* emphasizes the background for spirituals in preaching, p. xiii.

27. Raboteau, pp. 161–2. C. G. Woodson however sees this move to "religion without letters" as also regressive, backing away from earlier commitments to teach reading pp. 179–183. He recounts the convergence of economic and political factors which intensified opposition against slave literacy, p. 151–155.

28. Blyden Jackson notes how "without biblical scholarship" the spirituals were limited in their references by an illiterate population, seeing them as formulaic repetitions of characters and events. *History of Afro-American Literature* (Baton Rouge: Louisiana State University Press, 1989, Vol. I 1746–1895), p. 317. Cf. E. Franklin Frazier, on restrictions of access to the Bible, *The Negro Church in America* (New York: Schocken, 1963), p. 10; also John White, "Veiled Testimony: Negro

Spirituals and the Slave Experience" *Journal of American Studies* Vol. 17, 1983, 251–263.

29. Both Davies and Jones, for example, underscore Watts Jones, pp. 37, 265. Cf. Paul Petrovich Svinin records in his travel notes of 1811 how Holy Writ was disseminated in the form of "Watt's Psalms of David Imitated" which were read out line by line ("lined-out") Jackson, p. 232; cf. Ricks, *Some Aspects of Religious Music*, p. 7.

30. Charles C. Jones reports in his history of *The Religious Instruction of the Negroes in the United States*, the importance of "lining-out" the hymns for participation among congregants without access to the written text, The Reverand Samuel Davies specifically cites the *Psalms and Hymns* as central to his mission.

31. Southern notes that Watts *Hymns and Spiritual Songs* became "immensely popular in the colonies, especially among black folk," p. 35; also pp. 59, 146; Sobel, p. 222. Janet Cornelius cites the Watt's hymnal as central to black literacy, *When I Can Read My Title Clear*, p. 71.

32. See Shira Wolosky, "Rhetoric or Not: Hymnal Tropes in Emily Dickinson and Isaac Watts," *The New England Quarterly* 61:2 (June 1988), 214–232.

33. There are numberless discussions of typological structure in literary and American contexts. These include: Eric Auerbach, *Mimesis* (Princeton: Princeton University Press, 1953, 73–76; and "Figura," *Scenes from the Drama of European Literature*; Sacvan Bercovitch, ed., *Typology and Early American Literature* (Amherst: University of Massachusetts Press, 1972); Ursulla Brumm, *American Thought and Religious Typology* (New Brunswick: Rutgers University Press, 1970); Earl Miner, ed., *Literary Uses of Typology*, Princeton: Princeton University Press, 1977. See note 12.

34. See Marcellus Blount, "The Preacherly Text: African American Poetry and Vernacular Performance," *PMLA* (May 1992), 582–594, pp. 587–588.

35. Raboteau, pp. 4, 15, 250.

36. Levine, p. 76.

37. Raboteau, p. 147.

38. This link between slave rebellions and literacy laws is particularly examined by C.G. Woodson.

39. Thurman, p. 14; Laubenstein, p. 239; Sterling Brown, "Spirituals," *The Book of Negro Folklore*, eds. Langston Hughs and Arna Bontemps (New York: Budd Mead, 1958), p. 286; White, p. 261.

40. Raboteau, p. 251.

41. Levine, pp. 32–33.

42. William Warren Sweet claims that "the split between the churches was not only the first break between the sections, but the chief cause of the final break," *The Story of Religion in America* (New York: Harper & Brothers, 1930), p. 449.

43. John Lovell, Jr., *Black Song: The Forge and the Flame* (New York: Macmillan, 1972), p. 189; James H. Cone, *The Spirituals and the Blues* (New York: Seabury, 1972), pp. 24, 29.
44. Henry Louis Gates, Jr., *The Signifying Monkey* (New York: Oxford University Press 1988), pp. 79, 81, 86.
45. Douglass p.278. Cf Higginson: "dey tink de Lord mean for say de Yankees" and decodings: when singing "Ride on King Jesus, NO man can hinder Thee" the "paderollers told them to stop" p. 217
46. Fisher, pp. 25, 45; Frazier, p. 12.

7 WOMEN'S BIBLES

1. Elizabeth Cady Stanton and the Revising Committee, *The Woman's Bible* (Seattle: Coalition Task Force on Women and Religion, 1974).
2. Cf. Ilana Pardes, *Countertraditions in the Bible* (Cambridge, MA: Harvard University Press, 1992) on Stanton, pp. 13–17.
3. Carolyn De Swarte Gifford discusses the politics of Biblical interpretation in "American Women and the Bible," in *Feminist Perspectives on Biblical Scholarship*, ed. Adela Yarbro Collins (Cico, CA: Scholars Press, 1985), pp. 11–34, pp. 17–21.
4. Barbara Brown Zikmund, "The Struggle for the Right to Preach," in *Women and Religion in America* Vol. 1, eds. Rosemary Radford Ruether and Rosemary Skinner Keller (San Francisco: Harper and Row, 1981), pp. 193–241.
5. Nathan Hatch, *The Democratization of American Christianity* (New Haven: Yale University Press, 1989) describes American religious pluralism. Cf. Perry Miller, "The Puritan State and Puritan Society" *Errand into the Wilderness* (Cambridge, MA: Harvard University Press, 1956).
6. On Higher Criticism see Philip Gura, *The Wisdom of the Word* (Middletown, CT: Wesleyan University Press, 1981); Ira Brown, "Higher Criticism Comes to America," *Journal of Presbyterian History* 38 (1960), p. 206; George M. Marsden, "Everyone One's Own Interpreter? The Bible, Science, and Authority in Mid-Nineteenth Century America," in *The Bible in America*, eds. Nathan O. Hatch and Mark Noll (New York: Oxford University Press, 1982), pp. 79–100.
7. Nina Baym discusses women's Biblical participation, *American Women Writers and the Work of History, 1790–1860* (New Brunswick: Rutgers University Press, 1995), p. 47. Cf. Kathleen Kern, *We are the Pharisees* (Scottdale, PA: Herald Press, 1995).
8. See Mark. A. Noll, "The Image of United States as a Biblical Nation," in *The Bible in America,* ed. Nathan Hatch and Mark A. Noll (New York: Oxford University Press, 1982), pp. 39–58.

9. Mother as Christ figure is consistent with much sentimental religion in the nineteenth century. See Ann Douglas, *The Feminization of American Culture* (New York: Doubleday, 1977), Chapters 3 and 4.

10. For the relationship between abolition, religion, and women's movements, see, for example, James Brewer Stewart, "Abolitionists, the Bible, and the Challenge of Slavery," pp. 32–40, in *The Bible and Social Reform* ed. Ernest R. Sandeen (Philadelphia: Fortress, 1982).

11. Cf. Dorothy C. Bass, "Their Prodigious Influence: Women, Religion, and Reform in Antebellum America," in *Women of Spirit*, eds. Rosemary Ruether and Eleanor McLaughlin (New York: Simon and Schuster, 1979), 280–300; also Barbara Brown Zikmund, "Biblical Arguments and Women's Place in the Church," in *The Bible and Social Reform*, ed. Ernes R. Sandeen (Philadelphia: Fortress, 1982), 85–98; Martha Tomhave Blauvelt, "Women and Revivalism," in *Women and Religion in America*, eds. R.R. Ruether and Rosemary Skinner Keller (San Francisco: Harper and Row, 1981), pp. 1–45.

12. Gifford, "American Women and the Bible," pp. 17–19.

13. Cf. Yolanda Pierce, "African-American Women's Spiritual Narratives," *Cambridge Companion to Nineteenth-Century American Women's Writing*, ed. Dale Bauer and Philip Gould (New York: Cambridge University Press, 2001), pp. 122–142.

14. *Sisters of the Spirit*, ed. William L. Andrews (Bloomington: Indiana University Press, 1986); *Maria Stewart: America's First Black Woman Political Writer*, ed. Marilyn Richardson (Bloomington: Indiana University Press, 1987).

15. On Black women activists, see Frances Smith Foster, *Written by Herself: Literary Production by African-American Women 1746–1892* (Bloomington: Indiana University Press, 1993).

16. See Lawrence Buell, *New England Literary Culture* (New York: Cambridge University Press, 1986), pp. 166–190 on the Higher Criticism and literary developments.

17. Barbara Welter, "Something Remains to Dare," Introduction to *The Woman's Bible* (New York: Arno rept. 1974), p. xix.

18. Cf. Alicia Ostriker, *Feminist Revision and the Bible* (Oxford: Blackwell, 1993), pp. 63–67.

19. David Porter, *The Art of Emily Dickinson's Early Poetry* (Cambridge, MA: Harvard University Press, 1966), sees the hymns as a "constant occasion for irony," p. 55. Cristanne Miller discusses the hymnal basis of Dickinson's prosodies in *A Poet's Grammar* (Cambridge, MA: Harvard University Press, 1987).

20. Richard Sewall, *The Life of Emily Dickinson* (New York: Farrar, Straus Giroux, 1974), p. 119.

21. See chapter 2 above; *Emily Dickinson: A Voice of War* (New Haven: Yale University Press, 1984).

22. Ernest Lee Tuveson discusses the "Battle Hymn" and American Millennialism in *Redeemer Nation* (Chicago; The University of Chicago Press, 1968), pp. 197–202; cf. James Moorhead, *American Apocalypse* (New Haven: Yale University Press, 1978).

23. *Turning the World Upside Down: The Anti-Slavery Convention of American Women*, May 9–12 1837; *Introduction Dorothy Sterling* (New York: Feminist Press of America at the City University of New York, 1987), p. 13.

24. Quoted Gifford, "American Women and the Bible," p. 25. For discussion of the tensions between and within radical and conservative women's movements and specifically the WCTU, see Carolyn De Swarte Gifford, "Women in Social Reform Movements," in *Women and Religion in America*, Vol. 1, eds. Rosemary Ruether and Rosemary Keller (San Francisco: Harper & Row, 1981), pp. 294–303, pp. 301–302. See also Lori D. Ginzberg, *Women and the Work of Benevolence* (New Haven: Yale UP, 1990), pp. 205–206.

8   FRAGMENTED RHETORIC IN *BATTLE-PIECES*

1. As William Charvat sums up: "Melville's conflict with his readers lasted the whole ten years of his professional writing life and ended in defeat" *The Profession of Authorship in America 1800–1870*, ed. Matthew Bruccoli (Ohio: Ohio State University Press, 1968), p. 204.

2. Melville makes this comment about unpopularity specifically about "Clarel," Letter to James Billson, October 10, 1884 (*Letters*, New Haven: Yale University Press, 1960). On the reception of Melville's poetry, see Robert Penn Warren "A Note on this Book" *Selected Poems of Herman Melville* (New York: Random House, 1967, p. vii, and his "Introduction" (pp. 1–88).

3. Edmund Wilson, *Patriotic Gore*, p. 479. A. Robert Lee, who calls the volume an "historical retrospective" of events culled from the *Rebellion Record*, "Eminently Adapted for Unpopularity: Melville's Poetry," in A. Robert Lee, ed., *Nineteenth Century American Poetry* (New York: Barnes and Noble, 1985), p. 128; also Richard Harter Fogle, "Melville and the Civil War," *Tulane Studies in English*, Vol. 9, 1959, who sees *Battle Pieces* as "commemorative and historical," trying "to register in poetry the impact and scope of the Civil War in all its representative aspects," p. 63.

4. Daniel Aaron describes *Battle-Pieces* as "variations on the theme of order against anarchy," *The Unwritten War* (New York: Oxford University Press, 1973), p. 79. "Law and empire are the central theme of the collection" according to George Fredrickson, *The Inner Civil War* (New York Harper, 1965), p. 185. William Shurr divides the volume into a cycle of law and a cycle of evil in *The Mystery of Iniquity: Melville as Poet* (Lexington: University Press of Kentucky, 1972), p. 14. Robert Milder in "The Rhetoric of Melville's Battle-Pieces,"

Nineteenth Century Literature (September 1989), 44, sees Melville as affirming, if redefining, "the consecrating sense of historical mission" (p. 180) in terms of the need "to reconcile political idealism with moral and metaphysical realism" p. 181. For Joyce Sparer Adler, the poetry presents the war as an "historic tragedy" illustrating the "metaphysics of an evil universe" *War in Melville's Imagination* (New York: New York University Press, 1981), p. 133. Catherine Georg Ondaki, *American Transcendental Quarterly* 1:1 (1987), 21–32: "Battle-Pieces and Aspects of War: Melville's Poetic Quest for Meaning and Form in a Fallen World" argues that the poems "establish a moral and aesthetic order as the means of transcending the meaninglessness and disorder of the war," p. 21. Gail H. Coffler, "Form as Resolution: Classical Elements in Melville's *Battle-Pieces*," in *American Poetry: Between Tradition and Modernism*, ed. R. Hagenbuchle (Regensburg: 1984), pp. 105–121, argues for the "coherence" of Melville's poetry, with Melville accepting the necessity of "law" in order to achieve a greater good (105, 113).

5. Carolyn Karcher, *Slavery, Race, and Violence in Melville's America* (Baton Rouge: Louisiana State University Press, 1980), sees Melville as "caught between opposition to war and anti-slavery"(p. 262). Robert Milder sees the tension as between Union vs. Abolition (p. 178). Cf. Stanton Garner sees Melville's reference to "man's foulest crime" in "Misgivings" as referring "not to slavery but to the fratricidal battle which threatened "the Founder's Dream." (396). Bryan C. Short's claim about the *Confidence Man* applies no less to *Battle-Pieces*: that "when Melville's work " is ventriloquistic. It presents a variety of ethical stances other than Melville's own and it disperses authority among a number of voices," *Cast by Means of Figures: Herman Melville's Rhetorical Development* (Amherst: University of Massachusetts Press, 1972), p. 151.

6. *The Rebellion Record*, ed. Frank Moore (New York: Arno, 1977). Melville had available to him Volumes I through VIII, for the years 1860–1864. Hereafter cited as *RR*.

7. See, for example, *RR* Vol I: Doc 194, Jefferson Davis: "Knowing none but a just cause can gain the Divine Favor we would implore the Lord of Hosts to guide and direct our policy in the paths of right, duty, justice, and mercy." Cf. Doc 178, Vol. II: Abraham Lincoln, Proclamation of a Day of Fast and Prayer, August 12, 1861: "It is peculiarly fitting for us to recognize the hand of God in this terrible visitation and...to humble ourselves before him and to pray for his mercy."

8. Warren, p. 354.

9. On the use of divine mission both to sanction slavery and in support of abolition see Eric Sundquist, "Slavery, Revolution and the American Renaissance" *The American Renaissance Reconsidered* ed. Walter Benn Michaels and Donald Pease (Baltimore: Johns Hopkins University Press, 1985).

10. James McPherson, *Battle Cry of Freedom* (New York: Ballantine, 1988), pp. 653–663.
11. See Daniel Aaron on Milton's importance in Civil War writings, *The Unwritten War* (New York: Oxford University Press, 1973), p. 343. Cf. Henry F. Pommer, *Milton and Melville* (University of Pittsburgh Press, 1950).
12. Quoted Charvat, p. 235.
13. Helen Trimpi, *Melville's Confidence Men and American Politics in the 1850's* (Hamden, CT: Archon, 1987), p. 24.
14. The search for what Robert Penn Warren calls "the inner unity of the book" ("Introduction" p. 11) is pursued in Stanton Garner's extensive study of Melville, *The Civil War World of Herman Melville* (Lawrence, Kansas: University Press of Kansas, 1993), p. 392. But many commentators have remarked on the centrifugal force of rhetoric in the work—including William Bysshe Stein in *The Poetry of Melville's Late Years* (Albany: State University of New York Press, 1970), who observes that Melville's "rhetorical tactics cast doubt on exegesis which accept Biblical and Miltonic imagery" (p. 6); Carolyn Karcher, also remarks on the "striking range of viewpoints" she sees as a debate between dissenting factions, p. 263. Elaine Barry, in "The Changing Face of Comedy," *Herman Melville*, ed. Harold Bloom, Chelsea House, 1986, notes "persistent rhetorical play" p. 119. Cf. Richard Harter Fogle, "Melville and the Civil War," *Tulane Studies in English* 9 (1959), sees "Melville [as] sometimes merely the mouthpiece for the feelings the people," p. 71. Melville himself names this tension between part and whole when he describes *Battle-Pieces* as selections from "the events and incidents of the conflict, making up a whole, in varied amplitude."
15. On the divisive impact of rhetoric in the Civil War, see David Herbert Donald *Liberty and Union* (Boston: Little, Brown, 1978), p. 72. Cf. Donald Pease, *Visionary Compacts* (Madison: University of Wisconsin Press, 1987), p. 267.

9 Plural Identities and Local Color

1. William Newman, *American Pluralism* (New York: Harper and Row, 1973), p. 56. See also Milton Gordon *Assimilation* pp. 118–119, and p. 132 discusses the attempt by German groups to establish their own state and the defeat of this project.
2. The normative power of assimilation is a huge topic. See Andrew Greely, *Ethnicity in the United States* (New York: John Wiley and Sons, 1974), p. 17; See also Newman, p. 54; Gordon, p. 95; John Higham, *Strangers in the Land* (New York: Atheneum, 1975), p. 5. Michael Novak, *The Rise of the Unmeltable Ethnics* (New York: Macmillan, 1971). Jean Martin, "Ethnic Pluralism and Identity," *The*

Ethnic Dimension (Sydney: George Allen and Unwin, 1981) offers an overview.

3. Gordon and Newman both review what they call three philosophies of assimilation—"anglo-conformity," "amalgamation," or melting pot, and cultural pluralism: Gordon, p. 85; Newman p. 51. Higham's *Strangers* describes the dialectic of assimilation and nativism, p. 20. For a discussion of nativism, see Walter Benn Michaels, *Our America: Nativism, Modernism, Pluralism* (Durham, NC: Duke University Press, 1995).

4. Hans Kurath sketches the geography of language sectionalism in "Linguistic Regionalism," 297–312 in *Regionalism in America*, ed. Merrill Jensen (Madison: University of Wisconsin Press 1965), 297–312. See also Joshua Fishman, *Language Loyalty in the United States* (The Hague: Mouton, 1966).

5. Gordon, p. 94; Kammen, p. 74. Jefferson's *Notes on Virginia* supports ethnic homogeneity.

6. See John Higham. Cf. Marcus Hansen, *Immigration as a Factor in American History*, ed. Oscar Handlin (Englewood Cliffs, NJ: Prentice-Hall, 1959) pp. 10–15 identifies three waves: "Celtic" peoples (1830–1860)—Irish, Scotch, Welsh, German, Belgian, and Dutch; then by what has been called "Germanic" (1860–1890)—Prussians, Scandinavians, Austrian; and a third period (1980–1914) Mediterranean and Slavic.

7. Gordon remarks: "The melting pot concept may envisage the culture of the immigrants as "melting" completely into the culture of the host society without leaving any cultural trace at all...In this form, of course, the melting pot concept embraces a view of acculturation which is hardly distinguishable from that of Anglo-conformity," pp. 116, 125.

8. Higham traces pluralism and assimilation as constantly opposing and presupposing each other: "From the outset the belief that a democratic society should preserve the integrity of its constituent groups has unconsciously relied on the assimilative process which it seemed to repudiate." *Send These to Me*, p. 198. Cf. Michael Kammen, *People of Paradox*, p. 92.

9. Quoted Kammen, p. 72. See Verner W. Crane, ed: Franklin's The Internal State of America" 1786, *William and Mary Quarterly*, 3rd series, Vol. 15 (1958), 226. As Franklin wrote earlier, in "Apology for Printers" in *The Pennsylvania Gazette* (1731): "both sides ought equally to have the Advantage of being heard by the Publick....So many Men, so many Minds."

10. Michael Kammen, *People of Paradox*, Chapter 3. Oscar Handlin defines America as its pluralism, saying: "Immigrants were American history." *The Uprooted* (Boston: Little, Brown, 1952), p. 3.

11. Frederick Jackson Turner, *The Significance of Sections in American History* (New York: Henry Hold, 1907/32), pp. 287, 45. For Turner's sectional emphasis see: Howard Odum and Harry Estill Moore,

eds., "From Sectionalism to Regionalism," 35–51, in *American Regionalism* (Gloucester, MA: Peter Smith, 1966).

12. Horace Kallen, "Democracy versus the Melting Pot," *Culture and Democracy in the United States* (New York: Boni and Liveright, 1924) argues a unitary American identity would "violate" the fundamental "spirit of the American institutions." Instead, he envisions an "American civilization [as] the perfection of the cooperative harmonies of European civilization." Yet he also envisions cultural pluralism of ethnic groups in the form of a "federal republic" as a "democracy of nationalities, pp. 118, 124–125, 122. For a fuller discussion of Royce and James, see Wernor Sollors, *Beyond Ethnicity: Consent and Descent in American Culture* (New York: Oxford University Press, 1986).

13. For a critique of Kallen, see Wernor Sollors, "A Critique of Pure Pluralism," in *Reconstructing American Literary History*, ed. Sacvan Bercovitch (Cambridge, MA: Harvard University Press, 250–279). Cf. Philip Gleason, "American Identity and Americanization," in *Concepts of Ethnicity*, Cambridge: Harvard University Press, 1982, pp. 57–94, 96–99. Frederik Barth, *Ethnic Groups and Boundaries* (Boston: Little, Brown, 1969) argues for the central role of boundaries, even more than cultural content, in ethnic definition.

14. Gordon, pp. 132–33. Gordon comments: "Whatever ethnic communality was to be achieved...must be achieved by voluntary action within a legal framework which was formally cognizant only of individuals." Cf. Marcus Lee Hansen, *The Immigrant in American History*, ed. Arthur Schlesinger (New York: Harper and Row, 1964), p. 132.

15. Carl Degler discusses the meanings of "regions", "Northern and Southern Ways of Life and the Civil War," *The Development of an American Culture* ed. Stanley Coben and Norman Ratner (New York: St. Martin's Press, 1983), 112–144; also Fulmer Mood, "The Origin, Evolution, and Application of the Sectional Concept, 1750–1900), in *Regionalism in America*, ed. Merril Jensen (Madison: The University of Wisconsin Press, 1965), 5–99.

16. Robert H. Wiebe, *The Search for Order* (New York: Hill and Wang, 1967). Cf. John Higham, *Send These To Me* (New York: Atheneaum, 1975) describes the post–Civil War period as a time of "national integration" and a "quest for unity," p. 199.

17. Sandra Zagarell, "America as Community in Three Antebellum Village Sketches," *The Other American Tradition*, ed. Joyce Warren (New Brunswick: Rutgers University Press, 1993), 143–163 emphasizes tension between new national integration and old village diversity.

18. Richard Brodhead, *Cultures of Letters* (University of Chicago Press, 1993) discusses local color fiction in terms of "translocal agglomerations," p. 118. Alan Trachtenberg's *The Incorporation of America*

(New York: Hill and Wang, 1982) describes the consolidation in post-bellum America. Jay Martin, *Harvests of Change: American Literature 1865–1914* (Engelwood Cliffs, NJ: Prentice-Hall, 1967) sees local color as minimizing "basic differences and national identity as consisting of a harmony of regions," p. 25.

19. Larzer Ziff, *The American 1890s* (New York: Viking, 1966) calls local-color the "charms of diversity" in a reaffirmed Union (p. 296) that evades deeper social differences (p. 18). Benjamin Spencer's Cf. "Regionalism in American Literature," in *Regionalism in America*, ed. Merril Jensin (Madison: University of Wisconsin Press, 1965), pp. 219–260, similarly argues that the "nation, having solidified its political unity, could apparently abandon itself to delight in cultural diversity." p. 229. Cf. Benjamin Spencer, *The Quest of Nationality* (Syracuse: Syracuse University Press, 1957): p. 258. Robert Penn Warren's dismisses local-color on similar grounds, "Not Local-Color," *Virginia Quarterly* No. 1 (1932), 153–160.

20. Jay Martin, *Harvests of Change: American Literature 1865–1914* (Engelwood Cliffs, NJ: Prentice-Hall, 1967) reads local color more nostalgically, p. 83.

21. Howells, "American Literary Centres," *Literature and Life* (New York: Harper & Brothers 1902), 173–186, pp. 177, 175. See Jules Cametzky, "Our Decentralized Literature: A Consideration of Regional, Ethnic, Racial, and Sexual Factors," *Jahrbuch fur Americkastudien* (Heidelber), 17, 1972. Amy Kaplan, in *The Social Construction of American Realism* (Chicago: University of Chicago Press, 1988) sees Howells as responding to the "breakdown of traditional community" by seeking "to construct in realism new forms of social cohesiveness," p. 25.

22. Quoted Spencer, *Quest*, p. 259.

23. "Local Color in Art" *Crumbling Idols* 1894, quoted Claude Simpson, ed. *The Local Colorists* (New York: Harper and Bros., 1960), p. 1. Cf. Spencer, *Quest*, on creation of a national literature, p. 230. Cf. Martin, *Harvests*, p. 87 on Garland; cf. David Jordan (xi) "Introduction," *Regionalism Reconsidered* (New York: Garland, 1994), ix–xxi, p. xi.

24. On the relation between "Realism and Regionalism," see Eric Sundquist, in the *Columbia Literary History of the United States*, ed. Emory Elliott (New York: Columbia University Press, 1988), pp. 501–524. See also Eric Sundquist, ed. *American Realism: New Essays* (Baltimore: Johns Hopkins University Press, 1982).

25. Peter Revell, *James Whitcomb Riley* (New York: Twayne, 1970).

26. *The Best of James Whitcomb Riley*, ed. Donald Manlove (Bloomington: Indiana University Press, 1982), p. xvii.

27. Harriet Monroe, "James Whitcomb Riley," *Poetry: A Magazine of Verse* 8:6 (September 1916), 305–307.

28. Quoted Peter Revell, *James Whitcomb Riley* (New York: Twayne, 1970), p. 22.

29. Fulmer Mood, "The Origin, Evolution, and Application of the Sectional Concept, 1750–1900" in *Regionalism in America*, ed. Merril Jensen (Madison: The University of Wisconsin Press, 1965), pp. 5–99, especially pp. 14–16.

30. Quoted Spencer, *Quest*, p. 254; Hawthorne *Works* Riverside ed. (Cambridge, MA: 1914), X 456, XI, 470.

31. This is, of course, especially true of New England. See Spencer, *Quest*, p. 256.

32. James Whitcomb Riley, *Letters*, ed. William Lyon Phelps (Indianapolis, 1930), p. 102.

33. This argument has been made by, e.g., Marjorie Pryse, "Reading Regionalism: "The "Difference" It Makes," in *Regionalism Reconsidered*, ed. David Jordan (New York: Garland, 1994, 47–64, p. 48. See also Josephine Donovan, *New England Local Colorists* (New York: Frederick Ungar Pub., 1983); Marjorie Pryse and Judith Fetterly, *American Women Regionalists: A Norton Anthology* (New York: Norton, 1992). Richard Brodhead questions these claims in *Cultures of Letters*, pp. 144–146.

34. The question of market, and the place of regionalism within a culture of literary consumption is argued by Richard Brodhead, pp. 122 ff.

35. Shirley Marchalonis, "Lucy Larcom" *Legacy* 5:1 (Spring 1988), 45–51.

36. Marjorie Pryse and Judith Fetterley, "Profile of Alice Carey," *Legacy* 1:1 (1984).

37. Howells, *Literary Friends and Acquaintances*, "New England has ceased to be a nation unto itself and it will perhaps never again have anything like a national literature." See James Cox, "Regionalism: A Diminished Thing," *Columbia Literary History of the United States*, ed. Emory Elliott, pp. 761–784, p. 764. Cf. Ziff, on New England as become just a region, p. 17.

38. Greeley underscores such multiple affiliations, p. 27. Michael Steiner and Clarence Mondale, *Region and Regionalism in the United States: A Source Book for the Humanities and Social Sciences* (New York: Garland, 1988) call regional literature "the spatial dimension of cultural pluralism," p. x.

39. Novak, "Pluralism in Humanistic Perspective," pp. 27–56, *Concepts of Ethnicity* pp. 39–41. Novak calls this a "pluralistic personality" and associates it with voluntarism in which "individuals are free to make as much, or as little, of their ethnic belonging as they choose."

40. Milton Gordon proposes "structural pluralism" rather than "cultural pluralism" to indicate how individuals participate in "structurally separate subsocieties" that include religious, racial, and nationality groupings, p. 159. William Newman similarly emphasizes how in a highly differentiated, pluralistic society, members "continually cope with multiple realities, different majority and minority group interpretations of what it means to be a member of a given physical, cognitive, or behavioral minority," pp. 286–288; Kammen, p. 65

41. Higham, *Send These to Me*, p. 206.

10   EMMA LAZARUS' AMERICAN-JEWISH PROPHETICS

1. Marvin Trachtenberg, *The Statue of Liberty* (New York: Viking, 1976); John Higham, *Send These To Me* (New York: Atheneum, 1975).

2. Cf. Diane Lichtenstein *Writing Their Nations* (Bloomington: Indiana University Press, 1992), p. 38.

3. Esther Schor *Emma Lazarus* (New York: Schocken, 2006). See also Bette Roth Young, *Emma Lazarus in her World: life and letters* (Philadelphia: Jewish Publication Society, 1995).

4. Diane Lichtenstein makes this association with Deborah, but does not develop it, p. 37.

5. Sacvan Bercovitch, "The Ends of Puritan Rhetoric" in *The Rites of Assent* (New York: Routledge, 1993).

6. My thinking is based here in Michael Kramer's discussion of this poem in "How Emma Lazarus Discovered America in "1492," unpublished manuscript. Cf. Kramer on the relation between Christian and Jewish typology in "New English Typology and the Jewish Question," *Studies in Puritan American Spirituality*, Vol. III, December 1992, 97–124.

7. See Werner Sollors, *Beyond Ethnicity* (New York: Oxford University Press, 1986), pp. 84; 51.

8. See Shira Wolosky "Biblical Republicanism: John Cotton's 'Moses His Judicials' and American Hebraism," *Hebraic Political Studies* 4:2 (Winter 2009), 104–127.

9. Lazarus wrote accusingly to Emerson: "Your favorable opinion having been confirmed by some of the best critics of England and America, I felt as if I had won for myself by my own efforts a place in any collection of American poets, & I find myself treated with absolute contempt in the very quarter where I had been encouraged to build my fondest hopes" (Dec. 27, 1874), *The Letters of Emma Lazarus 1868–1885*, ed. Morris U. Schappes (New York: New York Public Library, 1949), p. 11.

10. Heinrich Jacob discusses Lazarus's earlier resistance to Rabbi Gottheil's efforts to involve her in Jewish culture, *The World of Emma Lazarus* (New York: Schocken, 1949), p. 80. Also Louis Harap, *The Image of the Jew in American Literature* (Philadelphia: Jewish Publication Society, 19xx), who quotes Lazarus to Rabbi Gottheil: "The more I see of these religious poems, the more I feel that the fervor and enthusiasm requisite to their production are altogether lacking in me," p. 286. In a similar vein, Edmund Stedman reports having said to Lazarus: "There is a wealth of tradition you are heir to and could use as a source of inspiration," to which she replied that she was "proud of my blood and heritage, but Hebrew ideals do not appeal to me." Harap, p. 289. See also the Lazarus biography by Esther Schor.

11. Jacob, p. 113

12. Zinaida Alexeievna Ragozin, "Russian Jews and Gentiles," *The Century Magazine* 23:1 (November to April), 905–920, p. 909.

13. Emma Lazarus, "Russian Christianity versus Modern Judaism," *The Century Magazine* 24:2 (May to October), 48–56, p. 49.

14. Yosef Hayim Yerushalmi, *Zakhor: Jewish History and Jewish Memory* (New York: Schocken, 1989).

15. Emma Lazarus, "The Jewish Problem," *The Century Magazine* 25:3 (November to April), 602–611, p. 602; Emma Lazarus, *An Epistle to the Hebrews*, Centennial Edition (New York: Jewish Historical Society of New York, 1987), p. 8.

16. Ziva Amishai-Maisels, "The Jewish Jesus," *Journal of Jewish Art* 9 (1982), 85–104, pp. 92–93.

17. See David Roskies for twentieth-century representations of the historical Jesus, *Against the Apocalypse* (Cambridge, MA: Harvard University Press, 1984).

18. Joshua Fishman, *Language Loyalty in the United States* (The Hague: Mouton 1966), p. 73.

19. John Higham, *Send These:* There was no Statue when the poem was written, and it was to be a monument not to asylum, but to Franco-American friendship. As James Russell Lowell wrote to Lazarus, "I liked your sonnet on the Statue much better than I like the Statue itself. But your sonnet gives its subject a raison d'etre which it wanted before quite as much as it wanted a pedestal.

20. Jacob, p. 209.

11 PAUL LAURENCE DUNBAR'S CROSSING LANGUAGES

1. Myron Simon, "Dunbar and Dialect Poetry," in *A Singer in the Dawn*, ed. Jay Martin (New York: Dodd, Mead and Co., 1975), p. 116. Cf. Darwin Turner, "Paul Laurence Dunbar: The Poet and the Myths," in *A Singer in the Dawn*, ed. Jay Martin (New York: Dodd, Mead, 1975) sees Dunbar's standard English verse as "talented but not exceptional," p. 72. Henry Louis Gates, Jr. discusses Dunbar in the context of black dialect in *Figures in Black* (New York: Oxford University Press, 1987), pp. 176, 179; and *The Signifying Monkey* (New York: Oxford University Press, 1988), pp. 173–176.

2. This question of dialect as compromised by the plantation tradition continues to be tied to arguments over Dunbar's racial identification or assimilationism. Sterling Brown, *Negro Poetry and Drama* (Washington, DC: Associates in Negro Fold Education, 1937) calls Dunbar's dialect pieces "a poetry of evasion," p. 41. James A. Emanuel "Racial Fire in the Poetry of Paul Laurence Dunbar," sees Dunbar's racial identity as ambiguous, *A Singer in the Dawn*, ed. Jay Martin (New York: Dodd, Mead, 1975), p. 78. Blyden Jackson and Louis D. Rubin, Jr., discuss the general problem of dialect as compromised by

the plantation tradition in "The Search for a Language," *Black Poetry in America* (Baton Rouge: Louisiana State University Press, 1974), and see Dunbar's dialect as a "folksy skepticism" that does not, however, deal with "the deep hypocrisy of political betrayal," p. 17. Bruce D. Dickson, Jr., however, in *Black American Writing from the Nadir 1877–1915* (Baton Rouge: Louisiana State University Press, 1989), sees Dunbar's dialect both as as subtly countering the plantation tradition, and as an emblem of Dunbar's racial ambivalence, pp. 58–59.

3. William Dean Howells, "Life and Letters," *Harper's Weekly*, Vol. 27, June 27, 1896; "Introduction" to *Lyrics of Lowly Life* (New York: Dodd Mead, 1896), p. xix.

4. James Weldon Johnson, *Along this Way* (New York: Viking, 1933), p. 160.

5. W.E.B. Du Bois, *The Souls of Black Flolk* (New York: Bantam, 1989), p. 3

6. Klaus Ensslen, "The Status of Black Poetry 1865–1914," sees Dunbar's standard English and dialect to "coexist as strangely unmediated and separate elements unbridged by even the slightest attempt at uniting them on the level of language." *American Poetry: Between Tradition and Modernism*, ed. Roland Hagenbuchle (Regensburg: Pustet, 1984), p. 146.

7. Darwin Turner emphasizes the conscious artistry of Dunbar's dialect pieces, p. 68, a position also explored by Ensslen, p. 153. This counters criticism of Dunbar's dialect as "not native" but only constructed, J. Sanders Redding *To Make a Poet Black* (College Park, MD: McGrath, 1939), p. 63. Cf. Benjamin Brawley, *Paul Laurence Dunbar* (Chapel Hill: University of North Carolina Press, 1936), p. 1; Cf. also Charles T. Davis, who sees Dunbar's term *Minors* as suggesting "problems about the poet's attitude about the use of dialect," *Black is the Color of the Cosmos*, ed. Henry Louis Gates, Jr. (New York: Garland, 1982), p. 134.

8. See Kimberly Benston on the complex issues of language inheritance in "I yam what I am: the topos of (un)naming in Afro-American Literature," in *Black Literature and Literary Theory*, ed. Henry Louis Gates, Jr. (New York Methuen 1984), pp. 151–172.

9. Johnson, p. 159.

10. Eric Sundquist, *To Wake the Nations* (Cambridge, MA: Harvard University Press, 1987) discusses Du Bois's complex views of the slave past, p. 470.

11. Quoted in Braxton, xiv. Dunbar wrote to Helen Douglass complaining of people "unable to differentiate dialect as a philological branch from Negro minstrelsy," quoted in Simon, p. 121.

12. Henry Louis Gates discusses the mask as "a coded, secret, hermetic world, a world discovered only by the initiate." *Figures*, p. 167.

13. Lawson, for example, sees Dunbar's as a sentimental representation of plantation life, *Dunbar Critically Examined* (Washington, DC: Associated Publishers, 1941), pp. 68–69. cf. Sterling Brown, p. 33.

Jean Wagner, *Black Poets of the United States* (Urbana: University of Illinois Press, 1973), pp. 81–82, criticizes Dunbar's as eliding "the misery ignored by plantation literature." Turner, however, sees Dunbar's images of the faithful slave as a reproach to whites abusing this loyalty, p. 70.

14. For discussion of the shifts in slave representation between antebellum and post-bellum slave narratives, see William L. Andrews, "Slavery and Afro-American Literary Realism," in *Slavery and the Literary Imagination*, ed. Deborah E. McDowell and Arnold Rampersad (Baltimore: Johns Hopkins University Press, 1989), pp. 62–80, pp. 65–67. See also Arnold Rampersad, "Slavery and the Literary Imagination," pp. 104–124, pp. 111–112 on Du Bois's responses to them.

15. Frederick Douglass, *My Bondage and My Freedom* (New York: Dover, 1969), pp. 441–45.

16. Victor Lawson emphasizes the Romantic background to Dunbar. Marcellus Blount, in "Caged Birds," in *Engendering Men*, ed. J.A. Boone and Michael Cadden (New York: Routledge, 1990) discusses Dunbar's use of the sonnet and its combinations of "both Euro-American culture and the Afro-American tradition." p. 232.

17. Houston Baker underscores the "energies of rhythmic song" as a central trope in Dunbar, *Blues, Ideology and Afro-American Literature* (Chicago: University of Chicago Press, 1984), p. 4, who treats the plantation heritage as a "liminal and inventive creator aware of a sharp dilemma and determined to express it in articulate form" p. 122.

18. Dickson discusses this critical stance of Dunbar against religion, p. 80.

19. See discussion of spirituals above, chapter 4.

20. For discussion of the apparent conflict and final ascendency of dance and song in black transformations of white religious forms see, for example, Sterling Stuckey, *Slave Culture* (New York: Oxford University Press, 1987), p. 25.

21. Mechal Sobel argues for the mutual influence of black and white religious forms in *The World They Made Together* (Princeton: Princeton University Press, 1987). See chapter 4 above on slave spirituals.

22. Marcellus Blount discusses these contexts for "An Ante-Bellum Sermon" in "The Preacherly Text: African American Poetry and Vernacular Performance," *PMLA* (May 1992), 582–594. See also Jon Michael Spence, *Sacred Symphony* (New York: Greenwood, 1988), on the relationship between sermon and spiritual.

23. Dickson makes this intensification of racism at the turn of the century an important interpretive frame for black writers, p. 5ff.

12   HARVARD FORMALISM

1. Van Wyck Brooks, *Scenes and Portraits: Memories of Childhood and Youth* (New York: Dutton, 1954), p. 106.

2. Robert Davidoff discusses this closeted homosexuality in *The Genteel Tradition and the Sacred Rage* (Chapel Hill: University of North Carolina Press, 1992). Cf. Daniel Cory, *Santayana: The Later Years: A Portrait with Letters* (New York: Braziller, 1963), p. 40.

3. George Santayana, *Persons and Places* (New York: Scribners, 1944), p. 119.

4. George Santayana, *The Genteel Tradition*, ed. Douglas L. Wilson (Cambridge, MA: Harvard University Press, 1967), pp. 40, 73.

5. Cf. Stow Parsons, *The Decline of American Gentility* (New York: Columbia University Press, 1973), pp. 274, 292. See also John Tomsich, *A Genteel Endeavor: American Culture and Politics in the Gilded Age* (Stanford: Stanford University Press, 1971), p. 186.

6. Lois Hughson, *Thresholds of Reality* (Port Washington, New York: Kennikat, 1977), p. 23.

7. George Santayana, *Persons and Places* (New York: Scribners, 1944), p. 51; and the chapter "A Change of Heart" in *My Host the World* (New York: Scribners, 1953) p. 5; Hughson discusses Santayana's "metanoia," p. 17.

8. Ivor Winters, "Foreward" to F.G. Tuckerman, *The Complete Poems*, ed. N. Scott Momaday (New York: Oxford University Press, 1965, p. xvi.

9. See Roland Hagenbuchle, "Abstraction and Desire: Dissolving Contours in the Poetry of F. G. Tuckerman," *American Poetry: Between Tradition and Modernism*, ed. Roland Hagenbuchle (Regensberg: Friedrich Pustet Verlag, 1984), pp. 70–86.

10. *Homage to Trumbull Stickney* ed. James Reeves and Sean Haldane (London: Heinemann, 1968).

11. *The Poems of Trumbull Stickney*, ed. A. R. Whittle (New York: Farrar Strauss and Giroux), 1966.

12. Stickney opposes Wordsworth against Euripides, whose side he favors, in a *Harvard Monthly* piece called "Nature Worship, Ancient and Modern" (Nov. 1894) (*Homage*, p. 5).

13. Santayana, *Sense.*

14. George Santayana, *Interpretations of Poetry and Religion* (New York: Harper & Row, 1957).

15. Santayana trots out Whitman routinely in his essays, most extensively in "The Poetry of Barbarism," and "Genteel American Poetry."

16. Cf. Santayana, *Sense*, 29; Santayana, *Genteel*, 82.

13   Walt Whitman's Republic of Letters

1. *Walt Whitman: The Contemporary Reviews*, ed. Kenneth M. Price (New York: Cambridge University Press, 1996). Cf. Betsy Erkilla, *Whitman the Political Poet* (New York: Oxford University Press, 1988), p. 238.

2. See Charles Feidelson, *Symbolism and American Literature* (Chicago: University of Chicago Press, 1953), for an early description of the poem as a "process" and "voyage," p. 18.

3. Cf. Stanley Cavell's discussions of Emerson's as a yet unattained America, especially in *Conditions Handsome and Unhandsome* (Chicago: University of Chicago Press, 1990).

4. Harold Bloom, "Introduction," *Walt Whitman* (New York: Chelsea House, 1985), 1–9, p. 2. This figural reading generally derives in Harold Bloom's poetics, from *Figures of Capable Imagination* (New York: Seabury Press, 1976) through his many writings on poetry.

5. Whitman is seen as egomaniacal self in D.H. Lawrence *Studies in Classic American Literature* (New York: Viking, 1961), pp. 163, 165; also Quentin Anderson's *The Imperial Self* (New York: Knopf, 1971), e.g., pp. ix, 93. Roy Harvey Pearce's reading of Whitman in *The Continuity of America Poetry* (Princeton: Princeton University Press, 1961) likewise sees Whitman's ideal as a "separate person sufficiently free...to let his ego roam"; pp. 164–165. David Simpson in *Nation and Narration*, ed. Homi Bhabha (London: Routledge, 1990) sees Whitman as an image of American imperialist aggrandizement, p. 177.

6. This recognition of "the creative participation of each reader" has, as does most Whitman commentary, a long history, as in R.W.B. Lewis discusses it in *Trials of the Word* (New Haven: Yale University Press, 1965), p. 11. Lewis compares this to Emerson's notion of "representativeness," as a democratic assertion of the "heroism implicit in each individual," p. 12. Cf. Gay Wilson Allen, *The Walt Whitman Handbook* (New York: Hendruck's House, Inc. 1962), p. 378; C. Carroll Hollis, *Language and Style in 'Leaves of Grass'* (Baton Rouge: Louisiana State University Press, 1983). Also Ezra Greenspan, *Walt Whitman and the American Reader* (New York: Cambridge University Press, 1990); Kerry Larson, *Whitman's Drama of Consensus* (Chicago: The University of Chicago Press, 1988).

7. For further discussion see Shira Wolosky, "Emerson's Figural Religion: From Poetics to Politics" *Religion and Literature*, ed. Paul Kane, 41:1 (Spring 2009), 25–48.

8. Betsy Erkilla's *Whitman the Political Poet* offers the fullest discussion of Whitman's political affiliations and their contexts.

9. Paul Zweig's biography, *Walt Whitman: The Making of the Poet* (New York: Basic Books, 1984) explores this period of Whitman's life with great insight. David Reynold's *Walt Whitman's America* (New York: Knopf, 1995) provides exhaustive biographical information.

10. Thomas L. Brasher, *Whitman as Editor of the Brooklyn Daily Eagle* (Detroit: Wayne State University Press, 1970), p. 20.

11. For discussion of Whitman's fiction, see Vivian Pollak, *The Erotic Whitman* (Berkeley: University of California Press, 2000), pp. 37–55.

12. On extension politics, see David Herbert Donald, *Liberty and Union* (Boston: Little, Brown, 1978), pp. 53–58.

13. Quoted from manuscript notes in Bucke memoranda, in Clifton Joseph Furness, "Walt Whitman's Politics," *American Mercury*, Vol. 16, 1929, 459–466, p. 2.

14. Edmund Morgan, *Inventing the People: The Rise of Popular Sovereignty in England and America* (New York: Norton, 1988).

15. "Protest," April 15, 1834, James D. Richardson, *A Compilation of the Messages and Papers of the Presidents,"* Authority of Congress, 1899, Vol. III, p. 90. On Jackson's claim to represent directly the whole people: Robert B. Remini, *Andrew Jackson and the Course of American Democracy* (New York: Harper and Row, 1984), Vol. III, pp. 154–9.

16. For discussion of Jackson's electoral reforms, see for example, Edward Pessen, *Jacksonian America: Society, Personality, Politics* (Homewood, IL: Dorsey Press, 1978), pp. 150–159; Robert Remini, *The Jacksonian Era* (Chicago: University of Illinois Press), pp. 24–27; 66; and Robert Remini, *The Legacy of Jackson*, p. 32, 36–37; John William Ward, "Jacksonian Democratic Thought: A Natural Charter of Privilege" in Stanley Coben and Norman Ratner, eds., *The Development of American Culture* (New York: St. Martin's Press, 1983), pp. 58–79; pp. 62–66.

17. Comparing Whitman with Lincoln is a topic unto itself. George Fredrickson succinctly but usefully discusses it in *The Inner Civil War* (New York: Harper Torchbooks, 1965), p. 66. For an extended discussion, see especially Allen Grossman, "The Poetics of Union in Whitman and Lincoln: An Inquiry toward the Relationship of Art and Policy," *The American Renaissance Reconsidered*, eds., Donald Pease and Walter Benn Michaels (Baltimore: Johns Hopkins University Press, 1985). See also Herbert Levine, "Union and Disunion in "Song of Myself," *American Literature*, Vol.59, No. 4, December 1987: 570–589.

18. Paul Zweig notes Whitman's general habit of self-description, p. 204.

19. Larzer Ziff, *Literary Democracy* (New York: Viking Press, 1981) comments: "he was celebrating the life of each of his country-men, not making peculiar claims for his own differences," p. 235. Donald Pease discusses the senses of national celebration in *Visionary Compacts* (Madison: University of Wisconsin Press, 1987), pp. 115–116.

20. Madison, for example in *Federalist* 14, speaks of the "turbulent democracies of ancient Greece and modern Italy" (New York: New American Library, 1961), p. 100. Cf. *UPP*, 159, where Whitman suggests that without "turbulence" a people is nothing more than a "race of slaves" in this phrase's republican, anti-British sense (*UPP*, 159).

21. Cf. In *Democratic Vistas* he speaks of "interminable swarms of alert, turbulent, good-natured, independent citizens...with none having yet really spoken, created a single image-making work for them (421).

22. For discussions of Whitman's construction of a "you" see C. Carroll Hollis, *Language and Style in "Leaves of Grass'"* (Baton Rouge: Louisiana State University Press, 1983); Ezra Greenspan, *Walt Whitman and the American Reader* (New York: Cambridge University Press, 1990); and Kerry Larson, *Whitman's Drama of Consensus* (Chicago: University of Chicago Press, 1988).

23. The relation between Whitman's term "adhesive" and a contemporary low-culture interest in phrenology has been discussed by Zweig and others, with special reference to Whitman's own homosexuality.

24. See note 28 below.

25. Allen Grossman, "The Poetics of Union in Whitman and Lincoln: An Inquiry toward the Relationship of Art and Policy," *American Renaissance Reconsidered*, ed. W. Benn Michaels and Donald Pease (Baltimore: Johns Hopkins University Press, 1985), pp. 183–208; Herbert Levine, "Union and Disunion in "Song of Myself," *American Literature*, Vol. 59, No. 4, December 1987: 570–589.

26. For discussions of American dissent, see Sacvan Bercovitch, *The Rites of Assent* (New York: Routledge, 1993); and Samuel Huntington, *The Disharmony of Politics* (Cambridge, MA: Harvard University Press, 1981).

27. David Reynolds, "Politics and Poetry: *Leaves of Grass* and the Social Crisis of the 1850s," *The Cambridge Companion to Walt Whitman* (New York: Cambridge University Press, 1995), 66–91: "Into the vacuum created by the dissolution of the nation's political structure rushed Whitman's gargantual 'I,' assimilating images... The healing of the divided nation, he had come to believe, could be best achieved through all-absorptive poetry," p. 67.

28. Peter Sacks, *The English Elegy* (Baltimore: Johns Hopkins Press, 1987) discusses the elegy as a public, communal ritual.

29. For Whitman's phallicism see Sandra Gilbert, "The American Sexual Poetics of Walt Whitman and Emily Dickinson," *Reconstructing American Literary History*, ed. Sacvan Bercovitch (Cambridge, MA: Harvard University Press, 1986), pp. 123–155; Harold Aspiz, who calls "A Woman Waits for Me" a product of "arrogant male chauvinism" (*Walt Whitman and the Body Beautiful* [Urbana: University of Illinois Press, 1980]), p. 140. Sherry Caniza reviews some of the issues involved in "Women's Response to the *Leaves of Grass*," *The Cambridge Companion to Walt Whitman* ed. Ezra Greenspan (New York: Cambridge University Press, 1995), pp. 110–134, but "sees Whitman's work as empowering le readers," pp. 113, 111.

Killingsworth sees Whitman's as a cross-gendered identity that strad-
dles male and female, pp. 66–69.

30. Hannah Arendt in *The Human Condition* (Chicago: University of
Chicago Press, 1958), describes political life as "a way of life in which
speech and only speech made sense and where the central concern of
all citizens was to talk with each other," p. 27.

POSTSCRIPT: CHARTING AMERICAN TRENDS: STEPHEN CRANE

1. Marston LeFrance's *A Reading of Stephen Crane* (Oxford: the
Clarendon Press, 1971) is essentially existential, seeing Crane's man
as "pursuing the ideal, the purpose and direction which make his
pilgrimage across the desert meaningful and distinguish him from
other animals," p. 137. Hyatt Waggoner negatively reads Crane as
foundering in "God's silence and nature's blankness; man's helpless-
ness and isolation," *American Poets* p. 249. Daniel Hoffman similarly reads Crane's poetry as dealing with "ultimate confrontations,
the individual alone against huge and inscrutable elementals... [and
without] the possibility of his finding the comradeship that redeems
man from ultimate isolation," *The Poetry of Stephen Crane* (New
York: Columbia University Press, 1957), p. 267.

2. Thomas Wentworth Higginson, who compared Crane to Dickinson
as poets whose formlessness would assure their literary doom, noted
Crane's as a poetry that "gives you a glance at [its thought], or, per-
haps two glances from different points of view, and leaves it there,"
Higginson "Recent Poetry" *The Nation*, Vol. 61, October. 24, 1896.
Reprinted in *Stephen Crane: Critical Heritage*, ed. R. M. Weatherford
(London: Routledge & Kegan Paul, 1973), p. 67. Cf. Max Westbrook,
"Stephen Crane's Poetry: Perspective and Arrogance," *Bucknell Review*,
Vol. 11, December 1963, 24–34; Ruth Miller, "Regions of Snow," in
Bulletins of the New York Public Library, 72, 1968: 328–349.

3. Quoted Katz, p. xxxv.

4. The desert does not, it seems to me, represent an existential "utter
indifference of the universe to the fate of the individual," as Katz
claims, "Introduction," p. xxii. Cf. Maurice Bassan, "Introduction"
Stephen Crane Twentieth Century Views (Englewood Cliffs, NJ:
Prentice-Hall, 1967): Crane's "surreal desert and mountain scenes,
with their pitiful, absurd, doomed figures engaged in dramatic confrontations with a terrible fate," present "the position of man, isolated from God and Nature [as] charged with a kind of existential
dread," p. 7.

5. Most commentators chart Crane's religion as rejecting his mother's
Wrathful for his father's Loving God. See Hoffmann for Crane's
father's theological notes.

6. Berryman, p. 92.

7. Harland S. Nelson underscores Crane's religious contexts, "Stephen Crane's Achievement as a Poet," *Texas Studies in Literature and Language*, Vol. 4, no. 4, Winter 1963: 568–582. Max Westbrook places Crane a "voice of perspective…characterized by humility, kindness, a quiet determination, and by a consistent belief in a truth which is symbolic, elusive, but always real;" as against a "voice of arrogance—representing the values Crane attacked in his prose and fiction as well as in his poetry—[and] characterized by pride, dogmatism, often by an aggressive manner, and by a stubborn insistence on a literal truth."

Sources and Abbreviations

Poems by women poets other than Dickinson can be found in:

Wolosky, Shira. *Major Voices: 19th Century American Women's Poetry*, London: Toby Press, 2003.

Dickinson, Emily (1830–1886) poetry is available in *The Poems of Emily Dickinson*, ed. Thomas H. Johnson, Cambridge, MA: Belknap Press of Harvard University Press, Copyright 1951, 1955, 1979; and *The Poems of Emily Dickinson*, ed. Bruce Franklin, Cambridge, MA: Belknap Press of Harvard University Press, 1998.

Sources of Poetry cited are:

Cary, Alice (1820–1871) and Phoebe (1824–1871). *The Poems of Alice and Phoebe Cary*, New York: Hurst and Co. Pub., 1850. *The Poetical Works of Alice and Pheobe Carey*, Boston: Houghton, Mifflin, 1892.

Crane, Stephen. *The Poetry of Stephen Crane*, New York: Columbia University Press, 1957.

Dunbar, Paul Laurence (1872–1906). *The Collected Poetry of Paul Laurence Dunbar*, ed. Joanne M. Braxton, Charlottesville: University Press of Virginia, 1993.

Gilman, Charlotte Perkins (1860–1935). *In This Our World*, New York: Arno, 1974; and *The Later Poetry of Charlotte Gilman*, ed. Denise D. Knight, Delaware: University of Delaware Press, 1996.

Harper, Frances Watson (1825–1911). *Complete Poems of Frances Ellen Watkins Harper*, ed. Maryemma Graham, New York: Oxford University Press, 1988.

Holmes, Oliver Wendell Sr. (1809–1894). *The Poetical Works of Oliver Wendell Holmes*, Boston: Houghton Mifflin, 1975.

Howe, Julia Ward (1819–1910). *Passion Flowers*, Boston: Ticknor, Reed, and Fields, 1853; *Later Lyrics*, Boston: J. E. Tilson and Company, 1866.

Jackson, Helen Fiske Hunt (1830–1885). *Sonnets and Lyrics*, Boston: Robert Brothers, 1887.

Lanier, Sidney (1842–1881). *Poems of Sidney Lanier*, ed. Mary Day Lanier, Athens: University of Georgia Press, 1981, with John Hollander's "Afterword," 265–272.

Larcom, Lucy (1824–1893). *The Poetical Works of Lucy Larcom*, Boston: Houghton Mifflin, 1868.

Lazarus, Emma (1849–1887). *The Poems of Emma Lazarus*, Two Volumes, Boston and New York: Houghton Mifflin, 1889; *Emma Lazarus: Selections from Her Poetry and Prose*, ed. Morris U. Schappes, New York: Emma Lazarus Federation of Jewish Women's Clubs, 1967. Also *Emma Lazarus, Selected Poems and Other Writings*, ed. Gregory Eiselein, Ontario: Broadview Literary Texts, 2002.

Longfellow, Henry W. (1807–1882). *The Complete Poetical Works*, Boston: Houghton Mifflin, 1922.

Lowell, James Russell (1819–1891). *The Poetical Works of James Russell Lowell*, London: Macmillan and Co., 1892.

Melville, Herman (1890–1891). Hennig Cohen, "Preface," *Selected Poems of Herman Melville*, New York: Fordham University Press, 1991, xii. For a review of the reception of the poetry, see Robert Penn Warren, "A Note on This Book," *Selected Poems of Herman Melville*, New York: Random House, 1967, vii, and his "Introduction," 1–88.

Piatt, Sarah. *Nineteenth-Century American Women Poets: An Anthology*, ed. Paula Bennett, Malden, MA: Blackwell, 1998.

Poe, Edgar Allan (1809–1849). *Complete Poems*, ed. Thomas Ollive Mabbott, Chicago: University of Illinois Press, 2000.

——— (1984). *Edgar Allan Poe, Essays and Reviews*, ed. G. R. Thompson, New York: Library of America, 1984, All citations from Poe's prose are taken from this edition, abbreviated as E.

Riley, James Whitcomb (1849–1916). *The Homestead Edition: The Poems and Prose Sketches*, New York: Scribners, 1904.

Santayana, George (1863–1952). *Poems*, ed. Robert Hutchinson, New York: Dover, 1970.

Sigourney, Lydia (1791–1865). *Select Poems*, Philadelphia: Edward C. Riddle, 1843.

Stickney, Trumbull (1874–1904). *The Poems of Trumbull Stickney*, ed. A. R. Whittle, New York: Farrar Strauss and Giroux, 1966.

Timrod, Henry (1828–1867). *Collected Poems of Henry Timrod*, ed. E. Winfield Parks and Aileen Wells Parks, Athens: University of Georgia Press, 1965.

Tuckerman, F. G. (1821–1873). *The Complete Poems*, ed. N. Scott Momaday, New York: Oxford University Press, 1965.

Whitman, Walt (1819–1892) works are notated as follows: *Uncollected Poetry and Prose*, ed. Emory Holloway, New York: Doubleday, 1921, as UPP; *Complete Poetry and Collected Prose*, New York: Library of America, 1982, as CPP; *Notebooks and Unpublished Prose Manuscripts*, ed. Edward Grier New York: New York University Press, 1984, as NM; *An American Primer*, foreward Horace Traubel, Boston: Small, Maynard and Co., 1904, as AP; *The Complete Poems*, ed. Francis Murphy, New York: Penguin Books, 1979, including the 1855 Preface, as P; *Democratic*

Vistas, in *The Portable Walt Whitman*, ed. Mark Van Doren, New York: Viking, 1945, as DV.

Whittier, John Greenleaf (1807–1892). *The Poetical Works of John Greenleaf Whittier*, London: John Walker and Company, n.d.

Wilcox, Ella Wheeler (1850–1919). *Poems of Progress*, Chicago: Conkey and Comp., 1909; *Poems of Passion*, Chicago: W. B. Conkey Comp., 1883.

Also: Making of America University of Michigan Web site.

INDEX